PERFORMATIVITY IN UK EDUCATION:
ETHNOGRAPHIC CASES OF ITS EFFECTS, AGENCY AND RECONSTRUCTIONS

EDITED BY
BOB JEFFREY AND GEOFF TROMAN

E&E
PUBLISHING

Printed and bound in the United Kingdom by
4edge Ltd, 7a Eldon Way Industrial Estate, Hockley, Essex, SS5 4AD.

E&E Publishing

We publish educational ethnographies of which this is our second.

Our first was Understanding Pupil Resistance: Integrating Gender, Ethnicity and Class
Lisa Russell

Other related publications
Ethnography and Education Book Series – Tufnell Press

The Ethnography and Education book series published by Tufnell Press aims to publish a range of authored and edited collections including both substantive research projects and methodological texts and in particular we hope to include recent PhDs. Our priority is for ethnographies that prioritise the experiences and perspectives of those involved and that also reflect a sociological perspective with international significance. We are particularly interested in those ethnographies that explicate and challenge the effects of educational policies and practices and interrogate and develop theories about educational structures, policies and experiences. We value ethnographic methodology that involves long-term engagement with those studied in order to understand their cultures, that use multiple methods of generating data and that recognise the centrality of the researcher in the research process.

The editors of this E&E ethnography and the Tufnell Book Series welcome proposals that seek to:
- explicate and challenge the effects of educational policies and practices and interrogate and develop theories about educational structures, policies and experiences,
- highlight the agency of educational actors,
- provide accounts of how the everyday practices of those engaged in education are instrumental in social reproduction.

The editors of this E&E ethnography and the Tufnell series are:
Professor Dennis Beach, University College of Borås, Sweden,
Bob Jeffrey, The Open University,
Professor Geoff Troman, Roehampton University, London and
Professor Geoffrey Walford, University of Oxford.

Titles in the Ethnography and Education series include:

Creative learning: European experiences
Edited by Bob Jeffrey

Researching education policy: Ethnographic experiences
Geoff Troman, Bob Jeffrey and Dennis Beach

The commodification of teaching and learning
Dennis Beach and Marianne Dovemark

Performing English with a postcolonial accent: Ethnographic narratives from Mexico
Angeles Clemente and Michael J. Higgins

How to do educational ethnography
Edited by Geoffrey Walford

Ritual and Identity
Christoph Wulf *et al.*

Young people's influence and democratic education
Elisabet Öhrn, Lisbeth Lundahl and Dennis Beach

Ethnography and Education Journal – Routledge Journals
www.tandf.co.uk/journals/reae
Ethnography and Education available from InformaWorld is an international journal that publishes articles to illuminate educational practices through empirical methodologies which prioritise the experiences and perspectives of those involved. We are open to a wide range of ethnographic research that emanates from the perspectives of sociology, linguistics, history, psychology and general educational studies as well as anthropology. The journal's priority is to support ethnographic research that involves long-term engagement with those studied in order to understand their cultures, to use multiple methods of generating data and to recognise the centrality of the researcher in the research process.

Contents

We dedicate this book to our academic colleagues, many of whom are referenced in this volume. With thanks and appreciation for the support given to our work and careers.

Introduction
Bob Jeffrey and Geoff Troman

This collection of articles across a wide range of educational sectors in the United Kingdom shows clearly the power and influence of performativity but also how people manage and cope with it. We agree that this supports a Foucauldian perspective, that power is more circulatory than presented in correspondence theories and that there are many acts of resistance and manipulation evident in actor's responses.

Performativity is underpinned by major social and educational policies intended to improve national economic status and social well-being. This is a market-based approach that encourages performance-based activity and the generation of a culture of performativity (Lyotard 1984; Ball 1998; Ball 2000). Lyotard's performativity is a different form to that of Butler, which Youdell (2006) notes concerns the nature of language and its relationship to the world in which a performative is 'that discursive practice that enacts or produces that which it names' (Butler, 1993: 13). Lyotard (1984) views performativity as a technology, a culture and mode of regulation that employs judgements and comparisons and displays the performances of individual subjects or organisations to serve as measures of productivity. In the educational field, the performativity culture is being used by government to raise standards in schools, to raise the educational achievement of the mass of the population. In setting targets for itself as government, for Local Authorities (LA) and schools it aims to develop a highly skilled workforce that can compete in what it sees as a new global industry – the knowledge economy. The underpinning assumption is that the higher the skills base and the higher levels of excellence achieved in knowledge acquisition and use, the higher the economic return will be for the UK.

Ball (1998) argues that performativity works in at least three ways. First it works as a disciplinary system of judgements, classifications and targets towards which schools and teachers must strive and against and through which they are evaluated. Second, as a part of the transformation of education and schooling, performativity provides sign systems which 'represent' education as self-referential and reified for consumption,

> And indeed many of the specific technologies of performativity in education (total quality management, human resources management, etc.) are borrowed from commercial settings. Both these aspects of educational performativity are linked to and 'valorised' within the market form in education. Teachers are inscribed in these exercises in performativity,

through the due diligence with which they attempt to fulfil competing imperatives and inhabit irreconcilable subjectivities. (ibid: 190).

Third, performativity also resides in the pragmatics of language. The linguistic discourse used to describe learning in these terms, by teachers and learners alike, becomes the norm, for example, 'The use of assessment statements, the language of inspection and the discourse of unsatisfactory teachers all have enunciative effects' (ibid: 191). In this particular case, when enunciations are declared by those with power such as political leaders and OfSTED inspectors, the language is taken up by those whose role it is to respond positively to powerful assertions and regulatory practices – teachers.

Performativity is a principle of governance which establishes strictly functional relations between an institution and its inside and outside environs (Ball 1998). In terms of a normalizing judgement, disciplinary power (Rabinow 1984) operates in the space that the law left behind, in the workshop, the school and teacher training. At the heart of all disciplinary systems functions a small penal mechanism. In education it is the teacher grading system or a failing school's reconstruction either by closure and reopening or through the reorganisation by special units. There is a penalty for non-observance as well as transgression, 'a pupil's offence is not only a minor infraction but an inability to carry out tasks' (ibid: 194).

In performative performance the technologies of power are the public league tables, targets and inspection reports that regulate practice, perceived by teachers to be high stakes due to the potential for judgments to be made about the quality of teaching and whether a school is successful or not (Scott 2006). They are devices for changing the meaning of practice and of social relationships, providing a new language, a new set of incentives and disciplines, and a new set of roles, positions and identities within which, what it means to be a teacher, student and parent, are all changed (Ball 2008).

Ball (2008) employs Willmot (1993) and Lyotard (1984) to show how performativity connects to self-interest (see Bright and Jeffrey and Troman, Ch. 9 in this volume). Within such areas of competition Willmott (1993: 522) suggests 'employees are simultaneously required, individually and collectively to recognise and take responsibility for the relationship between their employment security and contribution to the competitiveness of the goods and services they produce' (see Busher *et.al.* in this volume). New administrative procedures are generated that 'make individuals "want" what the system needs to perform well' (Lyotard 1984: 62) (see Jeffrey and Troman, Ch. 4, Perryman and Priestley *et.al.*, in this volume).

Teachers and learners are encouraged to see their own development as linked to and provided for by the 'growth' of the institution (Jeffrey and Troman 2012).

Advocates of the market tend to approach the issues of values in one of two ways: either as value neutral, as a mechanism for the delivery of education that is more efficient or responsive or more effective, or present the market as possessing a set of positive moral values in its own right – effort, thrift, self-reliance, independence and risk taking, what is called 'virtuous self interest'. Managers have become the technicians of transformation as Ball (2003) notes (May, 1994) (see Kakos in this volume). Ball (2008) argues that performativity has the capacity to reshape, in their own image, the organisations they monitor (Shore and Wright 1999) (see Priestley *et.al.* in this volume).

The operation of this technology of power (performativity) uses rationalised means to normalise individuals, showing how assessing one's own teaching quality through performativity testing can bring about new confidence, even to new entrants (see Jeffrey and Troman Ch. 4 in this volume). Continual improvement (Scott 2006) is a major feature of current testing (Rose, 2000) and a major element of a performativity text that helps sustain its power and force. Targets are not only met with final celebrations of a job well done but all target completion is met with another exhortation to continually improve, the individual, teacher, class and school performance (see Perryman in this volume). This is the heart of the performativity policy text, the power that circulates to the capillaries (Foucault 1980), in this case, educational practice. Professional assessments by teachers are used by auditors such as the LA and OfSTED in a critical mode exhorting them to improve upon them.

Lyotard (1984), as Ball (2008) highlights, introduces a law of contradiction in performativity where an increase in intensification of volume of first order activities (direct engagement, research, curriculum development) required by the demands of performativity, leads to an extension of the 'transaction costs', the costs involved in processing performative practices, a second order (time and energy collecting data, monitoring and reporting (see Busher *et.al.*, Haywood and Thomson, Perryman and Priestley *et.al.* in this volume). Acquiring information, necessary for perfect control 'consumes so much energy available for making improvement inputs' (Elliot, 1996: 15).

There are fabrications (Ball 1998; Ball, 2000), such as believing that Standard Assessment Tasks (SATs) used for national testing in schools are a test of a culmination of five years learning when they are clearly exam coached activities, and that the extensive preparation for OfSTED inspections represents reality (see Hayward and Thomson, Jeffrey and Troman Ch. 9, and Perryman in this volume). Fabrications are one version of an organisation that exists for effectiveness, not truthfulness (Ball, 2000). However, raising the level of achievement for all learners is a value adopted by all schools and the fabrications don't totally obliterate the ways in which teachers attempt to maintain a constant struggle to ensure that the performative aspects of a school's performance do 'not stand' for a day to day set of work practices (Ball 1998) by exhibiting a wide range of educative experiences (see Garland and Garland, Jeffrey and Troman, Ch. 4, Orr in this volume).

However, these performative technologies are not always solely reproductive for as Foucault (1980) recognises, reproductive power relations vary at different times and in different places due to the way the human subject is socially and historically constituted (see Bright in this volume). This capacity is the emergence of agency to adapt and reconstruct power relations. Freedom, according to Foucault, is a political skill or power to be exercised (Foucault 1979) and it is bought into existence when contradictory oppositions and alternatives are presented (see Menter, Priestley *et.al.* and Orr in this volume) or when historical memory contradicts immediate experience or in a more mundane experience with varying degrees of possibility within the immediate spaces of existence (see Hayward and Thomson, Garland and Garland in this volume). Freedom operates at different levels and carries with it varying degrees of risk. It constitutes a realised capability for both individuals and groups (see Orr in this volume). Its mainspring is not human nature but survival in a finite world of limited resources (see Bright in this volume).

According to Olssen (2006) Foucault argues that at certain levels and in certain contexts certain modes of determinism and free agency coexist and circulate. Foucault's view of power enacted through strategies in the model or metaphor of a game suggest as much. Like Bourdieu, Olssen (2006) goes on to argue, Foucault utilizes the concept of strategies to understand how practice is operationalised and how people act on their environments (ibid: 205) (see Jeffrey and Troman Ch. 9 in this volume). Strategies refer to the

> totality of the means put into operation to implement power effectively or to maintain it… They constitute modes of action upon possible action, the action of others… As such the concept of strategy is used to designate the means employed to attain a certain end, it is a question of rationality functioning to arrive at an objective…it is a question of the means used to obtain victory' (Dreyfus and Rabinow 1982, in afterword: 224-5),

or to develop counter movements (Troman *et.al.* 2007) (see Bright in this volume). To the extent that relations of power are open or fluid, there is a degree of instability permitting the possibility or reversal or modification by teachers and in some cases by students.

The data and analysis in the articles in this collection show up the contradictions of values, purposes, and management in everything schools do. They exemplify how, 'Management becomes ubiquitous, inescapable – part of and embedded in everything we do...Beliefs are no longer important – it is output that counts' (Ball, 2003: 223). However, they also find resolutions possible (see Garland and Garland, Jeffrey and Troman, Ch. 4, Menter *et.al.* and Orr in this volume). They show the complexity of institutional response, unpacked through ethnographic methodology to show how policy adaptations are not always highly structured or planned strategically (Brain, 2006).

Going beyond a sole concentration on discourse requires that we utilise a theoretical frame and methodology that can also support an examination of policy and practice. In this collection, therefore, we focus on how a range of performative policies play out in a range contexts of practice in the UK education system. Vanegas summarises the three interrelated policy contexts as follows:

> The 'context of influence' is where public policy is normally initiated; where policy discourses are constructed. In the 'context of policy text production' policies are articulated in the language of general public good; texts that represent policy are produced. In the 'context of practice', policy is not simply received and implemented, rather it is subject to interpretation and then recreated, Bowe *et.al.* (1992) argue that practitioners do not confront policy texts as naive readers, they come with histories, with experience, with values and purposes of their own. (Vanegas, 1996: 3)

It is important that policy, in the trajectory model, is seen as a cyclical and relational activity (Evans and Penney, 1994) which allows for 'negotiative power' from below (Woods, 1995). Although this model is rather more 'structured' than a strictly Foulcauldian model would allow, we benefit from the strengths of eclecticism. Empirical data which is generated in this type of policy ethnography is used to support the theoretical formulations of poststructuralist theorists and also, alternatively, examine the theories themselves.

Empirical work on performativity is rare, with most researchers concentrating solely on theoretical analysis of policy discourse. Current empirical studies of schooling do not often incorporate policy analysis with rigorous ethnographic enquiry.

This collection explores policy at the macro level, in the context of policy text production, and at the meso and micro levels in the context of practice. Its aim, therefore, is to combine policy analysis with ethnographic explorations of a range of educational sites in order to understand the impact of performative policies on the work of the Headteachers, teachers, lecturers and pupils/students. In order to view performativity from their perspectives, we use the methodology of ethnography.

This provides many advantages. Our focus is on how individual actors make sense of, analyse or interpret any given social situation. From this perspective, humans have the capacity to reflect upon their circumstances and because they have self-consciousness can see themselves reflected in other people's responses and reactions to them and can think about these reactions and act accordingly. Humans construct responses to situations rather than merely reacting to them.

Through interview, conversations and involved observation we also focus on actors' meanings, motivations and interpretations in the empirical world. Woods stresses the importance of the 'empirical social world', that is,

> the minute by minute, day to day social life of individuals as they interact together, as they develop understandings and meanings, as they engage in joint action and respond to each other as they adapt to situations, and as they encounter and move to resolve problems that arise through their circumstances. (Woods, 1996: 37)

The collection begins with two articles focusing on how research itself is influenced by the performativity discourse, and our second theme focuses on examples of the direct effects of performativity via inspections and testing upon school policymaking, practice and professional accommodation. The tension involved in the implementation of policy values in a context of performativity is then examined in our third theme, and the fourth theme of agency in performative cultures is then portrayed in two primary schools, Further Education, and youth outside mainstream education.

Busher *et.al.* (Chapter One) show how performativity shapes and determines, to some considerable extent, the boundaries of the research frame due to the necessity for a university to show performance according to criteria for future research funding and leads to, in some cases, superficial research findings. Menter *et.al.* (Chapter Two) focus on the same subject through an examination of Initial Teacher Educators' limits placed upon their research capabilities by the performative demands of their institutions. They show the contradictions in this situation and indicate the threat to academic and professional quality, but also highlight some lecturer strategies to ameliorate the situation, arguing that a 'will to act' is still present.

Our second theme focuses on the extent to which schools and teachers will go to satisfy the demands of performativity and are exemplified in the articles by Perryman (secondary), (Chapter Three), and Jeffrey and Troman (primary), (Chapter Four) and at the same time they show how performativity has the power to satisfy teacher and learner interests through success and achievement of the performative process and the effects on professional readjustment. Perryman (Chapter Three) details the fabrications entailed in carrying out the performative function of an inspection by merging the work of Butler (1990, 1993, 1997) and Lyotard (1984) in her notion of 'panoptic performativity', and Jeffrey and Troman (Chapter Four) show the way Foucault's governmentality works to ensure the reproduction of macro performative policies.

The next three articles, of our third theme, by Priestley *et.al.* (Chapter Five), Haywood and Thomson (Chapter Six) and Kakos (Chapter Seven) exemplify the contradictions and tensions exhibited by educational institutions' attempts to implement national policies in a culture of performativity and how these tensions are lived and felt by the teachers (see Wright Mills 1959). We gain insights into the lived reality of teachers' professional lives as they negotiate and act strategically, striving to implement the spirit of the policies in a context in which performative outcomes are paramount.

Although agency, our last theme, can be seen in all the articles in its various forms, Garland and Garland (Chapter Eight) Jeffrey and Troman (Chapter Nine), Orr (Chapter Ten) and Bright (Chapter Eleven) provide specific examples of the ways in which performativity is experienced and the effects on social relations, learner identity and alienated youth in attempting to deal with performativity, whilst recognising and appreciating the humanity of people's lives. Garland and Garland (Chapter Eight), from research in primary schools, show how the relationship between teachers and teacher assistants has altered to the extent that the human relations with students is often carried out by the latter and not the former, who are more focused on outcomes. Jeffrey and Troman's research (Chapter Nine), also in primary schools, focuses on those learners and how they cope with the pervasiveness of performativity by developing performative identities. Orr (Chapter 10) takes an initially pessimistic view, from his research in Further Education, suggesting that strategic compliance has also been marginalised in mainstream institutions, but that when loosely coupled from the main institution, creative practices can be implemented providing some performativity can be exhibited. Bright (Chapter Eleven) takes us right out of mainstream education to show the nature of disaffection of youth in performative dominated schools and how they react emotionally, how their social educational identities are readjusted by the situation, but also by them as they develop strategies to cope.

Ethnographic research is a major methodology, not only for re-presenting these acts of creativity and agency, but for challenging the immutability of dominant discourses and to show the complexity of policy and practice. The more ethnographies that are produced of the interstices of policy and practice, the more likely it is that powerful discourses such as performativity can be challenged and reframed in the wider interests of students. The raising of achievement, upon which some of the performative rhetoric is based, is a laudable policy but it needs to be based within a values framework and not disembedded and allowed to become the dominant, dehumanising discourse to which all education is now subject. This collection will aid this objective.

The costs to students and teachers of trying to raise achievement through performative discourses
Hugh Busher, Hilary Cremin

Introduction

Discourses of performativity which are constructed within educational sites, such as schools, shape the perspectives of participants such as teachers and school students, and gatekeepers to sites, such as head teachers and senior staff, as well as researchers who are taking part in ethnographic studies. Many national governments, often for claimed economic reasons, construct and police schooling and teachers' work using performative models of 'techno-bureaucratic managerialism' (Apple, 2000). In England, central government prescribe for state schools curriculum content, pedagogical approaches, student assessment and the assessment of teachers, all enforced through a punitive school inspection regime (Troman *et.al.*, 2007). Discourses of student voice (Flutter and Rudduck, 2004) and a recognition of the contribution students' perspectives make to constructing successful schools (DfES, 2008) resonate with wider notions of choice and discipline in education to emphasise students' needs as individual learners, parents' vested interest in their children's education, and to try to reduce student disengagement with schooling. These discourses influence how participants manage, resist, or perhaps act ambiguously to cope with them while struggling to assert their own values and interests and those of the people with or for whom they (claim to) work. These discourses also shape how researchers in educational settings, whose work is also shaped by these discourses, may design and carry out ethnographic studies on particular sites. This has implications for researchers' relationships with other participants in a study, as well as for their own careers.

These policy developments have taken place in the context of complex structural changes in the global economy, and the impact of globalization and regionalization at national and European levels (Dale, 2009). Changing global political and economic conditions have had a major impact on developing a common EU outlook, as has EU expansion eastward since 1989 since the collapse of Communism. The last has brought in to EU membership states with different historical 'social models', and different economic conditions, democratic structures and traditions of civil society, from those of the founding states of Western Europe' (Busher *et.al.*, 2011).

The power of the state is central to the construction of policy discourses in education and these influence the internal workings of schools. Schools are sites in which national policies and local perspectives are mediated by the boundary activities of their members (Wenger, 1998), especially those in formal leadership roles at several levels, to construct institutionally implementable educational policies and practices (Lupton, 2005) that reflect particular but contested values (Starratt, 2007). The importance of schools and schooling in shaping social constructions, such as society's views on identity, pluralism and social cohesion, has been increasingly acknowledged by national governments within Europe and by the EU (Dale, 2009).

Education is both a site and a conduit for struggles (Foucault, 1976) through which teachers and students can explore the tensions of being and becoming as they (re)construct their identities (Giddens, 1991; Kearney, 2003) in situational contexts. The pursuit and enactment of self-identity is central to the development of agency (Giddens, 1991) through which people interact with others and with constructed social systems/structures (Giddens, 1984). Consequently these processes are of central importance to students' and teachers' development of themselves as learners, community members of a school and citizens. However, schools often restrict democratic participation by students and teachers in shaping institutional practices, but expect them to adhere to policies (Deakin *et.al.*, 2004). In part this is because curriculum is tightly prescribed at national level in England and its implementation is policed by the Office for Standards in Education (OfSTED). School success is defined simplistically in performative terms of certain proportions of students in a particular school achieving particular grades, which places demands on teachers' work as well as on students. It emphasises corporate (school) productivity that can be evaluated by parents and government agents against other similar schools in school League Tables rather than focusing on individual (student) development, despite policies in English education fostering personalised learning and assessment as a vehicle for learning.

Dominant social discourses in England describe schools as institutions for controlling children and shaping them to become useful adult citizens. Schools are expected to discipline students to fit these norms through careful monitoring of their actions (surveillance) by adults, through regimentation (e.g. school uniform, school bells), through various manoeuvres (school timetables, examinations) and through punishment (detention, exclusion) which is in inscribed on their bodies, at least metaphorically (loss of time in detention, acting in ways prescribed by school rules) (Foucault, 1977; Paechter, 2007). In these processes, sometimes students are to some extent complicit by policing their own actions (Foucault, 1986) often with the encouragement of teachers (e.g. developing a school bullying policy). This reduces the risk of confrontation with students (Lenski, 1986) and helps students to believe they have some part-ownership of school processes.

Contestation of the dominant discourse of schooling is a normal part of the processes of membership of school institutions, not an indicator of pathology in an organisation (Bottery, 2003). The participants in a school include all staff and students and possibly other stakeholders, such as parents, too. Through struggling with national and local discourses on education, people construct their own particular cultures of and within institutions and their identities (voices) in the social, intellectual, emotional and political spaces of society (Bhabha, 1994) or of organisations such as a school. The struggle is particularly expressed through the cultures teachers and students construct collectively to delineate the values and beliefs that underpin their own practices whether in classrooms, subject areas or school generally. The 'small' cultures (Holliday, 1999) in classrooms and subject areas stand in tension and collusion with the dominant discourses of a school, incorporating elements of its organisational culture along with teachers' or students' own personal and work-related values and their shifting views of preferred practices. As in other institutions, especially those of a disciplinary nature, teachers and others in part control their own actions by monitoring them against the norms embedded in dominant discourses that impinge on their bodies in the way, for example, that they are allowed to use time and space (Foucault, 1977). Further, teachers who have ascribed authority to lead (Bourdieu and Passeron, 1977) have to sustain a school's culture to their own subordinates, the students, to maintain order in a less abrasive manner than that of more overt coercion (Lenski, 1986). In schools, teachers are both leaders and led, and face the tensions that occupying such ambivalent positions generates.

Teachers' views of their identities are closely bound up with their social and personal values and interactions with others and from the dispositions of knowledge, skills, values and experiences they carry with them, their histories (Thomas, 1995) as well as with the policy contexts in which they work (Hall and Noyes, 2009). Teachers' identities are (re)created through the interactions of their personal, situational and professional experiences (Day *et.al.*, 2005). The first is linked to teachers' lives outside school, with their families and social networks. Their daily work is 'socially and politically constructed' (Goodson and Numan, 2002: 272) in particular locations from the values and experiences they share with others in multiple communities (Wenger, 1998) and the influences of the dominant cultural and political discourses they encounter (Giddens, 1991). These are mediated by a teacher's location in a specific school that is influenced by local conditions (e.g. socio-economic status of a school's catchment area, school links with parents), quality of leadership (use of power) and the support they are given. The last includes the way that it is implemented by the Principal or other senior staff (Day *et.al.*, 2006a) and how feedback is given to teachers on their practices. Successful teaching seems to require positive support from school institutions both culturally and with resources (Bubb and Earley, 2010) to allow teachers to fully use their professional knowledge and skills (Day *et.al.*, 2006b). The broader cultural and policy discourses includes those of the state (Reay, 1998) which transit the semi-permeable boundaries of their institutions, as Riley *et.al.* (2000) point out, and infiltrate their personal lives.

Democratic participation of students can be fostered through institutional structures such as a school council, but school councils are often dominated by the agenda of senior staff (Fielding, 2004). Pupil consultation can lead to a transformation of teacher-pupil relationships, to significant improvements in teachers' practices, and to pupils having a sense of themselves as members of a community of learners (Ruddock and McIntyre, 2007). Further, Sebba and Robinson (2011) argue that children, under the United Nations Convention of the Rights of the Child, have rights to take part in decision making about their own lives, and that their involvement helps to create a culture of respect in schools. However, some authors have raised doubts about the authenticity of student 'consultation', considering that sometimes it may be tokenistic (Byrom *et.al.*, 2007) because staff are reluctant to engage with the heterogeneity of pupil voice (Arnot and Reay, 2007) and are unwilling to listen to some students' voices if they do not construct their views in ways expected of them by staff (McIntyre, *et.al.*, 2005). Adults control the metaphorical 'territory' of the child/student even though students have particular (legitimate) agendas (Hoyle, 1981, Busher, 2007) but are often only able to assert these in school through resistance or rule breaking.

There are clear advantages, too, for teachers of listening and talking to students about their perspectives on teaching and learning (Ruddock, 2004, Demetriou and Wilson, 2010). Students are experienced participant observers of teachers, teaching and schools (Riley and Rustique-Forrester, 2002). Many are able to articulate clearly what they consider to be effective and ineffective teaching and support for students, views that chime closely with the literature on effective teaching (Wragg *et.al.*, 2000). It can help teachers to improve teaching and the support of learning in their classrooms (McIntyre, *et.al.*, 2005) and meet the needs of all their students. Student voice can also contribute to the effective management of schools to meet students' educational needs, especially when schools work in economically and socially disadvantaged areas (Mujis *et.al.*, 2005).

This paper considers students' and teachers' awareness of the contradictions of policy, power and voice and of the official and unofficial discourses in a school, which Paechter (2007) argues reflect the interactions of agency and structure in particular policy contexts, and the influence of these on their constructions of their work-place identities and their school's organisational culture (Busher, 2006). It argues that even though English government investment in education in the mid-noughties possibly raised academic achievement in narrowly instrumental terms, it did so at a cost of disempowering many of the actors in schools, generating a sense of alienation and disengagement for some, teachers and students, from nationally sponsored performative discourses.

Methodology

The study was carried out in a multi-ethnic Secondary school in a largely economically deprived area of a Midlands English city. It set out to elicit the views of some students and teachers in the particular contexts of a school, which were investigated through the views of senior staff and school policy documents, about what it meant to be a participant in a school, especially for engaged and disaffected students, two categories that during the course of the study seemed to lack substance, since students said by teachers to be disaffected in one class were said by other teachers to be engaged in another. It used ethnography to investigate asymmetrical relationships between people (students, teachers) and senior staff in institutions and flows of power between people in situations in a case study that was bounded in time (2007-2009) and space (one school, one year group of students and their teachers in the school). Students' and teachers' views were triangulated with the official discourse of the school and with our own observations of classes and school life as we visited and worked with our participants in the school. Triangulation strengthened the credibility of a study by cross-referencing different perspectives on the social situation being studied (Flick, 2009).

Three groups of twelve students from Y9 (thirty six students in all), studying English and Citizenship, were selected, of whom eighteen were to be defined by their teachers as 'engaged' and eighteen as 'disaffected'. To construct the groups of students, their class teachers were to be asked to select those whom they thought were strongly engaged or disaffected, using indicators such as: attendance, punctuality, homework, participation in curricular and extra-curricular events, alignment with goals and aims of the school, and performance in line with expectation. To locate the students in one of their normal learning communities, twelve were to be selected from a top set in English, twelve from a bottom set and twelve from a mixed-ability tutor group (defined as a Citizenship teaching group). The 12 in each class were to be found by teachers selecting six students who were either engaged or disaffected from school, according to criteria derived from school documents. At the suggestion of one of the teachers from the school we also included a group of students with special learning needs (SLN).

Investigating students' views of their experiences of schooling can be seen as similar to investigating the perspectives of people who are or have been deprived of access to power in formal decision-making processes, effectively silencing their voices and denying their values except when they turn to resistance (Bourdieu, 1998), a form of asserting power. Research methodologies for these circumstances try to construct research through the standpoints of indigenous peoples as well as enabling their voices and values to be heard (Spivak in Morton, 2003). This approach seems applicable to school students, who inhabit the metaphorical 'territory' of the child but are ruled over by adults who impose their norms and values, arguably a form of colonisation.

The study drew on the work of Thomson and Gunter (2005), who worked with a small group of students as consultants to develop a 'students-eye' set of evaluative categories and questions, and Riley and Rustique-Forrester (2002), who asked young people to use visual methods to represent their views of their life in school. We asked participants to take photographs to illustrate this, then make them into scrapbooks and talk with us about them. Visual ethnography is a well-recognised group of methods (Prosser, 2009) for capturing participants' views of their experiences. Photo-records can communicate the feeling or suggest the emotion imparted by activities, environments, and interactions with people and provide some tangible evidence of these (Prosser, 2006). Photo-records, like other visual displays, also embody the values and beliefs their makers hold (Howells, 2003). Interviews based on such representations can help elicit people's views of schooling (Croghan *et.al.*, 2008).

Visual and interview data was analysed qualitatively and quantitatively as Wall and Higgins (2009) suggested it might be. The qualitative analysis used open coding (Flick, 2009) to construct patterns of perceptions among students and teachers. The quantitative analysis merely counted what artefacts appeared in the photographs taken by students and teachers (Busher and Cremin, 2009). Instead of counting the objects and location of objects students placed within each photograph, as Prosser (2009) suggested researchers might do, we counted how many times particular objects appeared as the main focus of each photograph taken by the student participants in the study, as Wall and Higgins (2009) did – see Table 1 overleaf. Although this content analysis could not answer questions about why participants had made their choices of objects, it did provide a mute testimony to what students appeared to think was important in their relationships with the school as an institution and with the people with whom they worked in it (part of their brief for taking photographs as a visual record of their experiences of school).

It gave us an indication of what aspects of schooling the thirty six students thought were more or less important in their school lives, something we followed up in more detail with seventeen of them through interviews based on their scrapbooks (see below).

Table 1: Extract from the content analysis of student photographs in the scrapbooks

Main object of photograph	Boys (23) Photos (234)	Girls (13) Photos (149)	'Engaged' (17) Photos (160)	'Disaffected'(16) Photos (208)
Male peers	23	16	6	26
Female peers	9	30	8	28
Males (N)	32	23	7	36
Females (N)	12	53	14	44
Teachers	11	14	14	9
Other staff	5	4	4	4
Classrooms	39	4	8	25
Teaching Block	35	15	23	26
Year base	0	3	3	0

Having gained access to the school, late in the Autumn term, after interviewing senior staff and collecting school policy documents on inclusion and discipline, the academic researchers trained the selected students in a series of lessons to carry out visual research ethically, including constructing a story board using photographs to show themselves in school and to think about their identities in school. During one of the lessons just before Christmas they took photographs round the school showing their relationship in it and with it. These tasks were closely related to elements of the National Curriculum in English and Citizenship which these students had to study. The students were trained in the ethics of visual methods since taking any pictures around a school could involve, intentionally or unintentionally, capturing images of people. The actions of students as researchers using photography is potentially ethically problematic (Allan and Cullen, 2008) and raises questions about what documents might be ethically used and what might constitute informed consent amongst young people.

The scrapbooks (storyboards) were constructed during three lessons in January 2008, supervised by the teachers and academic researchers, and became the property of the students as they were told when they took the photographs for them. They were used as the basis of reflexive interviews with seventeen students drawn from across the four classes (including the SLN group) with the research team in the Spring 2008 and with three of the teachers who taught the students in the Summer 2008. Prosser (2009) describes this as photo-elicitation. As Pink (2001) points out, what is often conveyed in images is not the objects that are seen but the meanings they represent. These can only be gleaned by talking with the creators of the images about them and their intentions when constructing them.

These reflexive interviews were intended to encourage participants to explain their taken for granted intentions and ideas (James and Busher, 2006) rather than be introspective stimulated recall interviews to explore participants inner cognitive processes (Lyle, 2003). They aimed to explore participants' values and perspectives when thinking about their relationships with other people in school and with the school as institution, similar in manner to the way in which James and Busher (2009) used email-based interviews to explore the views of professional workers about their experiences in different academic work settings. It assumes that research cannot be value free, i.e. is inevitably subjective (Greenbank, 2003), so it becomes important to understand the values carried by participants when trying to make sense of their understandings of situations if the outcomes of research are to be credible (James and Busher, 2009).

A final data collection phase of the project also used the student photographs to construct group posters in the July 2008 to try to interrogate students' group views to see if these differed noticeably from students' individual perspectives. Focus groups and group interviews are often used to investigate group perspectives on social situations and how these differ from individual perspectives on the same situations (Flick, 2009). Visual methods can be used in a similar manner. Patience (2007) used a participatory group video to allow a group of low-achievers in a Secondary school to gain self-esteem in their academic capacity. At this time, too, the English and Citizenship teachers, in whose classes we worked, asked to carry out a similar process to that of the students. After taking their photographs of significant sites and other people for them in the school, teachers were interviewed in the same manner as the students.

The lived experience of the research was more fraught than this apparently smooth narrative suggests, in part due to the pressures of performativity that invaded the school, and is discussed below. However, anecdotal evidence from teachers and students suggests the students welcomed this study and saw themselves benefitting from it. This and the development of knowledge related to the formal curriculum of the school helped to give benefit to the students taking part in the research as Pink (2001) suggested research should do to be ethical.

Findings

The findings from this study help to develop an understanding of how discourses of performativity enshrined in English central government education policy 2007-2008 affected the cultures of schools and classrooms and the practices of individual teachers and students, whether or not the practices were directly linked to public examinations or the subject curriculum. The discourses of performativity appear to have permeated every aspect of school life and the relationships of participants in it through influencing the culture of the school and the values enshrined in it because of the importance ascribed to those discourses by key players in the school. Firstly, this section investigates teachers' and students' perspectives of how national and local policy contexts pervaded their learning opportunities in school. Then it considers how these discourses played out in the internal policy processes of the school and how teachers and students responded to and coped with them to try to maintain their own agenda. The initials after quotations indicate which participants, staff or student, produced which perspective, but the initials are fictitious.

The impact of performative discourses on participants in a school
Central government policy
Teachers thought education policy discourses strongly shaped their work and constrained their relationships with students (pupils).

> It's the idea of you have to get this exam. Pressure it put on the [students] and they switch off. (Staff PH)

National Curriculum structures were transmitted through its examination processes, the Standard Assessment Tests (SATs) which students had to take and pass at certain levels in particular Core subjects at the end of Key Stage Two (when they were 11 years old) and Key Stage Three (when they were 14 years old), and the school leaving examinations (GCSEs) which all students were required to take when they were about 16 years old.

> Part of the way that the school is judged is by the percentage of kids getting three A to A* [at] GCSE. We were appallingly low at this. (Staff CS)

Schools were expected to gain certain percentages of children passing examinations (GCSE) or achieving particular attainment levels in the SATs, as well as many other targets, if they were to be deemed effective by OfSTED. The school in this study was not deemed effective.

> The government says 639 or 638 schools are failing. We are on that list. Most teachers in the school think that we are successful but we realise that the standards that we achieved in OfSTED on the national scale, aren't that good. (Staff CS)

The benchmarking of school performance emphasised the importance of the C/D grade boundary in GCSE. This led to teachers making great efforts to get students to pass at grade C, arguably to the detriment of other students, especially those in need of additional support to achieve the best grades they could. This emphasis on achieving particular examination grades appeared to affect relationships between teachers and students and the culture of the school.

> Other teachers are quite strict and they want you to do the work – but I s'pose that's because they want us to get good grades. (Student AR).

Students acknowledged that they had to accommodate to the system if they wanted to achieve their own agenda.

> No matter how much I dislike it, I have to do it [French] for GCSE because you have to have at least one modern foreign language to get in. (Student CA).

School examination results were monitored by the central government system of school inspection, OfSTED, and published in annual National League tables to allow parents to compare the achievements of different schools. To meet some inspection targets related to levels of student exclusion, school discipline policy was moderated for malcontent students:

> Something called persistent defiance which you can permanently exclude for, but we don't and we should. And it's always been, oh OfSTED's coming and we don't want our exclusion rate up. (Staff PH)

If a school failed to meet its inspection targets it could be required to amend its policies by the inspectors. High rates of exclusions were said to affect the popularity of a school and the attractiveness of it to local parents.

Government investment in education focused on targets that it perceived the public thought were important.

> So the government invested masses of money in able and talented [students], via the Excellence in Cities programme. (Staff CS).

This included trying to raise students' aspirations to go to university regardless of their social class or ethnic background.

> We are trying to increase aspiration. I am responsible for 'Aim higher, widening participation' programme'. (Staff CS).

It also included improving the physical environment of a school, as some participants illustrated through their photographs.

> It's a big sports hall because apparently we got the smart choice between sports hall and a swimming pool ... our other two gyms ain't that nice. (Student CP).

> That's the DT block ... it's a Technology College ... And we've got good equipment. (Student MK).

This investment seemed to have improved student performance and the reputation of the school locally.

> The GCSE grades ... were really bad when I came to the school and now they're getting better. (Student MK).

Government policy of increasing parental choice of school for their children was said to increase parents' and students' engagement with schools. However, one student pointed out,

> [I]don't like coming to [school] ... it's not a very nice atmosphere really. It wasn't <u>any</u> of my choices [of school]... that doesn't help at all. (Student CA)

Researchers' activities were also affected by the performative culture of schools. Teachers in the school's English and Citizenship departments wanted to work with the research project because it was related strongly to elements of the National Curriculum in their subjects for Year 9 (Y9) students. However, they perceived two major problems: which Y9 students should take part; Y9 students had to take Standard Assessment Tasks (SATs) at the end of their studies for Key Stage Three of the National Curriculum in late May 2008. SATs results were reflected in the school's performance in National League tables and poor performance would make the school look unattractive to potential parents compared with other local schools.

As teachers feared that selecting a few students in each class would prevent the others from benefiting from the aspects of the project related to the Y9 National Curriculum, teachers asked the researchers to work with whole classes, groups of at least 18, much larger than the project had planned or were easily manageable. As the timetabling of school curriculum to meet National Curriculum targets was very tight, students could not afford to miss any lessons so could not be taken out of lessons for the project. Teachers thought that alternative lunchtime 'meetings' for the project would not attract disaffected Y9 students.

Teachers thought Y9 students needed the period from February to May to revise for their SATs, so requested that the last phase of the research (making group posters) happened in July 2008, nearly six months after students finished constructing their scrapbooks and being interviewed in early February 2008. By then, students and teachers were close to the end of the school year. Students appeared to have lost enthusiasm for the project and they and their teachers tended to see the construction of the posters as an 'end of term' time filling activity.

In Autumn 2008, according to several staff the school's Senior Management Team (SMT) became nervous about how the school's image amongst the local community might be affected by findings from the study reflecting students' views of the school, although SMT welcomed the findings themselves and thought them helpful. Consequently, despite explaining the importance to the trustworthiness of research of getting participants to check researchers' emergent findings, researchers were not allowed to present the project findings to staff and students.

Parents and the local community

The importance of the views of parents and local communities to the school was shown by the efforts made by teachers and senior staff to keep parents involved with their children's progress.

> I mean [parents] get reported to every half term. So six sets of tracking
> plus a parent's evening [each year]. (Staff PH)

This element of school policy reflected long term perspectives on the importance of the relationship between home and school as well as current policy discourses.

> When it was [a] secondary modern ... there have always been students who went to university from our local predominantly historically white council estates. (Staff CS).

However, the changing social mixture of the school's catchment area had made teaching much more challenging.

> With our mixed racial and indigenous population ... possibly the biggest challenge for most of the white students ... is no aspiration or low education generally. For the other students [it] is adapting to life in a new city, with different conventions, rules and different possibilities. (Staff CS)

Consequently some senior staff and teachers welcomed government investment in widening aspiration programmes, while students welcomed any investment that improved how the school was perceived by local people.

> I want to make it a better school for other people com[ing] up in Year 7, who never wanted to come to the school ... getting a good mark in my GCSEs, making the teachers look good, making the school look good. (Student MK)

Several students were concerned about the image of their school locally, and used photographs to illustrate this.

> It feels quite safe – no-one's going to get in and no-one's going to get out, but ... it don't look nice. All you see is a load of spikes and poles ... It's more like a prison than a school." (Student CP)

Some resented how the actions of other students damaged the school's image. One pointed out "a graffitied door ... which is not really good." (Student MR). While another acknowledged, "there's quite a lot of rubbish everywhere – and there's bins in every Year Base but people just can't be bothered to use them. (Student SY).

Adapting to performative discourses
Internal policy process:
The internal policy processes of the school reflected and enacted national and local performative discourses. The head teacher altered the school hierarchy, creating "a non-teaching post ... to work with C/D borderlines and people who aren't in Year 10 and 11." (Staff PH). This concern led to a constant scrutiny

of students' performance to identify which ones needed special support to help them achieve what examination grades they could.

> We identify the [students] ... if they have not done SATS/Teacher assessments ... as soon as they arrive we do reading/spelling tests. (Staff JT).

The curriculum became a disciplinary regime for teachers and students as staff sought to gain the examination grades the school needed to maintain its standing in the League Tables.

> How can you get kids to sit down for an hour. What gives us the right? And then to say ... put your hand up, bubble bubble, but [actually] repress. (Staff PH).

It also led to increasing pressure on teachers to adapt their pedagogy to suit the learning needs of all students to help them achieve better examination results by, "doing a lot of special needs workshops this year. Trying to get the [teachers to] ... differentiate the work [more]." (Staff JT). Although this might be interpreted as government policies helping to improve teachers' practices, some teachers thought it was merely re-inventing people-centred modes of teaching and learning.

> But we're just re-inventing. ... Personalised Learning, what was it called, a long time ago when I did my PGCE, it was called MIXED ABILITY [teaching]. (Staff PH).

The apparatus of the 'state'
Senior staff organised a system designed to create productive docile bodies that would allow the school to meet its performativity targets.

> If he's [Vice-Principal] strict, then the kids will all be scared of him and they will do what he asked them to do. (Student AH).

One aspect of this was depriving students of control of access to knowledge without any explanation.

> They've just shut off Google, because there were things last year ... which is quite annoying. We haven't really been told [why]. (Student CA).

Another aspect was limiting students' control of their bodies, e.g. by preventing girls, "wearing more jewellery and pushing the uniform. [Disaffected girls] are more likely to be more physical, just walking down the corridor ... linking arms or pushing" (Staff PH), and sometimes threatening embarrassment through normal bodily functions.

> Toilets ... are always locked, so if you really need to go, then you have to [like] walk all the way over to a place where you can get the key to a toilet. (Student SY).

School and curriculum activities were tightly timetabled, too, depriving students and teachers of control of time and space. This system was implemented through a surveillance regime to monitor the actions of students and staff. One aspect was that of active observation.

> Part of our Head's attempt to tighten things up ... he is waging a war on uniform ... when students come in between 8:15 and 8:45 the doorways are monitored to check that they are coming in appropriately [dressed] but quite a lot of students circumvent that by coming in late, so every day between 8:45 and 9:45 a member of senior staff sits there. (Staff CS).

This included staff patrolling corridors and playing fields during lessons and break times.

> I do one [break duty] down in the hall, and one up on the field, which is basically telling all the smokers to go further away ...If I can see who they are I will report them. (Staff PH).

A second aspect, to some students' annoyance, was the use of CCTV.

> I didn't even know we had it until we went into the staffroom ... we could be talking about ... something private and stuff! (Student NR).

A third aspect, as one student recorded in a photograph, was a teacher carrying, "a walkie-talkie and a bunch of keys. I think she was trying to sort out a problem ... someone might have run away ... from a lesson or something like that." (Student SY). The school had a recognised punishment regime to enforce the system. This included that of legitimated verbal force.

Most of the [teachers] just shout and they're mean ... don't like the way they treat you and the way that they teach the class. (Student CT).

Some students perceived this practice as one of intimidation because, "everybody's [like] scared of him 'cos if they go to see him they know they're going to get yelled at really badly" (Student CT) and thought it humiliated them.

There was a scale of penalties for different misdemeanours that was recognised by staff and students.

By stage three [students] are sent outside [classrooms] to cool down for a few minutes and ... they can then be removed to a stage four or a stage five. (Staff ER).

One of my friends, she went in to Stage 5 – she was wearing jeans. (Student SP).

He was put on report for bullying ... you either get a green, orange or red report and greens [when] you haven't done something serious, but it can be hurtful. (Student MR).

If I don't get [my homework] in I get detention. I don't really like getting detentions. (Student RI).

When students misbehaved seriously parents were brought in and, "the bill goes home and [students] have day seclusion or are suspended for a while." (Staff JT).

Some students acknowledged the legitimacy of this 'state' apparatus, particularly welcoming it when it gave them support – 'Everyone has a named teacher, or a tutor ... if there's anything you want to talk about, they'll ask you to see if you're alright' – or kept them out of trouble – '[in] our [subject] area where we hang around ... staff are there to keep an eye on you ... just in case something does happen' (Student AR) – or helped them to learn successfully. However, other students not seem to be unduly deterred by the system punishment regime. 'But if you get caught [smoking] more than twice ... you get some letters sent home ... they show you some video on smoking' (Student JD). Staff, too, recognised the surveillance regime was not entirely effective, but offered no alternative. 'A smashed window! We have cameras in all the rooms, so I don't know how...'

Some staff recognised that they could work with students to sustain the school system, especially when it focused on intra-student relationships.

The anti-bullying policy ... We deliberately went to kids with that. And they in fact designed [it]. (Staff ER).

Teachers' views of the other: perceptions of students

Teachers were very aware of the need to ensure that students performed as well as possible in public examinations, including SATs: "You know it's an exam factory and you must get them through exams." (Staff ER). Consequently, they tended to categorise students in terms of whether or not they were willing to collude with teachers in achieving the performative objectives of the school. Collaborative students, they thought displayed certain behaviours: "...won't have the jewellery. ... are much less likely to be sitting on the corridor." (Staff PH). Some teachers translated the performative discourses of government into a perception of students as consumers of education:

> I see our students really as the customers ... [who] tell the management or the teachers things that they would like, things that they think could be improved, things that they're happy with. (Staff ER)

Other teachers perceived students as victims of their circumstances.

> We have a lot of naughty children. [Their] behaviour comes from the fact that they can't access much and frustration and things like that. (Staff JT). I think its home expectations possibly. (Staff PH).

In this view, students' anti-social behaviour was mere criminality rather than any deeper sense of alienation. Staff needed to get, "students to respect [the environment] a lot more. Stop wrecking the display boards" (Staff ER), perhaps in part by taking responsibility for it. "We tried painting the [toilets] as part of the student council." (Staff ER).

However, some teachers thought students' behaviour reflected the way in which they were treated by staff and how the broader regime of the school disempowered them from taking many decisions about their own lives:

> There are teachers in this school who will pick on jewellery 'right take that off'... And you see some teachers take pupils outside to shout at them for five minutes just because it's easier to do that than engage with the rest of the class. (Staff PH).

Students' perspectives of teachers

Students' perspectives of teachers were ambivalent. Although they recognised the hierarchical nature of schooling through which teachers legitimately exercised control of the school and of students' work, they generally resented the unfair way in which control was implemented.

> I don't like DT. The teacher's a bit moody ... one day she'll be alright with me but [then] be a bit sarcastic and stuff like that sometimes. (Student AK).

They also disliked perceived incompetence by teachers, including not being able to control a class, even when sometimes teachers were absent from lessons because of their other, often pastoral, duties.

> [The teacher] wasn't around a lot in the DT class and I used to think, "Why is she never there?" and, you know, we used to just do random things in our lessons and we didn't really learn anything. We just went around doing stuff. (Student AH).

Alongside this, students developed an utopian view of the 'good' teacher who could accurately interpret student behaviour – "your teachers know ... if [pupils] are playing games and not do[ing] their work" (Student AH) – and helped students learn successfully – "he helped me a lot to get ... a level 7 in my mock SATs" (Student AH). Such teachers developed respectful and caring relationships with their students. "There's always a nice atmosphere when you go into that room ... she's always really happy and really nice about things and you" (Student CT). They were trusted to work in a collaborative but focused way and "sit with your friends and get on with your work, and they're not always telling you off and [like] give you detention for no reason" (Student SY).

Conclusion: What was the impact of performative policies on the experiences of education and implications for educational futures and local cultures?

The findings from this study show how students and teachers in this school perceived the impact of national and local discourses on education. Staff and students recognised that they were disciplined by these discourses, and that this discipline was inscribed on their bodies (Foucault, 1977, Paechter, 2007) through them being expected to act in certain ways to meet the performative norms embedded in government education policies. Not only were teachers able clearly to indicate how particular national discourses and local habitus (Bourdieu, 1986) led to particular institutional policies and practices, but students recognised some of these, too (impact of National Curriculum on teachers' behaviour, impact of technology college policy on resources to which they had access, concern about local community perceptions of school). Consequently students did not blame teachers for acting as agents of school policies and dominant discourses. Indeed they acknowledged that teachers' work, when carried out successfully, helped them to meet their own agenda of attaining particular careers.

The processes of surveillance (Foucault, 1977) that the adults in the school used to keep control of the students is clearly visible – the use of CCTV, of patrolling teachers with walkie-talkies – as well as the conventional processes of teachers being on patrol at break and lunch times and being with classes during lessons, although some students suggested that this was not always the case when a teacher was drawn into taking disciplinary action against students in other classes on behalf of teacher colleagues. There is also evidence of students being drawn into the complicity of self-surveillance through helping teachers to develop an anti-bullying policy in school and through preferring to be supervised indirectly by teachers at lunch times to avoid being the butt of other students' aggression. In part this seemed to be an attempt to meet their own agenda (Busher, 2006) as much as them accepting dominant social perspectives on the purposes of schooling. Other students recognised that, however alienated they felt by school system, they had to comply for their own benefit – gaining the GCSEs they needed for preferred careers.

Students and teachers showed clear awareness of the punishment regime of the school, how it was implemented and what was the tariff of penalties for particular actions and how that affected how they might control themselves. This, students and teachers thought, was clearly linked to the performative norms faced by students and teachers. Whilst some students did their best to act in ways to avoid punishments, such as detentions that they did not like, others seemed to regard the risk of being punished as something worth chancing in order to act in particular ways with their peers (smoking). However, some students also showed resentment of some punishments – teachers shouting at them, in particular – which impinged on their person, creating docile bodies (Foucault , 1977). Some teachers also expressed concern at the violence that was shown to students by some of their colleagues, particularly over aspects of personal adornment which challenged dominant norms of how children in school should dress.

The impact of performative discourses seem to support the view that education is both a site and a conduit for struggles (Foucault, 1976; Hall and Noyes, 2009) through which teachers and students explore the tensions of being and becoming (Giddens, 1991; Kearney, 2003). There seemed to be considerable stress amongst the teachers and conflict between teachers and students as a result of performative discourses, as Hall and Noyes (2009) noted. Teachers felt they had to do everything possible to help students to attain the best academic grades they could, especially above the C/D GCSE border line. The consequences for not doing so threatened the standing of the school with parents and, potentially, ultimately their jobs, but also their sense of professional pride in what it meant to be a teacher. The students were aware of the pressures on the teachers and on themselves to attain these grades, but resented the emphasis on control rather than collaboration that many teachers seemed to prefer to try to achieve this.

The study supports the view of Riley and Rustique-Forrester (2002) that students are experienced observers of teachers, teaching and schools. If teachers had a stereotypic view of what was the 'good' student – docile, enthusiastic, hardworking, quiet – which did not match what they regularly experienced in the classroom, students, too, had a view of the 'good' teacher who was friendly and supportive and helped them achieve good results through carrying out interesting work in a well-organised manner in collaboration with their colleagues. They discriminated clearly between the teachers they liked and those whom they liked less, and articulated what separated the former from the latter. Had the teachers listened more carefully to the students' views on schooling and lessons, as Rudduck (2004), Demetriou and Wilson (2010), McIntyre *et. al.* (2005) suggested, they might have learnt a lot about constructing successful lessons with collaborative cultures that minimised dissonance and maximized performance.

The performative policies in education of central government in England in the noughties had a considerable cost socially. The need which teachers perceived for tighter control of students in order to achieve the performative targets they faced led to students with jaundiced perspectives of schooling and teachers, teachers who were seriously stressed because of the demands of performativity (two of those involved in this study left the school in 2008), a sense of loss of empowerment by teachers, and a discouragement of collaborative approaches to work. Students learnt to be part of a production process in which they themselves were produced and controlled, rather than being encouraged to be creative collaborative citizens and producers.

Correspondence: Hugh Busher, School of Education, University of Leicester, 21 University Road, Leicester, LE1 7RF, UK, email: hugh.busher@le.ac.uk

Acknowledgement
The 'Voices' project, 2007-09, on students and teachers understandings of

schooling, was funded by the British Academy, Award Number: LRG-45482 The researchers were:

Dr Hilary Cremin, University of Cambridge (hc331@cam.ac.uk)

Dr Hugh Busher, University of Leicester (hugh.busher@le.ac.uk)

Concluding Research Assistant: Dr. Carolynne Mason, University of Cambridge (cljm2@cam.ac.uk)

Performance in teacher education and research – a double whammy for teacher educators?

Ian Menter[a], Moira Hulme[b] and Pauline Sangster[c]

Introduction

Teacher educators in universities across the world work in constantly changing contexts. The performativity agenda that has been experienced throughout most sectors of the economy, including the public services, developed in particularly interesting ways in teacher education. This chapter looks at two relatively distinctive strands in these developments as they have affected university-based teacher educators in the UK. We examine and consider the effects of how the introduction of standards in teaching has changed the language and practices of teacher education before then, exploring the effects of the research assessment agenda in university departments of education (UDEs). For many staff these pressures create something of a 'double whammy', and a need for professional reorientation. The second half of the chapter looks in particular at the lived experiences of teacher educators in two 'ancient' Scottish universities to explore how this double whammy impacts on their professional identities.

Thus the overall purpose of the chapter is to explore the combined effects of two major aspects of policy in education on the working lives of teacher educators based in universities. These two aspects are critical in their influence on the professional identities of the staff concerned, even though they may impact on them in different ways, depending on their backgrounds, experience and career aspirations. The chapter begins by examining these two particular manifestations of performativity as policy developments, before moving more directly into the 'real world' of two institutions. By doing this we seek to explore how teacher educators have responded to the changes that have been imposed on them. In the concluding section we offer some reflections on the implications of these insights and some suggestions about how – collectively – teacher educators might seek to regain some greater control of their professional lives.

At the outset it is important to acknowledge that the staff working in UDEs can rarely be seen as a homogenous group either in respect of their backgrounds or in respect of their employment contracts. Typically the full complement of staff includes people who are employed on a temporary basis, sometimes on secondment from school teaching or local authority posts, people who have been

a: University of Oxford; b: University of Glasgow; c: University of Edinburgh appointed recently largely for their research experience or potential and others who may have been working in the higher education sector for a considerable time, as well as people who have been recruited directly from school teaching in order to bring their current professional experience to bear in the training of teachers. In Becher and Trowler's (2001) terms, we have not so much a single 'academic tribe', but a number of 'sub-tribes' (Menter, 2011). Members of each sub-tribe may well experience a different mix of pressures of the kind referred to above.

UDEs have a fairly difficult history in higher education and there have been contrary trends in different times and places over more than a hundred years (Robinson, 2004; Furlong and Smith, 1996). Even within the contemporary UK we can see opposite tendencies in England and Scotland as demonstrated by the near-exclusion of universities from the White Paper *The Importance of Teaching* (DfE, 2010) at the same time as the Donaldson Report, *Teaching Scotland's Future* (Donaldson, 2011) puts universities at the very heart of teacher development. The uneasy positioning of UDEs committed to professional education and to educational research has also been noted in North America (Labaree, 2004; Lagemann, 2000). The valorisation of 'the practical' and instrumental within Anglo-American policy discourse on teacher training stands in contrast to the 'Bildung' tradition in Germany and the Nordic countries (Ulvik and Smith, 2011:517), and this exacerbates tensions for UK teacher educators straddling the dual worlds of the school and the academy.

To use Bourdieu's term, the habitus occupied by teacher educators is a complex and somewhat fractured one, overlapping as it does the two professional worlds of schools and of universities. The cultural and social capital that individual teachers may have developed within the school system (Allan *et.al.*, 2009) may seem to reduce in its value quite sharply when they move into higher education where the scholarship of teaching remains 'an emerging concept' (Nicholls, 2005:55). The contentious case of 'professional education' for new university teachers – including teacher educators – through certificated programmes aptly illustrates the separation of research and teaching roles and identities in universities and the different value attached to different areas of academic work (McLean, 2006). The language of credentialism, standards and competencies, that is a now feature of workforce development for the school and college sectors, does not readily lend itself to critical deliberation in the context of university pedagogy. The rise of audit regimes and entrepreneurial activity in schools and universities are parallel developments that present significant challenges for university-based teacher educators and their managers. As 'a particular type of academic' (Murray and Male, 2005:136), teacher educators work within 'multiple communities' and 'multiple workplaces' (Harrison and McKeon, 2008:166). Goodlad's (1994) description of 'hybrid educators' is useful in describing the complexity of roles that are always 'on location' within evolving partnerships and subject to the 'performative turn' in both fields.

Teacher education policy

The steady encroachment of performance management into education, sometimes described as performativity (Gleeson and Husbands, 2001), sometimes as (new) managerialism (Gewirtz, 2002), has been documented and explored by a number of scholars. Its components typically include performance pay, incentivisation, appraisal or performance review and new 'advanced' teaching grades. Such moves are consistent with the development of a high accountability, low trust culture. As Olssen *et.al.* put it:

> The specification of objectives, performance reviews and other management techniques may encourage teachers to behave in ways that are antithetical to certain fundamental educational values such as altruism, intellectual independence and imagination. Moreover, we argue that the restoration of a culture of trust and professional accountability within all educational institutions is a necessary prerequisite for the maintenance of a robust and prosperous democratic society (Olssen *et.al.*, 2004:197)

Such developments have required a scheme of measurement in order that teachers may be judged in a transparent and consistent way. Such schemes have usually been cast in the shape of teaching standards or competences. Early central intervention in teacher preparation in England and Wales came with Circular 3/84 (DES, 1984), further strengthened by Circular 24/89 (DES, 1989) which established for the first time a national Council for the Accreditation of Teacher Education (CATE). These circulars also required Teacher Education Institutions (TEIs) to design and deliver programmes 'in close working partnership with schools' (DES, 1984). The realisation of this policy goal was slow and until the early 1990s universities remained the 'dominant' partner (Furlong *et.al.*, 1996:36), prompting further government intervention. Circular 9/92 (DfE, 1992) and Circular 14/93 (DfE, 1993) introduced competence-based teacher education for the primary and secondary phases and stipulated the need for 'joint' contractual partnerships with schools. Compliance was monitored through inspection of Initial Teacher Training by the Office for Standards in Education (OfSTED). The creation of the Teacher Training Agency in 1994 (subsequently renamed the Training and Development Agency for schools), and the disbanding of CATE, led to the development of a framework of national standards for Qualified Teacher Status (QTS) between 1994 and 1998.

There was considerable debate on this at the time, with some commentators arguing that it was not possible to encapsulate the complex nature of teaching in a list of observable behaviours and traits and others arguing that such an approach would diminish creativity in teaching. The imposition of the Standards and curricula for Initial Teacher Training (ITT) (subsequently abandoned in 2002 and replaced with the *Qualifying to Teach* framework, (TTA, 2004)) was regarded by many as a form of political over-regulation. The standards were seen as a means of standardising and regulating practice through closer monitoring of performance through bureaucratic (rather than professional) control. Critics suggested that the specificity of the standards (and the subsequent development in England of standardised pedagogies associated with the national literacy and numeracy strategies) represented 'pedagogical deskilling' (Robertson, 1996), a form of 'practical fundamentalism' (Goodson, 2003; Reynolds, 1999).

Lawn (1996:71) argued that the reforms of the 1990s were responsible for 'reducing training to subjects, substituting school teaching apprenticeships for pedagogical and educational studies'. Nevertheless, competences were introduced into ITT and were subsequently developed into a series of standards that had to be met in order for trainees to achieve Qualified Teacher Status (Mahony and Hextall, 2000).

Similar developments took place in Scotland and were also met with degrees of scepticism and opposition (Stronach *et.al.*, 1994). In Scotland however, there was an attempt to combine the definition of professional competences with the development of the 'subject benchmark' for Education which were being developed by the Quality Assurance Agency (QAA) as part of the HE sector-wide development. That development itself could also be seen as another element in the wider technicisation of HE. The Scottish approach was to establish a working party comprising key stakeholders. The working party developed proposals compatible with the wider quality assurance framework that was being developed for the full range of higher education.

In contrast to the direction of travel in England, the Scottish document stressed the intellectual grasp and theoretical understandings that teachers were expected to demonstrate. ITE courses should 'provide opportunities for students to engage with and draw on educational theory, research, policy and practice; [and] promote a range of qualities in students, including intellectual independence and critical engagement with evidence'. Furthermore, students should be encouraged to 'engage with fundamental questions concerning the aims and values of education' (QAA, 2000:5) (see Menter *et.al.*, 2006).

Reactions to the introduction of standards among teacher educators did vary and a comparative study of policy and practice in England and Scotland found some resistance from university-based teacher educators in both countries (Menter *et.al.*, 2006). A lecturer in an English university college acknowledged that:

> We work within particular constraints. Clearly there are certain things even under Qualifying to Teach that have to be in the course in order for us to reach the standards … These are a given in a sense. (Menter *et.al.*, 2006: 50)

And in England, the 'policing' of this compliance was being undertaken through the OfSTED inspection process:

> Each institution is responsible for its future and we're not going to change our procedures if we think that's going to be detrimental to our OfSTED outcome. You can see the dilemma, can't you? (ibid., 51).

In Scotland, although there was also resistance to such developments (as noted above), there were those who saw the introduction of the Standard for Initial Teacher Education as a positive step. This was perhaps because of the greater flexibility and the less stringent surveillance and control that operated north of the border:

> I think both the academic things has been strengthened and that has been helped by the new professional profile for ITE in Scotland, with a triangle of professional knowledge and understanding and professional skills and values, and the values sit with traditional study in universities. Because it is a professional course we have these three elements and I think that gives strength to the academic [aspect] and what it is to be integrated, and I think it is a very good way forward. (ibid., 46-47)

So, by the first decade of the 21stcentury, with similar developments in Northern Ireland and Wales (Hulme and Menter, 2008), it became the case that teacher education and training practices across the UK were dominated by standards schema. In Scotland there are four published standards: the Standard for Initial Teacher Education; Standard for Full Registration (induction); Standard for Chartered Teacher (for experienced and accomplished teachers); and the Standard for Headship. In England, as we write, the standards (revised in 2007) have again been under review. The recently-appointed Secretary of State for

Education, Michael Gove, found that what existed was over-complex. Launching the review of Teachers' Standards, the Department of Education insisted that '[i]nstead of focusing on the essential skills of great teaching, the current standards are a vague list of woolly aspirations' (Department of Education press notice, 11 March 2011). to the publication of the first report of the review group, Michael Gove argued that '[t]he old standards placed a premium on bland statements and platitudes over practical use for teachers' (Department of Education press notice, 14 July 2011). In accepting the recommendations of the review, Gove suggests that core Standards to be implemented from 2012 'set clear expectations about the skills that every teacher in our schools should demonstrate ... They will make a significant improvement to teaching by ensuring teachers can focus on the skills that matter most' (ibid.).

In one sense then England is moving to an even more reductionist, apparently simple definition of teaching, although there is a view among some teacher educators within the academy that such a minimalist approach provides an opportunity to develop a much more open and extended approach. The interpretation of the revised Standards, within increased provision for employment-based and school-based teacher education, that is also signalled in the White Paper, is less certain. Notwithstanding, it can certainly now be suggested that such has been the effect of the standardisation on teacher education that a Foucauldian 'Panopticon' approach has been put in place, initially through the heavy surveillance of OfSTED inspections (in England) and more recently through more effective self-surveillance by teacher educators. Teacher education across the UK, but especially in England, has been subject to a relentless series of increasingly self-managed technologies of control. What we are suggesting here is that the regulatory processes have been increasingly embedded within the processes of teacher education and the exercise of power and control has been widely incorporated into the thinking and practices of university-based teacher educators themselves. This is an excellent example of the application of 'governmentality' (Dean, 1999), that is the intersection of 'practices of government' with 'practices of the self.'

It is difficult for teacher educators to work against the grain of the competencies discourse (Ellis *et.al.*, 2011b). Standards are productive as well as evaluative, providing parameters for officially endorsed action or ways of being a 'good teacher' (Moore, 2004). It is in this productive work that they bring about their performativity. Roberts *et.al.*, (2006) have explored the ways in which demonstrating achievement of 'the standards' involves careful acts of 'fabrication' (Ball, 2001). Although, as McNally (2006) and others have argued, it is the emotional and relational rather than competence-related dimensions of professional learning that present the greatest challenge in the early experiences of teaching, it is the performative dimensions that strategic learners attend to as they work with mentors to achieve performances that 'meet the standards' – carefully assembling together presentations of the 'performing' and 'conforming' teacher. Clandinin and Connolly (1995) have described the 'secret', 'sacred' and 'cover' stories that teachers tell as they move across the different spaces on the professional knowledge landscape. The public choices between teaching personae that are available in an audit culture invoke the production of performative selves (Ball, 2003; McNamara and Brown, 2005). The challenging tasks of teacher education in problematising practice, cultivating an 'inquiry stance' and promoting (socially) critical reflection are all the more difficult within performance cultures that value a different model of professionalism. Enhancing professional learning and assessing competence is open to multi-form responses. Self-options encompass creative, proactive and optimistic 'activism' (Sachs, 2003) – expressed for example in positive readings of the diminution of the teaching Standards in England. However, arguably Casey's (1995:163) depiction of the 'colluded', 'defensive' and 'capitulated self' also applies when reflecting on responses to the 'inventorial' (Moore, 1996:204) turn in teacher education over the last two decades.

Research assessment

Over the past twenty years the significance of research assessment in the UK has steadily increased. There may only be an assessment exercise every 5-8 years but the influence of the process is now more or less continuous. Impact has differed in different institutions, but the way in which the 2008 Research Assessment Exercise (RAE) was structured did mean that most university Departments of Education across the UK made a submission and many more subsequently received research income (the so-called 'QR' element of funding) than had previously been the case, even if for some it was on a very small scale (Gilroy and McNamara, 2009).

UDE staff recruitment practices did change significantly in many institutions over this period. Where there had been an emphasis during the 1980s and 1990s on 'recent and relevant experience' of teaching in schools, more posts were advertised during the first decade of the new century with criteria which focused on research experience or achievement and, even where professional experience was still prioritised, many posts made reference to 'research potential' in their criteria (Ellis *et.al.*, 2011a, 2011b; Menter, 2011). For those people who were research active and productive, the RAE was not necessarily a negative experience. However, in a study of the impacts of RAE 2008 Oancea (2010:7) found that a number of:

...other staff (including some who had been submitted as research active to RAE 2008) reported a sense of struggling to work and develop in what they described as a negative work climate, and of being hindered in their engagement, at a good level of quality, in other academic and academic-related activities, in particular in teaching. They reported negative impacts on their morale and motivation, on the quality, focus and breadth of their research publications, and more generally on their career development opportunities...

Many people employed in Education Departments are active researchers and many seek to become active. However, there are also staff, including some who may have been working in teacher education for a number of years, whose professional identity is much more tied up with the commitment to 'excellent teaching practice'. That is, there are many people working in UDEs whose professional *raison d'être* is to pass on their professional expertise to pre-service and in-service teachers. For such people, the expectation and/or requirement that they should become research active is a threat and a challenge they find unwelcome. In several institutions, including some 'research-intensive' universities, a way of responding to this has been to create two different kinds of academic contract: one is a teaching-only contract, the other a research and teaching contract.

In the 'new' universities, which tend to have much less of a research tradition, but where most of the staff have spent the majority of their time teaching, the pressures from the research agenda may be experienced even more intensely. This is certainly what Sikes (2006) found in her case study of one such institution:

> Whilst there were many different cultures within the School of Education at New University, there was an overall understanding that everyone shared. This was to the effect that the demands made upon them were conflicting, excessive and were, in large part, the consequence of the push for New University to compete with 'traditional' universities. (Sikes, 2006: 566)

Many of these new universities have large Faculties of Education and so the 'double whammy' in those contexts may well affect large numbers of people.

Given the dual pressures on staff to teach and to research it is not surprising that one of the responses in many UDEs has been to encourage staff to research in their own field of practice, that is teacher education and/or their own subject or other specialism. There has therefore been a rapid expansion of teacher education research in the UK over recent years. However, much of this has been small-scale and short-term (Menter *et.al.*, 2010) and the most recent RAE panel reported some disappointment that there was little evidence of improved quality in teacher education research (HEFCE, 2008).

Identities in conflict – managing, performing and researching teacher education

The following section draws on a pilot study of strategies being used to promote research engagement among teacher educators in two research-led universities in Scotland (2009-2010). The study involved semi-structured interviews with a purposive sample of twelve 'early career stage' researchers with teacher education roles (nine female and three male) and seven senior managers (three female and four male) with responsibility for the strategic development of research capacity among ITE staff (for details see Hulme and Sangster, in press). All of the early career stage participants were employed on permanent contracts; research active with a developing record of publications; but, had not yet acted as principal investigator on an externally-funded research council project. Previous research has focused on the challenges of building research capacity in UDEs in new (post-1992) universities. However, few studies have addressed the particular challenges facing teacher educators employed by research intensive universities. On the one hand, there are clear advantages in entering UDEs where research is esteemed and supported; on the other, as Menter (2011) has noted, teacher education comprises 'sub-tribes', indeed 'hierarchies' of academic workers (Ellis, 2011a:25). Navigating this terrain as an early career researcher is challenging, particularly in the current climate where service to the profession and the academy can appear to be in constant tension. The effects of UK research quality audits and the desire to climb global university rankings, combined with uncertainty around the outcome of reviews of national systems of teacher education and the likelihood of a lengthy period of challenging economic circumstances, create new challenges for university-based teacher education.

Here we examine how these challenges play out in the day-to-day experiences of teacher educators as reported by our sample. Consideration is given to how contradictory tendencies are negotiated and the likely consequences of current trajectories. An obvious implication of the merger of Colleges of Education with universities in Scotland in the 1990s was that research should feature in the future work of teacher educators. Universitisation was a long-held ambition of the Educational Institute of Scotland, the largest teachers' union, supported by the General Teaching Council of Scotland which was established in 1965. Popular support for the development of research-led teaching and a stronger intellectual basis for teacher education were counter-balanced against the demands of participation in the Research Assessment Exercise, albeit within negotiated targets. Senior managers contended with the dynamics of institutional mergers and a significant cultural shift in expectations.

> The teaching profession needs to have high intellectual aspirations and is better therefore placed in the university sector where it is surrounded by and imbued with research activity. That is better for teaching and the better for the quality of education. (Senior manager)

> The merger took place when the university was itself looking to its research credibility...We had to turn scholarship into research. In the merger discussions in the Senate that was an issue that arose on more than one occasion. Would the taking on of the College be a drain on the resources, and be an embarrassment in terms of the Research Assessment Exercise? (Senior manager)

Aspirations to build research capacity among the full contingent of education workers in the new Faculties were rocked by sometimes rapid fluctuations in student numbers. One senior manager reported that during periods of expansion 'some colleagues who maybe don't feel so comfortable with a research or enquiry agenda have been fully stretched in order to deal with the teaching of the ITE students'. The cover system of 'please takes' which is widely used in Scottish secondary schools, was introduced in one institution, supported by digital surveillance of staff diaries. Demands to meet teaching commitments with an expanding role allowed the continuation of established college practices and ways of working within university structures. One strategy to address role ambiguity (and to make it possible to cope with these tensions) was the creation of 'university teacher' posts, followed by 'senior university teacher' posts to provide opportunities for career progression. With hindsight, the formal bifurcation of career pathways and priorities, which was intended to provide equity and incentives, was not wholly supported by our interviewees as teacher education confronts new challenges.

> You could get a personal chair on the strength of your research no matter how mediocre a teacher you were...It ought not to be a continuing slog against those who say research gets all the prizes...My own view is that now, as I reflect on these things, there has been a disassociation between teaching and research. It has been reinforced in the university. The teaching function – engaging with learners and classrooms – has become

disassociated from research and enquiry in education. (Senior manager)
Rather than fetishising posts like university teacher because even the noun
has a kind of resonance with something that schools would recognise, we
ought to have been capitalising on the growing appetite for research-led
practice in schools themselves... Pragmatically we may see the end of the
school visit or the traditional teaching practice. There is everything to
play for in terms of the continuing link between higher education and the
development of teachers. (Senior manager)

Former college staff who participated in interviews expressed a strong
service ethos and consistently prioritised ubiquitous student needs above
commitment to developing a research profile. Teacher educators and senior
managers agreed that in the early stages post-merger, research development
was characterised by 'a fairly *laissez-faire* approach' that had not moved 'rapidly
enough' (Senior Manager). Although programme documentation indicated
that research and scholarship underpinned all degree programmes, engagement
with (consumption) was not, on the whole, matched by active engagement *in*
research (knowledge production). Lamenting a reported lack of strong central
intervention, early career stage researchers noted that '[y]ou do tend to be left
to your own devices to do it'; and consequently '[i]t's one of the first casualties.'
A developing (individual) research identity was frequently subordinate to a
(collective) commitment to the student body. For some, research continued
to be seen as separate from, rather than integral to, the core tasks of teacher
education.

If we have students coming or we have a class that is our priority. We are
very student orientated. If a student knocks on your door and you are
supposed to be doing your research project or your reading, you will stop
that and deal with that. People do not want to lose that. A lot of people
who have come through being a teacher don't like the fact that a lot of
these elements are disappearing from the courses. (Teacher educator)

I've got to do my teaching first. People have come and paid to be taught.
That's where my first responsibility lies. (Teacher educator)

If you come from teacher education you come with a commitment that
it is the learner who is most important. I put the students first and then
my own research. Whatever happens, I won't disadvantage the students.
(Teacher educator)

Espoused commitments such as these were approached with a degree of benevolent scepticism by some managers. In the view of one manager, teacher educators oppressed themselves with an attachment to outmoded and uneconomic practices – 'the timetable is like a school timetable' – and a nurturing disposition ill-fitted to the needs of the entrepreneurial research-led university. The feminisation of teacher education was identified as a problem that contributed to workload issues: 'In my view, certain of the programmes rely on what I would call maternalistic teaching'.

> There are colleagues whose fundamental overwhelming concern for students goes way beyond the call of duty. All that extra work is wonderful for students. I'm not saying we forget students – we forget students at our peril because they are the bread and butter of our existence – but life is about choices. A lot of our colleagues have elected to go down a route that has implications. You can't consciously make that choice and then complain about the implications. (Senior manager)

There was an initial expectation among some senior staff, as well as among those newly-appointed, that teacher educators appointed to positions in UDEs would embrace opportunities for 'reinvention' and professional growth. These expectations were not always met. It was suggested that in making the transition from a school/college to a university location, 'hybrid educators' (Goodlad, 1994) might navigate successfully the many challenges to research development in heterogeneous workplace cultures. The volume of entrants to the 2008 RAE, staff completion rates for research degrees and productivity in terms of contract research, records the success of many individuals and assembled teams in navigating this new terrain. Despite such achievements, progress was uneven and this was reflected in a 'long tail' in research productivity and enduring divides between teaching-oriented and research-oriented staff. A reported consequence of 'intensification' was disenchantment and retrenchment for some and increased tensions between staff.

> There are two tiers in my department. There's a teaching pathway and a research pathway and there are two sides. If you talk about research sometimes people roll their eyes. (Teacher educator)

> People in the staff room aren't talking about research. They're talking about their teaching and it becomes very like a primary school staffroom mentality. (Teacher educator)

Performing teacher education involves multiple demands: working creatively within the Standards framework, sustaining strong partnership networks, satisfying teacher quality and research accountability regimes. The regulation of teacher education in Scotland involves accountability to the General Teaching Council (which monitors, reviews and accredits university programmes of teacher education) and the Scottish Government and is subject to periodic 'aspect' review by the inspectorate (now a part of 'Education Scotland'). Increasingly, teacher education providers are asked to produce not only auditable records of compliance with regulations but evidence of the impact of their activities on teacher quality and school students' learning. Forms of regulation for teacher education are supplemented by the 'codes of conduct', 'programme specifications' and 'benchmarks' of UK higher education (McLean, 2006). Relations with students are rendered calculable through constructs of quality such as the National Student Survey (for final year undergraduate students). Individual research productivity is monitored through the monthly audit of 'research returns and evidence of esteem' and through participation in a cycle of institutional 'mini-REF' reviews, which may lead in some cases to selected staff being enabled to 'buy themselves' out of teaching in order to complete the writing of a high quality research output.

Professional Development and Review (PDR) processes seek to align personal, professional and institutional objectives through annual target setting. A culture of self-evaluation – operating at organisational, departmental and individual levels – promotes continuous self-improvement monitored through standardised performance indicators. Staff are also subject to a regular self-reporting audit of relative time spent on teaching, research and administration, known as TAS, the Time Allocation Survey. Such is the range of procedures and processes which impinge on the university teacher educator's professional life. Constant 'identity work' is needed to craft a coherent identity simultaneously as an accomplished teacher, teacher educator, academic and emerging researcher. In expressing a commitment to scholarly agency, interviewees told of the personal, emotional and financial costs of over-commitment. They described their frustration at being 'caught between two stools', engaged in the 'constant battle of the research and teaching'.

> At the moment I am drowning. You feel like you've given up every ounce of your life to your job. (Teacher educator)

> I can see the impact on my family. My kids have been home and I never even noticed. (Teacher educator)

I only work part time and that gives me a bit more time to do the research that I want to do, although it is in my own time. I just don't know how I could do that if I was working full time. (Teacher educator)

Interviewees described the micro-politics involved in working across diverse micro-communities and reported both inclusive and exclusionary practices. Constant assessment of the value of participating in different activities was a common thread through the transcripts, indicating an increasing commodification of academic work as a calculable practice. Opportunities for participation in the full range of activities undertaken by UDEs were underpinned by implicit and explicit cost-benefit calculations (self-audit). These were reinforced and formalised in one institution through the construction of a pilot 'workload matrix' that itemises and awards weightings (in terms of credited hours of work) to a range of tasks organised in three established 'workload areas': (1) teaching activity; (2) research and knowledge transfer activity; and (3) administration and approved service. For example, ten hours are awarded for supervision of an undergraduate dissertation over one semester; four hours for delivery of a half-day CPD workshop; one hundred hours for a published referred journal article; and twenty-five hours for undertaking the role of Adviser of Studies. The effect of such practices is to render visible, commodify and quantify academic labour. The need for intervention is presented in terms of equity and transparency; the outcome is further regulation and the generation of new data sets for the purposes of differentiation.

Contributions to the corporate good were commonly expressed in terms of the potential for income generation through research, consultancy and the provision of CPD services. The development of modularisation and the promotion of short courses increases the volume and pace of course 'delivery'. Academic staff participate in marketing, branding and budgetary management in an increasingly competitive field. The resources available to local and national government to support CPD and to commission research are reduced. Funding for research – especially in the humanities and social sciences – from UK research councils, European funding streams and philanthropic bodies is similarly under strain. In such straitened times, technical-rational considerations can carry greater weight than ethical-political concerns. Building capacity for inquiry among an inclusive community of scholars, especially directed at questions of pedagogic quality, can appear subordinate to demands for success measured in terms of hit rates, through-put and revenue.

If you're bidding competitively you'll want to put forward a very strong team and funders are not generally concerned about capacity development. (Senior manager)

There are people who work in the same area within the school who have been unsupportive. They've formed their own clique and go in for research grant applications together and don't tell me they're doing it.... They build up their own teams and my face didn't fit. (Teacher educator)

I do believe that I can pay my own way in this faculty. I give a lot back in terms of income generation through CPD but I don't do as much of the traditional university model of research and scholarship. (Teacher educator)

This exploratory study of researcher development in UDEs portrays a shifting and contested landscape. It was undertaken at a time of transition in Scottish education (with full implementation of the new school curriculum, *Curriculum for Excellence*, 2010) and teacher education (following the announcement in November 2009 of the Review of Teacher Education in Scotland). Tensions were exacerbated by the formation of redundancy and structural change committees in both institutions. These were formed to consider how best to sustain the activities of UDEs in the face of a challenging set of external circumstances, including dramatic reductions in student places for initial teacher education in Scotland (SFC, 2010) and uncertainty around the future direction of education policy as a result of parliamentary elections. University reshaping has included school-level re-organisation into explicit research themes, cost reduction strategies and further changes to the teacher education workforce through voluntary severance and retirement. One likely outcome of recent deliberations is a much more selective approach to submissions for assessment under the Research Excellence Framework, 2014 (HEFCE, 2011).

Institutional responses in UDEs are somewhat Janus-faced as a result of pressure to raise research quality. On the one hand, there is widespread public acknowledgement that 'the relationship between teaching and research has to be a much more equal one in terms of intellectual credibility and esteem' (Senior manager). On the other, strategic responses to support improvements in research quality have increased the strain towards separation (of the 'professional' from the 'academic') rather than integration. The re-allocation (or 'farming out') of teaching and supervision to those who have signed teaching-only contracts, or who form part of the flexible workforce of temporary 'associate tutors', moves responsibility for core teacher education tasks to the most 'vulnerable university teachers' (Nelson and Watt, 2004). The prospects for research-informed professionalism within this mix are uncertain.

One of the major tasks of the short to medium term will be a much bolder differentiation between teaching activities and research activities at the level of management and planning...a culture where teaching and research are esteemed, where they interact creatively with one another, but where the deployment of staff to particular activities makes much more effective use of their expertise. (Senior manager)

There are colleagues that are never going to research and therefore we should not be affording them any time to do so. A fairly clinical decision has to be made about the extent to which the School can actually afford that time with no end result...Those colleagues can support the development of research by doing more teaching. The time has come for them to be much more managed than they have been... There is an instinct in higher education to allow people to be individual, self-expressive, self-directing and that's okay if you are a traditional academic. If you are what I would describe as more of a professional you've got different priorities and that has to be oriented in different ways. (Senior manager)

It appears that the future may contain ever stronger demarcations between the 'research active' and 'research inactive' (Lucas, 2006). The usual claim in such situations is that different categories of academic workers are to be equally esteemed. However, according to one recent study there appears to be a refusal in some HEIs to continue to support teacher educators as an 'exceptional category', whose work as university teachers is not valued equally to the work of research active colleagues (Ellis, 2011a:20). Recent developments, in response to the research agenda, appear to be marked by a movement away from an internal commitment to capacity building ('grow your own') to an external appointment strategy ('buy them in'). One senior manager noted that '[w]e are beyond the stage now of recruiting staff in whom we need to invest for five years before we get a return.'

As an outcome of restructuring and changes to research funding priorities, UDEs are in closer relation to other faculty and subject to pressure to develop a stronger interdisciplinary portfolio. Rather than attention to personal 'reinvention', contemporary rhetoric is of organisational reinvention. At the same time UDEs are urged to increase the relevance, visibility and impact of their research in relation to professional practice. Such exhortations come from within the research community (Gardner, 2011) and from the policy community (Donaldson, 2011). The process of transition creates new challenges, including the capacity of research active post-doctoral appointees without teaching experience to undertake teacher education roles as secondee numbers contract and former college staff retire. One possible strategy might include retrenchment to post-graduate, post-qualification provision. Reducing pre-service commitments reduces the impact of fluctuating ITE student numbers (and income derived from ITE funding streams) that has impeded capacity building in Scotland. It would also distance some UDEs from an obligation to focus on the delivery of centrally generated policy agenda for schools. Such moves would represent a significant change in direction in the on-going process of universitisation in Scotland. The hybrid educator of the future may have fewer borders to cross if Education as a university subject has a different relation to teacher education.

Conclusion

The professional identities of university-based teacher educators tend to be complex. We have seen how the respective worlds of the school and the university create tensions for many of them. Both of those worlds are in a continuing state of flux, so it is unlikely that any stable settlement can be reached either for individuals or for the wider group. The double whammy of formal policies such as standards for teaching and research assessment is only the visible expression of deeply conflictual experiences for many teacher education staff. The emotional and psychic conflict is conveyed by some of the voices cited above, but also in the expressions of disenchantment and alienation that so often characterise the discourse of corridors and common rooms in UDEs. The habitus of teacher educators in the UK has been disrupted for many years now, and the link between social structures and social practices which habitus represents (O'Brien, 2011) has become attenuated, or in some cases severed.

As long ago as 1998, Murray was arguing the following:

It may be that the dual demands of being both teacher and active researcher reinforce the sense of teacher education as the impossible job. ... But they also offer the opportunity to explore and re-define the relationship between teaching and research... (Murray, 1998:157)

Certainly, in some institutions there are attempts under way to redefine roles and responsibilities in such a way that these tensions can be addressed, if not resolved. It is our view that the way forward lies in further developments in the relationship between research, policy and practice in education. At present, small-scale research carried out by educational practitioners (whether located in schools or in universities) is not valued highly within the academy, because it tends not to be rated highly within assessment exercises. But it remains the key interface within professional education.

In the light of our analysis in this chapter one response is to call for much more recognition of the broad base of what should count as educational research. Not only should the full range of educational research be acknowledged but it should also be recognised that research carried out in a professional context can also be research that is excellent (or not!). Indeed, although the latest innovation in research assessment in the UK, the introduction of an 'impact factor' into the Research Excellence Framework (HEFCE, 2011) has not been universally welcomed, perhaps educationists should see it as a space within which greatly-increased priority and recognition can be attached to that research which is carried out in interface with practice.

But such developments alone are unlikely to be sufficient, for we need to return to our early discussion on the nature of teaching and the ways in which teacher education practices are also constrained through the performative agenda in school teaching. At the same time as we seek a redefinition and revaluation of the research-teaching interface, we need to work together to secure much greater scope for professional autonomy and imagination in teaching and teacher education; indeed we need space for much greater agency. This will be dependent on reconstructing a relationship of trust between teachers and the wider community of parents, students and politicians and policymakers.

Acknowledgements
The authors would like to thank the current and former staff in both universities who gave their time to be interviewed.

3

Inspection and the Fabrication of Professional and Performative Processes

Jane Perryman, Institute of Education, London University

Introduction

This chapter is about how English schools perform for inspection. During an inspection a school can become 'an organisation for the gaze' (Ball, 1997: 332), with teachers preparing for inspections by 'performing the good school'. The chapter is based on research conducted in a school during the aftermath of the intensive inspection regime of Special Measures and its subsequent OfSTED inspection. I interviewed middle and senior managers' about their recollections of life under Special Measures, in effect the time in which they learnt to perform. I then use data from time spent in the school before and during the school's OfSTED inspection, and discuss inspection as performance. I found that at the case study school, teachers fabricated the situation in order to meet OfSTED requirements, but this fabrication led to inspection of the performance, not the reality, and a sense of alienation and cynicism about the result.

I start by examining the research context, explaining how the case was selected, and my relationship with the school and the role I played as researcher. I then discuss the theoretical context. This chapter is routed in a number of theoretical concepts. I discuss Foucault's (1963, 1977) ideas about disciplinary power, and the role of discourse and normalisation in making schools conform to what is seen as school effectiveness. I argue that surveillance is an important technology of this discipline using the metaphor of the Panopticon (Bentham, 1787) to illustrate the experience of inspection. I also discuss theories of performativity, inspired by Austin's (1962) work on the nature of performative acts, subsequently developed by Lyotard (1984) and Butler (1990), and explain how I see this as an important element of the performance for inspection.

Within this context I will examine how the school performed for inspection, through fabrication of documentation, teaching to a strict recipe, rehearsing meetings and interviews with inspectors and preparing the school as one would a stage prepared for a performance. I discuss how conspiring to create a successful performance led to cynicism about the result, and explore the other consequences of performing for inspection. Finally I consider how recent changes to the inspection framework will affect the performing school.

The research context

Northgate[1] is an English mixed inner-city comprehensive for pupils aged 11-16.

---

1. This is a pseudonym to protect the school

The pupils come from a four mile catchment area of significant economic and social deprivation. During its most recent inspection, there were 865 pupils on roll, 75% of whom were from minority ethnic groups. There were thirty seven languages spoken at the school, and 10% of the pupils were at the early stages of English acquisition. 30% of pupils had Special Educational Needs, 50% of the pupils receive free school meals[2], and there were around fifty refugees[3].

It would be disingenuous to suggest that Northgate was carefully selected after other sites had been considered and rejected. I worked at the case study school before coming into higher education, and used my contacts at the school to gain access to a site which gave me a unique opportunity to study the impact of inspection regimes over a period of three years. Immersed in the situation as the researcher often is, a case study researcher could face accusations of bias. The question is often asked 'has the researcher been able to create the objective distance necessary?' There are advantages to insider-research including intimate knowledge of the context of the research and the micro-politics of the institution, and I detail these elsewhere (Perryman, 2011). Essentially I contend that as long as I do not claim to be asserting an objective truth, then the advantages of my knowledge of the school and the willingness of participants to speak to me outweigh the potential problems. For most insider researchers the advantages of knowledge of context and micro-politics plus a sense of 'street credibility' (Robson, 1993) outweigh the issues of potential bias and lack of objectivity. As Smythe and Holian (2008: 38) suggest 'the trick is to work out how to try to derive maximum benefits whilst minimising the negative side effects on the researcher, the researched and the research outcomes'.

Opportunity not withstanding, Northgate was a particularly interesting site as, having failed an OfSTED inspection, it had been under Special Measures for eighteen months, during which time it was monitored by frequent inspections by Her Majesty's Inspectorate (HMI). OfSTED was established in 1992 to devise a framework for school inspections and to oversee a system of inspections of schools. It was based on an explicit framework and required extensive classroom observation. It was to be undertaken by a team of independent inspectors trained for the task, with each team led by a registered inspector and required to include a layperson. Following the inspection, a school would be required to produce an action plan.If a school was not seen to be providing an acceptable standard of education, it would become subject to Special Measures and subsequently receive termly visits from Her Majesty's Inspectorate to monitor progress.

---

2. A benchmark for measurement of poverty
3. All statistics from the OfSTED report, date withheld

If a school was judged to have made sufficient improvements it would be removed from Special Measures following a full inspection. In extreme cases, if OfSTED did not observe improvement, the school would be closed down. Northgate was in Special Measures for two years, then improved sufficiently to be released from the regime shortly before I started my research. It underwent another OfSTED inspection almost two years later. The research in this chapter focuses on the time after Special Measures, and the preparation, experience and aftermath of the subsequent OfSTED inspection.

In order to protect the anonymity of the school, the actual dates of the relevant OfSTED inspection have been withheld. The key methods used were interviews with middle and senior managers, observation and participation in an inspection week. In summer year 4 (so called as it was the fourth year after the opening of the school), I interviewed 12 teachers about how they had learned to perform during Special Measures. They were three senior managers, three heads of faculty, four heads of departments and two year heads. I returned in autumn, year 5, for a more limited session. Teachers had started to realise that OfSTED would return sometime in the next term, as schools released from Special Measures must have a full inspection within two years (so they had until the following May). I was able to gather data about how middle and senior managers felt about the imminent OfSTED inspection. By now, of the twelve I had interviewed in June, two more had left. I realised I would need to widen my sample, and so for this set of interviews added two more middle managers. I interviewed one head of faculty, three heads of department and three heads of year.

In spring, year 5, I was able to negotiate access to the school for the month before its OfSTED inspection, and for the OfSTED week itself. I offered to help prepare some of the newer teachers for the inspection in exchange for access to the school for the month before and during OfSTED week. Hence, this research period is not just based on interviews, but on my own participation and observations. I worked at the school for three days a week for the four weeks before and during the week of the OfSTED inspection. As I was working with the senior management team I observed similar working hours, arriving at the school at 8.00a.m for morning briefings, and leaving at around 6.00p.m. During the OfSTED week, I attended every day except the Wednesday, which included arriving at the school at 7.45a.m on the first day. Before the inspection, I attended meetings and advised on classroom practice. During the inspection I acted as 'an extra pair of hands' in making sure things ran smoothly, as well as attending meetings with the inspectors and participating in countless staffroom conversations. I also conducted 17 interviews during this period including ten of my original cohort. There were two senior management, one head of faculty, eight heads of department, five heads of year, and one non-teaching staff member.

In summer, year 5 I returned to the school the term after its inspection, which had been, in their terms, very successful. I interviewed seventeen middle and senior managers, specifically four senior management, three heads of faculty, seven heads of department and two heads of year. I asked them to reflect retrospectively on the OfSTED inspection, and also to comment on how the school seemed now the middle and senior managers believed that the threat of inspection had been removed for the foreseeable future. Finally, in spring year 6, I interviewed twelve people, including the original cohort and anyone else I had previously interviewed. They were four senior managers, three heads of faculty, three heads of department and two heads of year. I asked how the school had fared in the year since OfSTED, focussing again on the nature of inspection as performance.

Inspection and disciplinary power

Before discussing my findings, I will turn to the theoretical context. I locate inspection within notions of power-knowledge (Foucault, 1963, 1977), discourse and discipline. If inspection is primarily about gathering knowledge of schools, then, to Foucault, it must be intrinsically linked to power. Knowledge can be seen as a necessary dimension of power because our perception of the created truth can constrain how we act. Foucault argues that those who have power have specialist knowledge. Thus in the field of mental illness, psychiatrists hold unique power because of the knowledge they hold, and this knowledge is created by specific discourses about mental illness. Psychiatrists have the power to diagnose a condition because they command a specialist discourse. I place inspection systems firmly within the power-knowledge metaphor because is primarily about gathering knowledge of schools and then making judgements about them, and is therefore intrinsically linked to power. In terms of inspection, the power of knowledge is held by the inspectors. They hold, it seems, the sacred truth about effective schools, and make their judgements accordingly. It is not for teachers or management of schools to judge, but the external and omnipotent forces of inspection. It is the power wielded by inspectors that can make schools feel that a performance is necessary as the consequences of failing an inspection are severe.

Institutions become successful insofar as they educate people to accept particular regimes rather than subject them to coercion. Foucault argued that the mechanisms by which this 'education' is achieved are hierarchical supervision, normalising sanctions and examination. In modern institutions such as schools, control of the institution is maintained through monitoring and supervision and the constant gathering of knowledge about its effectiveness. Not only are pupils being educated to certain regimes, but the teachers and management of the school need to be 'educated' into accepted modes of successful practice. Inspection plays a key role in this discipline, and interestingly the balance between supervision and the gathering of knowledge has shifted since the 2005 Inspection Framework was introduced. Now the evidence-gathering by the staff of the school itself has acquired great importance, increasing the sense that schools are policing themselves.

Discourse and normalisation

Normalisation, which can be defined as the modification of behaviour to come within socially acceptable standards, is a powerful mechanism of power, as the nature of power is no longer about coercion and control over our bodies, but is increasingly about the control of minds. This is achieved through the hegemonic internalisation of discourses of control. In general, this means that those who are subjects of power internalise expected behaviours, and learn these behaviours through acceptance of a discourse. In an inspection context, normalisation describes the process by which schools operate within the accepted norms of an 'effective school', a concept dictated by the discourse of school effectiveness research. This was led largely by the work of Sammons, Hillman and Mortimore (1995), whose study of fifty randomly selected London primary schools studied the progress of two thousand children over four years and identified thirteen characteristics of effective schools. They identified the following factors; leadership, shared vision and goals, an orderly learning environment, emphasis on learning, purposeful teaching, high expectations, positive reinforcement, monitoring of pupil progress, a high level of pupil involvement in the life of the school, positive home-school partnerships and an ethos which enables the school to become a learning organisation (Sammons *et.al.*, 1995: 8). This research has been appropriated by OfSTED to provide a rigid recipe for how an effective school should be run. Discourses endow those who have specialist knowledge with power and in terms of inspection, this knowledge is provided by the school effectiveness discourse, and inspectors have the power to enforce adherence to its doctrines. Phrases such as 'experts say...', 'studies show...', and 'research has concluded...' give power to those who hold the knowledge and decide how it should be acted upon. Thus Foucault claims that:

> The judges of normality are everywhere. We are in the society of the teacher-judge, the doctor-judge, the educator-judge, the social worker-judge; it is on

them that the universal reign of the normative is based; and each individual, wherever he may find himself, subjects to it his body, his gestures, his behaviour, his aptitudes, his achievements (Foucault, 1977: 304).

Ball explains that this is because 'discourses constrain the possibilities of thought. They order and combine words in particular ways and exclude or displace other conditions' (1990: 2). Gold and Evans (1998: 9) agree, writing of discourse construction in education that 'dominant discourses are often so powerful that the dissenter finds it hard to voice dissent articulately or objectively'. The key issue is why some things are chosen as dominant discourses at certain times and, in the arena of my research, why certain approaches to schools and teachers are accepted as 'effective' and why others are not. Thus, according to Ball (1990: 162) 'Teachers are trapped into taking responsibility for their own disciplining through schemes of self-appraisal, school improvement and institutional development'.

Inspectors see their work as neutral and objective, as it is assumed that there is a measurable reality that is possible to 'know'. Thus, according to Jeffrey and Woods (1998: 84), teachers feel that when inspected 'they are under examination in a disciplinary exercise where their humanistic morality has been replaced by one centred on technology'. The pre-eminence of effectiveness is a classic example of the use of knowledge to convey power. Walkerdine (1988: 188), writing of the use of discourse in general explains that 'the imposition of this discourse onto the world therefore renders to the mathematician, scientist, psychologist, linguist or whatever an incredibly powerful position. For s/he produces statements which are taken to be true'. I would add 'inspector' to that list of those in a powerful position due to the imposition of their version of truth. Thus, according to Morley and Rassool (1999: 13):

Underpinning the entire movement on standards, standardisation and school effectiveness is the assumption that once a set of educational 'truths' has been established, they hold good for all teachers, schools, children, parents and communities. School Effectiveness can represent an epistemology of closure and certainty. It is both a homogenised and homogenising discourse.

Jeffrey and Woods (1998: 106) argue that the school effectiveness discourse as policed by inspectors has lead to a colonisation of schools, as 'although the OfSTED team are seen once and rarely again, the discourse of inspection and accountability remains with the school'. Thus having learnt the accepted modes of behaviour, schools continue to perform the good school between inspections until that becomes how the school functions all the time. This links with normalisation, the process of ensuring that behaviour judged as normal becomes the only acceptable behaviour. As Walsh (2006: 113) comments 'the criterion of "school effectiveness" with its panopoly of performance management mechanisms has redefined the terms by which the social worth of education is now routinely evaluated within the education system. Dissenting opinions are now labelled "excuses".

In these terms school effectiveness research often creates an over-mechanistic approach – if schools do not meet a rigid set of criteria then they are not effective, and if improvement is to occur it must be aimed at replicating the effectiveness factors in the school. Morley and Rassool (1999: 1) assert that while the research 'poses as a counterpoint to fuzzy thinking and imprecision in education and promises success criteria, with blueprints and taxonomies for the effective school', it actually leads to 'binary thinking', where schools can be categorized as effective or failing, and teachers as good or bad.

The discourse of OfSTED involves standards, quality, efficiency, value for money and performance. In order to be successful, schools need to accept that this discourse is the way forward, especially if they are in danger of failing. There is no room for schools to 'do their own thing' in terms of improvement. If a school is to be judged as effective, it must demonstrate that it has met pre-determined criteria which are set to judge a school, irrespective of the socio-economic environment, and it is the need to demonstrate effectiveness according to external success criteria which leads to the performance culture as a reaction to inspection. Thus all schools have the potential to be normalised, and those that are deemed to be abnormal can be labelled as failing and subject to harsh regimes in the hope that they will improve. Performativity becomes the mechanism through which schools demonstrate, through documentation and pedagogy that they have been normalised, inspection, through surveillance and panoptic techniques, examines this process. In order to explore this further, I would now like to turn to the role of observation and the Panopticon.

Performativity in the Panopticon

So many powers, from the slow illumination of obscurities, the ever-prudent reading of the essential, the calculation of times and risks, to the mastery of the heart and the majestic confiscation of paternal authority, are just so many forms in which the sovereignty of the gaze gradually establishes itself – the eye that knows and decides, the eye that governs (Foucault, 1963: 88-9).

Normalisation is policed through hierarchical supervision and examination. Thus surveillance is an important technology of the maintenance of power. I follow Foucault in using the metaphor of the Panopticon (Bentham, 1787) to illustrate surveillance as a form of discipline, and apply this to inspection. The Panopticon is an architectural mechanism for total control via a seemingly inescapable and unrelenting gaze. In the Panopticon, prisoners are never sure if they are being watched or not, so learn to behave as if they are being watched all the time. This surveillance is a commonly used managerial technique in call centres, where workers know that all calls are recorded but not which ones will be listened to 'live' or later, so must behave at all times as they have been trained to do. I do not, of course, maintain that the Panopticon is anything other than a metaphor for control in education, but argue that its very real twenty-first century equivalent is the culture of performativity.

The idea of performativity originated in Austin's (1962) work on performative utterances and was developed by Lyotard (1984) and Butler (1990), who approached it from different angles, Lyotard writing of a culture of enhanced efficiency, and Butler of stylised acts. I believe these ideas come together in the idea of 'panoptic performativity'. In terms of inspection this can describe the way that teachers, particularly those considered to be in challenging circumstances, or undergoing Special Measures, experience inspection as if they are constantly being observed, subjected to a seemingly relentless gaze, and perform accordingly in order to be successful. It is through the increasing culture of performativity and accountability that conformity, discipline and normalisation is ensured, as teachers learn to police themselves, and to perform the successful inculcation of the normalised behaviour.

The accountability culture in schools lends itself well to the metaphor of the Panopticon and thus, as Harland (1996: 101) notes, 'the exercise of continuing surveillance through the process of monitoring and evaluation means that those concerned also come to anticipate the response...to their actions past, present, and future and therefore come to discipline themselves'. Wilcox and Gray (1996: 120) also link inspection with disciplinary mechanisms, 'as it requires a school to undergo an exacting discipline which extends over a period considerably longer than that of the inspection week and may also lead to a school being disciplined'. They locate the Panopticon with the handbook which continues to influence schools in between inspections and is used as a management development tool. Thus, as Troman (1997: 349) describes, 'inspectors are the absent presence in the school'.

The panoptic metaphor is useful for the experience of being inspected for a number of reasons as it can describe the experience of constant, returning inspection, as under Special Measures, or the constant threat of no-notice inspection as under the recent inspection frameworks. Teachers in schools in danger of 'failing' inspection need to behave as if they are being inspected all the time so the performance becomes second nature, and thus the disciplinary mechanism is internalized. There is also the experience of inspection as not just constant but all-seeing. To use the panoptic metaphor, even if a school is not being officially inspected, 'the dark central tower' of OfSTED is always invisibly watching. The result is increasing conformity to perceived expectations, the acceptance of the discourse as demonstrated through performativity.

Inspection seems a constant threat and teachers can feel they need to modify their behaviour in a permanent way 'because the constant pressure acts even before the offences, mistakes or crimes have been committed' (Foucault 1977: 206). During OfSTED inspections, 'the nature of the audit influences performance, and schools change their practices to conform to what they think the inspectors inspect' (Earley, 1998: 172). Thus a school becomes 'an organisation for 'the gaze' and for the avoidance of 'the gaze'' (Ball, 1997: 332).

Performance and performativity

Performativity is a complex and contested term and it is difficult to find a finite definition. I define it as a disciplinary technology that uses judgements and comparisons against what is seen as efficient as a means of control. A culture of performativity leads to performances that measure efficiency. It is also the modern equivalent of the Panopticon, or rather the panoptic metaphor made real.

The term performative was introduced by J.L. Austin (1962) when he talked of 'performative utterances', words which describe an action as the action is happening, or 'saying as doing'. Examples of performative utterances are 'I promise', 'I dare', 'I bequeath'. Performative utterances in education can be seen in terms of labelling theory, such as labelling certain students as 'A' grade, or, in the arena of my research, labelling schools as 'failing', or 'effective'. Marshall (1999: 316), writing about teacher appraisal, says that performative language acts in appraisals to normalise individuals and 'the appraisals themselves, masquerading as descriptors, in turn mask the underlying power-knowledge in the force of performative utterances'.

From the word 'performative' comes 'performativity'. There are many, often confusing uses of the term 'performativity'. In the field of performance studies it is used as a definition of the theory of performance, or analysing performance. Indeed when reading about performance studies, it is quite hard to differentiate where the boundaries are between performance and performativity. Goffman (1959: 15) defines performance as 'all the activity of a given participant on a given occasion which serves to influence in any way any of the other participants'.

This is such a broad definition that it must include performativity. Schechner (2002: 110) uses performative as an adjective which 'inflects what it modifies with performance-like qualities' and says that performativity is the extension of performance into all areas of everyday life. Hence performativity is 'like a performance without actually being a performance in the orthodox or formal sense'. So in other words, when an action or situation is performative, it is not performance as we traditionally understand it, as according to Alexander, Anderson and Gallegos (2005), the concept of performance implies an audience; that which is performative is performance taken beyond its formal setting. That is my understanding of performative within the theory of performance. It is also useful to consider performativity as used by Judith Butler (1990; 1993) and Jean Francois Lyotard (1984).

Butler (1990, 1993) draws on Austin's work when she argues that gender can be performative, socially constructed, learnt in stylised and repeated acts. She uses 'performative' to describe a discursive practice which enacts what it names, and that performativity describes the construction of social realities. Women, for example, enact their gender through repetition of 'feminine' acts which appear authentic and natural but are in fact learnt. In her words;

> Performativity consists of the reiteration of norms which recede, constrain and exceed the performer and in that sense can not be taken as a fabrication of the performers 'will' or 'choice'; further what is performed works to conceal, if not to disavow what remains opaque, unconscious, unperformable (Butler, 1993: 234).

This definition resonates, as when ascribed to education this way of defining performativity can describe the performance of what is seen as effective within education. Alexander, Anderson and Gallegos (2005: 4) maintain that 'teaching is a performance event as well as being a performative event'. Nowhere is this more apparent than when teachers are 'performing the good school' during an inspection. Wilcox and Gray (1996: 56) describe an inspection week as a performance;

> ...the school's 'performance' during the inspection week is a more chancy affair. It is subject to the subtleties and vagaries of the key participants, the extent to which the teachers 'rehearse' and the coherence of the teachers and senior managers 'direction'. What emerges, pursuing the metaphor of the drama is a 'performance'. That performance is the product of numerous interactions between teachers, pupils and inspectors each of which is subject to interpretation. Circumstances may well arise in which

the (mis)interpretation of nuance upon nuance results in an inappropriate picture being given of the whole institution.

Alternatively, Lyotard (1984) uses 'performative' to refer to a method of maximising efficiency through a culture of controlled outcomes and accountability. He argues that power depends on the optimisation of performance. Lyotard's version of performativity obscures differences, requiring everything to be measurable and all to be accountable against the same standards. Thus 'an equation between wealth, efficiency and truth is established' (Lyotard, 1984: 46).

In the performative accountability culture of education in the first part of the twenty-first century, 'concepts like efficiency are treated as though they were neutral and technical matters, rather than being tied to particular interests' (Ball, 1990: 154). In other words, the hegemonic belief is that efficiency is seen as 'a good thing' irrespective of the cost to people – intensification, loss of autonomy, monitoring and appraisal, lack of decision making and lack of personal development are not considered. Gewirtz (1997: 219) says that the language used to describe and promote change and innovation in teaching is not neutral, but 'forms part of discourses which function as powerful disciplinary mechanisms for transforming teacher subjectivities and the culture and values of classroom practices' thus, and learning must be determined in accordance with learning outcomes and objectives. Trainee teachers are typically required to document their practice with detailed lesson plans; this preparation, it is implied, is the key to good teaching itself. Teaching and learning in this manner matches inspection and accounting and the efficient use of resources. The teacher becomes a learning resource, a facilitator, and teaching is theorised as fixed recipes. The variety of good practice can be suppressed, and according to Alexander *et.al.* (2005: 211) 'new practices based on surveillance and performativity encourage the targets of power to collude in their own disempowerment'.

In education, performativity is manifested by the culture of outcomes, efficiency and accountability which has swept through education in England and Wales since the 1988 Education Reform Act. The performance context is also relevant, as it is repeated and stylised actions which enable schools to perform this efficiency. Performativity is about performing efficiency in a publicly accountable way, a second layer of unreality. Morley (2003: 71), writing about the process of Quality Assurance in Higher Education writes that:

...performativity involves a damaging process of ventriloquism and impersonation as academics and managers attempt to represent themselves in a language that quality assessors will understand and value.

Hence, universities and schools are not only 'performing the good school' but being seen to do so. To use the analogy of the driving test, in order to pass the driving test the driver not only needs to look in her mirror, but make sure the instructor sees this happen. I am not, of course, suggesting that drivers only look in the mirror when being tested, but the quick flick of the eye lids necessary to look in the mirror is not sufficient when one is being watched, and is replaced by an exaggerated stylised gesture.

Performativity is a technology of power and normalisation. Avis (2005: 211) says that 'performativity becomes embodied in a regime of truth that refuses other conceptualisations of good practice, which therefore become silenced and are denied legitimacy'. This connects with the idea of accepted forms of School Effectiveness, evaluation as a form of control and the way schools must now conform to one accepted recipe of a 'good school'. Lyotard, (1984: 50) writing of the spread of performativity in higher education, argued that 'even if the performativity principle does not always help pinpoint the policy to follow, its general effect is to subordinate the institutions of higher learning to the existing powers.'

Performativity is intrinsically linked to the emergence of the power of the evaluative state, accountability in education policy and transparency to the public gaze. Elliot (2001: 194) says that 'performative cultures presume that the performance of core activities within organisations can be made transparent to the public's gaze on a continuous and sustainable basis through the technologies of audit'. OfSTED is the organisation through which the gaze is maintained. Performativity is a regime of rituals such as inspection, audits, interviews and routines such as meetings and record-keeping (Ball, 2001).Power (1994: 7) argues that performativity 'signifies a displacement of trust from one part of the economic system to another from operatives to auditors'. This issue of trust is important. Mahony and Hextall (2000: 102) characterise the education system as a 'high surveillance/low trust' regime. The performance is not as important as the mechanisms to ensure the quality of performance. It is not just about public, external discipline, but a constant state of readiness and meticulous preparation etc. In Ball's words:

> It is the database, the appraisal meeting, the annual review, report writing and promotion applications, inspections, peer reviews that are to the fore. There is not so much, or not only, a structure of surveillance, as a flow of performativities both continuous and eventful that is spectacular. It is not the possible certainty of always being seen that is the issue, as in the Panopticon. Instead it is the uncertainty and instability of being

judged indifferent ways, by different means, through different agents, the 'bringing off' of performance (2001: 211).

The performing school

In this chapter, in order to illustrate the issue of inspection as performance, I describe in detail the preparation for and experiences of the OfSTED inspection that Northgate went through in spring year 5, as well as middle and senior managers' reactions to the previous Special Measures regime. I argue that inspectors do not see the real school because of the level of stage management, game playing, performance and cynicism engendered by the panoptic regime. Ball describes this as fabrication, arguing that 'fabrications are versions of an organisation (or person) which does not exist – they are not 'outside the truth', but neither do they render simply true or direct accounts – they are produced purposely to be accountable' (Ball, 2001).

This argument that inspectors see a school as a performance rather than reality is echoed elsewhere. In Chapman's (2002: 261) research, teachers told him that OfSTED had failed to pick up on many important issues for the school:

> Senior teams reported that they attempted to minimise their vulnerability to variability of inspection teams or poor timing of an inspection through rigorous planning and thorough preparation of staff... One middle manager reported 'they are critical times for the head and he will do everything in his power to present the school in the best light'.

Similarly, Burns (2000: 26), interviewing teachers in schools which had just undergone OfSTED inspections, found responses such as, 'I think OfSTED week was like a performance...a play and we acted very, very well...it wasn't the real school'. In another example, a deputy head told Jeffrey (2002: 543) that 'you have to actually catch on to what it is they want...and then perform it'. One headteacher told Plowright (2007: 382) 'we'd trained our staff well. I used one or two tricks that I knew would go down well'.

De Wolf and Janssens (2007: 382) found that 'gaming' or 'intended strategic behaviour' as a response to inspection is not unusual:

> The most well known form of intended strategic behaviour is 'window dressing'. This means the creation of proactive ad reactive arrangements which are generated simply and solely to be assessed more favourably by the supervisor.

The performance presented by a school undergoing inspection is usually set within the rigid parameters governed by the discourse around what constitutes a good school. This change of behaviour can be seen in terms of fabrication of documentation, staging and game-playing before and during inspection, and a deal of cynicism about the whole process.

Fabrication of documentation

In experiencing the panoptic performativity of Special Measures, the staff of Northgate had learned how to perform the good school. At Northgate, under Special Measures, teachers accepted that they must act as if they were being inspected all the time, in order to train themselves and pupils into expected modes of behaviour, and so that the arrival of an inspector would be to deal with, and part of the routine. Ball's phrase 'an organisation for "the gaze" and for the avoidance of "the gaze"' (1997: 332) very appropriate for Northgate, which, during Special Measures and before and during its OfSTED inspection, seemed like an organisation existing purely for the purposes of passing an inspection. Indeed 'the school became a sort of apparatus of uninterrupted examination' (Foucault, 1977: 186), although in this case the examination was of teachers and not of pupils.

Documentation was used to both inculcate and demonstrate a discourse of effectiveness. Ball (2003: 8) remarks that under inspection 'what is produced is a spectacle or what we might see as an 'enacted fantasy' which is there to be seen and judged'. He goes on to say that 'the heart of the educational project is gouged out and left empty. Authenticity is replaced by plasticity'. Under an inspection regime, a school's documentation becomes part of the surveillance. This is not unusual, as Duffy (1999: 110) notes:

> Some of the documents generated by a school for an inspection may have the aim of giving the best possible impression to the inspectors, and the school might not be so prolific in its production of policy statements or so up to date in its handbook if the inspection was not imminent.

In schools this can be seen in constant clarifications of policies and procedures, in departmental handbooks, school and departmental action plans. Ball (1997: 319) notes, 'documents produced in these technologies become increasingly reified, self-referential and dislocated from the practices they are 'meant' to stand for or account for'.

This is mirrored in Morley's comment about universities having to demonstrate the norms of Quality Assurance just as schools reproduce the norms of School

Effectiveness. She writes that 'the hyped text is complicit in the reproduction of quality norms' (Morley, 2003: 71). This is also an example of what Sparks (1987) called 'strategic rhetoric'. Researching a school whose Physical Education department felt marginalised during the major curriculum reforms of the late 1980s, he discovered 'the strategic use of certain language forms in relation to the proposed innovation, as a means of enhancing the status of their subject within the school' (ibid.: 37). This involved 'the use of concepts from educational theory such as 'developing the whole child', 'core experiences', 'individual learning styles' and 'relevant life skills" (ibid.: 42). Thus the department was able to leave its practice unchanged whilst giving the impression change had occurred, and gain space on the new curriculum despite its perceived low status. In most schools, the arrival of OfSTED heralds a period of over-work, in preparation. MacBeath (2004) writes:

> OfSTED. For teachers, there are few words that carry the same emotional impact and weight of expectation. For a generation of school staff it has signalled time to set aside learning and engage in tactical manoeuvres designed to impress, if not outwit, their uninvited visitors. Preparing for inspection becomes, for three months or more, an overriding obsession.

Northgate was reinspected within two years of coming out of Special Measures, as is necessary in such circumstances. The school had learned its lessons well. As was usual under the 2003 Inspection Framework, the school had eight weeks' notice. Documentation was prepared, schemes of work and lesson-plans revamped and the full performative environment recreated. Extensive documentation was produced at department level:

> Well I think that our handbook is the biggest handbook that I've ever put together in my life so far. That's taken a week to pull together. (Janice, middle manager, spring year 5).

In addition to department documentation, for the inspection the school had to produce a self-evaluation document called the S4, which under the 2003 OfSTED model, was very important. OfSTED would use the S4 to plan their visit, as the school would identify strengths and weaknesses. This was not a straightforward process, and would be the first time the game metaphor was made explicit:

> A visiting governor, with OfSTED experience, made it very clear to the senior team that they had to play a clever game. Strengths had to be identified, but not overplayed; weaknesses discussed, but in the light of

planned improvements. If OfSTED agreed with the self-evaluation, it was implied, then all would be well (field notes, spring year 5).

I became involved in the preparation of the S4 as part of my role as temporary member of the senior management team. There were eight sections to the S4. These were: overall evaluation; the achievement of pupils; pupils' attitudes and personal development; teaching and learning (including assessment); the curriculum and accommodation; pupil support; partnership with parents and the community; and leadership and management. Each section was split into three or four sub-sections, following the pattern of identification of strengths, evidence for these strengths, identification of weaknesses and plans for improvement. The form took eight people ten hours to complete, working in two 4pm to 9pm sessions. Filling in the form was not just arduous, but a subtle and careful game in which strengths must not be overplayed and weaknesses disguised yet simultaneously admitted.

In the 2005 framework the S4 was replaced by the even more stringent SEF which served as the main document that OfSTED used to prepare its inspection of the school. The problem with self-evaluation documents produced for evaluation is that an honest warts-and-all approach is simply not possible. Over-emphasise strengths, and a school could be criticised for complacency with a management team unable to plan for progress, but identify too many weaknesses and there is a risk of giving a skewed picture which may influence the judgement of the inspectors negatively. Mel describes similar dilemmas with her subject documentation:

> I'm worried that if I put that in the Department Review and say 'I'm going to do this, I'm going to do that' there will be too much 'I'm going to' rather than I'm there doing it. (Mel, middle manager, spring year 5).

Was Mel to admit she hadn't started many of her well-intentioned plans, or pretend everything was in hand? This approach does have implications for a school's improvement, because if a school disguises serious faults in order to avoid going into Special Measures, then it will not receive the support it may need.

Fabricating the stage
Before the OfSTED inspection of spring year 5, normalisation (i.e. preparing the school to demonstrate its fit with the normalising School Effectiveness discourse and thus passing the inspection) was also accomplished by putting up displays, selecting work to show the inspection team and making internal judgements about teaching and learning. Senior management activity before the inspection

was directed towards observing and grading lessons.

The school had a special INSET day, specifically set aside for departments to work together on their lesson plans for OfSTED. There was a general air of exhaustion, combined with frenetic activity. Displays were being created and erected. The Registered Inspector had requested work to be collated for six pupils per year into subject boxes; two from pupils of higher ability, two medium and two lower. There was frantic activity after school as departments selected their book samples. They were playing the game of selecting two 'low achievers'' books that 'aren't too low'. As someone remarked, 'If someone is 'low', won't their book be really shit?' (field notes, spring year 5).

In the week before the inspection, Lola, a head of department, wearily listed the extra work she'd had to do, and expressed the desire to just get it over with:

> We've had to be observed and jump through the hoops for the observations. We've had to put a lot of unnecessary paperwork and things in place that were in place, but it's now decided that it's got to be done in a certain format, because everybody's got to use the same format. (Lola, middle manager, spring year 5).

This is an example of the drive towards normalisation. Everyone had to use exactly the same lesson plan format, schemes of work were written to a rigorous formula. There was no room for deviation, as anything not normal runs the risk of being pathologised, seen as ineffective, or even sick and in need of intervention. Dave describes the pressures of this drive to perfection:

> I wouldn't want to have OfSTED all the time because I think that you can't teach to that intensity all the time, every day. No one does that in their daily lives, everybody has a bad day in the office or a day that isn't running that smoothly. I don't think teachers can be expected to be anything different, but OfSTED forces you into this kind of 'I am a perfect teacher'. (Dave, middle manager, spring year 6).

Playing the game

This drive to perfection intensified as the shadow of OfSTED loomed. Preparing the stage went far beyond just the physical environment. There was a real sense from middle and senior managers that they were playing a game. This not only involved jumping through the prescribed hoops, teaching lessons in the correct manner, presenting all the correct documentation etc, but also suppressing negative thoughts and comments – and even hiding some pupils! The inspectors intended to comb through the school very thoroughly, so preparations had to be extensive. Apart from lesson observations, the inspectors would be speaking to around seventy pupils and stressed that it was important to have quality time with them. The meeting schedule for teachers was organised. There were twenty eight meetings organised for the Monday, all looking at specific issues such as standards and achievement, pupil attendance, year 11, parental links and various initial faculty meetings. These involved twelve different inspectors, twenty six different members of staff and three governors.

On the Tuesday there were nineteen meetings, looking at issues such as behaviour, health and safety, literacy and assessment and pastoral meetings. These involved six inspectors, eighteen staff and one governor. Five inspectors would also meet with selected pupil representatives, probably about forty in total. Wednesday only had four meetings scheduled, as this was the day when inspectors would be starting feedbacks to heads of faculty. Meetings were rehearsed, and these findings are echoed by Grace (Jeffrey and Woods 1998: 155), 'We practised ensuring that we presented a consensus for any interviews we had. It was very helpful. I want them to say that the Senior Management Team has a shared clear view'.

It was in the stage-managing of the morning briefing that the performance seemed really blatant. Morning briefing occurred at Northgate before the beginning of every school day, as the whole staff met to hear and give announcements (such as timetable changes, staff absences etc). The inspectors would expect to attend briefing, and my field notes remark on the way in which there was a rehearsal of how the first morning meeting in the presence of the inspectors would go, and its subsequent success.

During the inspection week, I wrote:

> The staff briefing goes as rehearsed. The room is very crowded, with the addition of thirteen inspectors. Lots of 'showy' things said, most of which were already announced on Thursday – football scores, a cricket award and a year 9 trip to the Globe Theatre. One head of department said 'It's all so bloody false. I'd like to know what people are doing this week that they're not normally doing'. (field notes, spring year 5).

This head of department's remark calls to mind Goffman's (1959: 108) comment, 'since we all participate in teams we must all carry within ourselves something of the sweet guilt of conspirators'. Similarly, Zoë's views below are linked to Goffman's work on 'dramaturgical loyalty'. She points out:

They are obviously really worried that people are going to say the wrong thing, so they are saying that you have to follow the party line and the party line is this. (Zoë, middle manager, spring year 5).

Indeed, Goffman (1959: 207) remarked that, 'it is apparent that if a team is to sustain the line it has taken, the team must act as if they have accepted certain moral obligations. They must not betray the secrets of the team when between performances whether from self-interest, principle or lack of discretion'. I did indeed note a sense of peer pressure in which everybody was expected to play the game. This was not enforced by senior management, but by the teachers themselves. This mutual panopticism ensured that OfSTED inspectors were presented with a unified staff, presenting a consistent image of the work of the school. Interestingly this approach led to suspicion from the inspectors:

I meet senior management in the morning to hover in a corridor. There is much less tension than yesterday, and the Head has had his initial feedback from the inspector and has been told that yesterday was 'good for a Monday, but a bit stage-managed'. (field notes spring year 5).

The inspector's comment about stage-management seems odd. Inspection teams are surely aware of that there is a stage-managed nature to an OfSTED week, but surely can not really expect anything else.

Resistance and cynicism

Exploring the issue of resistance under this model, Foucault writes, 'my problem has always been…the problem of the relationship between subject and truth. How does the subject enter into a certain game of truth?' (in Bernauer and Rasmussen, 1988). Resistance is integral to Foucault's theories of power. In schools, resistance to a technology such as performativity is not easy, as it is so rooted within the discourse of what is acceptable, and those in power will often be the defenders of the discourse. The hint to how it may be achieved is in the use of Foucault's phrase 'game of truth'. Ball (2001) notes that 'tactics of transparency produce a resistance of opacity, of elusivity' and labels such tactics 'fabrications'; which he says 'are versions of an organisation (or person) which does not exist – they are not "outside the truth" but neither do they render simply true or direct accounts – they are produced purposely 'to be accountable'" (2001: 216). Morley (2003: 72) concurs, writing that 'as with any powerful meta-narratives assuming "truths", other "truths" are silenced and excluded from the quality discourse.' In my research, resistance to inspection is the cynical 'playing of the game', putting on an act. Teachers cannot refuse to be inspected, but can resist it in how they perform and stage manage what is seen, and in their grudging response to inspectors' judgements, with 'failing' viewed as political construct, and 'success' greeted with cynical snorts.

In one example of resistance, some of the performance went as far as actually fooling the inspectors, just as it had during Special Measures. As Helen reflected a year later;

> I think the problem is that it is too easy to fool OfSTED. I think it is very easy to present them with superficialities in terms of paperwork that they are impressed by, and then when they go away you know that this is just a façade and therefore you have no respect for the whole process and that is how I feel about it. (Helen, middle manager, spring year 6).

The issue of having no respect for the process can explain the cynicism about the result. I have witnessed this both in schools and in higher education. If there is a bad report from OfSTED, then teachers can suggest that the inspectors do not know what they are talking about. If the report is good, then participants congratulate each other on fooling the inspectors. A principal lecturer in a new university told Morley (2003: 57) that they had not been totally truthful in their preparation for Quality Assurance, saying that, 'I mean I'm not saying that we told lies, but we cemented over certain issues, and those weren't picked up'. A school middle manager told Stoll and Fink (1996: 5), 'I thought there were a lot of issues both good and bad that the OfSTED report hadn't even touched on here... it didn't focus very deeply on issues which affected the school'. This is an important issue as, if schools are hiding their weaknesses (and thus their real development needs) from inspectors, then real progress and improvement will be severely hampered. Plowright (2007: 384) found that the school he researched covered up its real problems, one head of department complaining 'each time...they paper over the cracks and it looks fantastic on the report. Whereas you only have to go a little bit deeper and there are real problems'. Hence, as Ball (2001: 217) notes 'crucially and invariably acts of fabrication and the fabrications themselves act and reflect back upon the practices they stand for. The fabrication becomes something to be sustained, lived up to...all of this keeps the gaze in place'.

Continuing the theme of fooling the Inspectors, was the issue of the rather sinister sounding 'redirected pupils'. Around 20 of the most troublesome students were being sent off on various activities during OfSTED week, some on a residential trip to an outdoor activity centre, others on a programme of educational day trips with their learning mentors, some of which would lead to

Duke of Edinburgh Awards. This is not an unusual strategy adopted by schools during inspection. A correspondent on the *Times Educational Supplement* forum comments:

> The pupils were well behaved, which the inspector commented on. This is perhaps not surprising, as due to a reciprocal agreement with heads of other local schools, many of the most challenging pupils were on 'step out' visits for the duration. A large number of others ended up on temporary exclusions ('halfmeltedsnowman' in M. Duffy, 2005).

Macbeath (2004) concurs, noting of one Hertfordshire secondary school under inspection that 'troubled students were sent away to an outdoor pursuits centre to partake in a week long alternative education system'. This fooling of the inspectors can be linked into Foucault's ideas about resistance, and Butler's (1997: 86) view that 'the psyche is what resists the regularisation that Foucault ascribes to normalising discourses'.

In another manifestation of resistance, middle and senior managers started to make judgements in return about the inspectors' experience, conduct, and the discrepancies between them:

> And also comparing your OfSTED with colleagues' OfSTEDs in different schools you are aware of how there is no ... it is totally arbitrary, it depends on which team you are getting. (Helen, middle manager, spring year 6).

This reaction is not unusual. Stoll and Fink (1996:75) also 'found genuine concern regarding the variation in the quality of inspectors both within and between teams'. Middle and senior managers constantly questioned the ability of the inspectors to make judgements:

> It was horrible because everyone judged you and you thought 'what d'you know, you've been in the room 20 minutes! (Zoë, middle manager, spring year 5).

> They can't really see how you do actually do assessment through oracy and through what you say to the kids all the time, and how you bring them on and progress them, and they don't really take into account all the social settings, even though they say they do because they looked at base data. (Mel, middle manager, spring year 5).

Criticism of inspectors is not uncommon. Troman, in his research into a primary school undergoing inspection noted one headteacher who told the teachers that:

>...this inspector couldn't work in a primary school and that 'he wouldn't like him working in his school because he couldn't organise a piss-up in a brewery'. He then referred to all the local inspectors: 'They're all auditors, they're all accountants, they know nothing about primary schools.' (Troman, 1997: 359).

There was also resentment of the enormous amount of preparation which people had undergone:

>The head of department said that OfSTED had not seemed interested in their documentation and handbooks and they 'might as well not have bothered'. The inspector even left lesson plans behind (field notes, spring year 5).

>He never looked at any of the schemes of work. I took the schemes of work and handbook over and he said to me 'once you've seen one hand book you seen them all, once you've seen one set of schemes of work you've seen them all'. He didn't look at anything. I went across with a huge box and he looked at absolutely nothing. (Lola, middle manager, summer year 5).

>Yes, there was some stuff around which showed some evidence, that I did get out and show him some evidence, but it wasn't asked for. (Lynn, middle manager, summer year 5).

>OfSTED was a huge effort for one week, it was very stressful on most of the staff, unnecessarily so, people worked very hard and made a lot of effort and it was a huge event for the school. (Mark, middle manager, summer year 5).

This view was backed up by other comments about the fact that the inspectors had not really concentrated on the paperwork. Such comments are, 'Doing the schemes of work and the handbook has turned out to be a waste of time'. 'I did hours and hours and hours of work on stuff that was never needed'. Zoë describes her frustration with the process as follows:

>When I look back, I think 'why did I do so much work?' because it was really easy, because when they came in they didn't ask to see half the

things, they didn't ask to see CATs[4] things, the statistics or anything. (Zoë, middle manager, summer year 5).

This was reflected in cynicism about the eventual result:

They said we look like a good school and things are not happening, if you scratch a little bit you can see they are not happening. (Lynn, middle manager, summer year 5).

The head of department says 'I wish they could have told us that at the beginning and we wouldn't have had to do so much work' (field notes, spring year 5).

I think if we had failed all the staff would have left as well so I don't think they would have failed us. (Dave, middle manager, summer year 5).

It is interesting how in being complicit in putting on a successful performance for the OfSTED inspection in year 5, the middle and senior managers were unable to take the outcome seriously. Possibly all teachers express cynicism about the results of an OfSTED inspection (whether good or bad), but cynicism seems particularly widespread in this case.

The future

Plowright (2007: 384) writes that inspection is 'a game that is understood by all parties…schools ignore playing the game at their peril'. It is unlikely that more recent inspection regimes will make this situation any better. In 2004, David Bell, the head of OfSTED, announced 'we're exchanging a searchlight for a laser' (Slater, 2004). In terms of inspection itself, the most significant change from the previous framework was the reduction in the notice-period for inspections, from eight weeks to as little as forty eight hours, which on the one hand could stop schools over stage-managing the event, but on the other may cause the school to run a completely panoptic regime internally, so that they are in a state of perpetual readiness.

The inspection framework of 2005 (OfSTED, 2005) was designed to curb this over-preparation by giving schools very short notice. I argue that schools will need to be in a state of constant readiness, or the 'constant state of activation engineered by the gaze of OfSTED' (Elliott, 2001: 197). Goffman wondered

---

4. Cognitive Assessment Tests, which pupils sit at the start of their secondary school to provide basic data about their literacy, numeracy and thinking skills.

to what extent this 'easy access' would affect any organisation undergoing inspection:

> When inspectors have easy access to the place where a team carries on its work, then the amount of relaxation possible for the team will depend on the efficiency and reliability of its warning systems. It is to be noted that thorough-going relaxation requires not only a warning system but also an appreciable time lapse between warning and visit, for the team will be able to relax only to the degree that can be corrected during a time-lapse (Goffman, 1959: 222).

To return to Foucault, it is possible that under the new system, because of the fact that inspectors could arrive at any time 'what was fundamentally invisible is suddenly offered to the brightness of the gaze' (Foucault, 1963: 195). Bentham (1787: 9) noted 'the less the inspector is really present, the more he is apparently omnipresent; or more precisely, the inspector is apparently omnipresent precisely insofar as he is not really present'. I have the uncomfortable feeling that for schools in challenging circumstances like Northgate, having a permanent threat of inspection at any time would almost be like a return to Special Measures, with the whole school built around passing inspection, with little or no space for any initiatives, schemes or plans which were not directly related to the OfSTED agenda. Schools in challenging circumstances would be most likely to fall into the ominous 'cause for concern' category mentioned above and face no-notice inspections. It could be a particularly punitive system for such schools, whilst welcomed by more successful schools, confident in their results, reputations and self-evaluations and relishing the lighter touch.

The threat of a punitive inspection surely militates against an honest appraisal of a school's strengths and weaknesses. Swaffield and MacBeath (2005: 242) agree, saying that 'external inspection and honest disclosure by schools are unlikely bedfellows'. They go on to say that 'in a policy climate in which self-evaluation is mandated and subject to external evaluation the role is more politicised and the stakes are higher' (ibid.: 249). In other words, how can any 'self'-evaluation be on an agenda dictated externally, and for the judgement of external eyes? To me this seems the essence of the subject disciplining itself, as in order to produce a self-evaluation that presents the school in the best (to OfSTED) light 'the knowing subject reorganises himself, changes himself, and begins to function in a new way' (Foucault, 1963: 90). Hence Laar (2006: 5) writes that 'from now on the school is the inspector', but even this is understating the power of self-evaluation. The teachers (or rather management) are indeed inspectors, but without the power to make judgements. They are merely the warder, not the director of the prison with the power to liberate or punish.

Recent frameworks seems to be more about self-inspection than self-evaluation. Under the new system, the role of management could be almost wholly directed towards creating the model school. MacBeath (2004) argues that:

> Senior managers become resident inspectors, gathering and assembling data annually in order to complete the self-evaluation report, a story told in lifeless data and dry prose, concealing more than it reveals, tailored to what OfSTED wants to hear rather than what the school could, in less constrained circumstances recount.

Thus as Avis (2005: 218) argues, 'this move beyond performativity is mealy mouthed and is a conditional trust based upon sustained performance'. The key word here is performance – I believe that the self-evaluation document combined with the constant threat of no-notice inspection creates the perfect state of panoptic performativity.

Conclusion

In this chapter I have attempted to demonstrate how an inspection regime can invite a school to fabricate a performance. This is achieved through manipulation of documentation, and management and staff uniting in a game which presents the school in its best light, and can even border on deception. The staff of Northgate in particular, because of the experience of Special Measures, became adept at playing the game. Documentation was enhanced, lesson plans created, pupils temporarily disappeared. Briefings were rehearsed, displays embellished, and meeting records amended. A distorted, yet successful school is presented to inspectors, who write their report accordingly. It is no wonder that many were cynical about the final outcome.

This is not therefore likely to be the best system for engendering long-term improvement. Alexander, Anderson and Gallegos (2005: 215) reached the conclusion that 'ironically a performance culture often lessens efficiency rather than increases it'. Helen, below, expresses the dilemma which schools find themselves in – that if they put on their best show they can not expect proper help and guidance, but if they reveal their weaknesses too honestly they may face more punitive inspection regimes:

> The problem, and we said this before about OfSTED, is that if they do examine you warts-and-all, then they need to understand the size of

the problem, and the gap of trust between us and them is that do they really understand the size of the disaffected student problem? Do they understand it? Do they know how big it is, how deep it is? If they did we would be saying 'Come in and look and help us!' (Helen, middle manager, spring year 6).

Learning to perform the 'good school' can be damaging. As detailed here, in performing for inspectors, management and staff become adept in disguising the real problems and issues which face the school. This can mean that these issues do not get the attention and support they require. Subsequent inspection frameworks aimed to address the problems of over-preparing and putting on a performance by cutting down the notice period for inspection to a couple of days and relying heavily on school self-evaluation. I wonder if, with the emphasis shifting to the schools to maintain the gaze, this will merely ensure the permanence of the performing school. The performative culture is so deeply ingrained in schools and education systems that I can foresee a game of permanent artifice, where schools squeeze their individual circumstances into a self-evaluation document designed solely to impress inspectors, and hold themselves in a state of perpetual readiness to live up to their claims, the model prisoner. In this context, 'bleak indeed is the desire for perfection' (Marshall, 1999: 310).

Acknowledgements

This chapter was originally published in **Perryman, J (2009) Inspection and the fabrication of professional and performative processes.** *Journal of Education Policy 24:5 609-629*

Governmentality in Primary Schools in England

Bob Jeffrey and Geoff Troman

Context

The European Commission put an end to the debate on whose educational principles should be prominent in 1995 when it stated that education policy was in the service of economic imperatives (Ball, 1998). Since the 1990s there has been an epidemic of educational policy of which the common global themes are economic, increasing criticism of schools, reduced funding, changes in governance, increased use of market approaches and an emphasis on standards and achievement (Levin, 1998).

In the 1990s the UK government adopted a centralist approach: introducing a National Curriculum; institutionalising OfSTED inspections with public reports on achievement, progress and standards of achievement; setting Local Authority (LA) targets (see Glossary); producing tightly constituted literacy and numeracy programmes and established a national testing programme with the data available enabling comparison of school performance. This centralisation of policy prescription focused on an effective school approach based on the ideology of good schools defying disadvantage, which now appears to have failed and the discourse of diversity and choice that ran alongside the centralised programmes is now being extended (Harris and Ranson, 2005). Raising standards is now the responsibility of schools (Woods, 2004) and pragmatism and compliance are the enforced strategies (Alexander in Woods, ibid.).

There has therefore been a shift from government to governance – of a unitary state to governance of and by networks – new architecture or regulation based on interlocking relationships between disparate sites, in and beyond the state, controlled decontrol, the use of contracts eg: such as those with independent School Improvement Partners (SIPs) targets and performance monitoring, to steer from a distance rather than use bureaucratic systems to deliver policy (Ball 2008), and as Ball notes, a 'polycentric state' and 'a shift in the centre of gravity around which policy cycles move' (Jessop, 1998: 32).

Policy texts such as the 2005 White paper on education (DfEE, 2005) make it clear that choice and diversity is the new mantra on which to base an education policy. The transparent ideology behind the economic and educational models that now seem enjoined is a public market (Woods, 1998) in which there is choice of school, diversity of provision based on demand driven funding and school self-determination. These policies of choice and competition encourage schools to market themselves more effectively to target parents as consumers and competition and rivalry intensifies (Bagley, 2006).

LAs in conjunction with professional experience and expertise, which crossed institutional and regional boundaries largely determined educational values and policy prior to the 1990s. From 1990 the English government took a more centralised micro management approach and lately the emphasis has shifted to schools to deliver basic education and performance but with some limited freedom to respond to market preferences.

This article examines, through an ethnographically based ESRC research project (RES-000-23-1281), the ways in which primary schools incorporate government policies and market values and some of the ways the schools use their responsibility to appropriate them to develop their own interests. Specifically, we focused on the discourses of performativity and creativity.

Theoretical Frame

Central government educational policy texts in England have dominated schools in recent times, including: the introduction of National Curriculum in 1989, used to plan teaching and learning; national assessment testing; inspection reports (OfSTED); Qualification, Curriculum and Assessment Authority (QCA) guideline; national reports and the publication of school standards. These written texts contain values and beliefs about the role of education in society and the economy. As Ball (2008) notes, policy discourses privilege certain ideas and topics and speakers and exclude others, organise their own specific rationalities, making particular sets of ideas obvious, common sense and 'true' (5). They mobilise truth claims and constitute rather than simply reflect social reality, 'Language is deployed in the attempt to produce certain meanings and effects' (Edwards *et.al.*, 1999: 620). Policies are very specific and practical regimes of truth and value and their vocabularies, are part of the creation of their acceptance and enactment. These discourses bring objects into being, they form the object of which they speak (Ball, 1993), such as policy texts, and they construct particular types of social relation through the relative strength of the practices they determine. The recognition of policy texts as discourses opens up greater possibilities of interpretation and action than a more prescriptive approach to policy analysis allows.

The research explores the way in which governmentality (Foucault, 1979a) works at the micro level though examining local discourses, the kinds of power relations established and the emergence of agency through the strategic practices that Foucault maintains dominate local situations as Thrift (2000) notes, 'To govern human beings is not to crush their capacity to act, but to acknowledge it and to utilise it for one's own objectives' (Rose, 2000: 4).

One of the main vehicles for the governance turn (Ball 1998) has been the use of performativity. It is underpinned by a major policy to improve economic status and social well being, a market-based approach that encourages performance-based activity – the generation of a culture of performativity (Ball, 1998, Ball, 2000, Lyotard, 1979). The performativity of Lyotard is a technology, a culture and mode of regulation that employs judgements and comparisons and displays the performances of individual subjects or organisations to serve as measures of productivity. In the educational field the performativity culture is being used by government to raise standards in schools through national inspections in England (Jeffrey and Woods, 1998, Perryman, 2006) and to raise the achievement of the mass of the population through target setting and testing. In setting targets for Local Authorities (LA) and schools, government hopes to develop a highly skilled workforce that can compete in a new global industry – the knowledge economy. The higher the skills base and the higher levels of excellence achieved in knowledge acquisition and the best use of that knowledge, the higher the economic return for the UK. According to Olssen (2006) an explanation of how new forms of power shape and govern the individual, involves supplementing, in Barry Smart's words:

...the state/civil society dichotomy by an analytic focus upon the governmentalisation of power relations, that is the development of individualising techniques and practices which are reducible neither to force nor to consent techniques and practices which is transformed by political conflict and struggle through the constitution of new forms of social cohesion. (Smart, 1986: 162)

This research explores the way in which governmentality (Foucault, 1979a) works to transform schools and teachers.

Methodology
This ethnographic research took cognisance of the structural influences in situations and the dilemmas, tensions and constraints under which primary teachers work and the way they manage and cope with their situations. To understand the complexities of what is happening we needed to employ a qualitative approach, which 'captures and records the voices of lived experience... contextualises experience...goes beyond mere fact and surface appearances... presents details, context, emotion, and the webs of social relationships that join

persons to one another' (Denzin, 1989: 83). Data needed to be collected within the school context, since experiences, perspectives and identities are strongly shaped by their context (Rosenholtz, 1989).

Our ethnographic approach of spending time in the field using three different time modes – compressed, selective intermittent and recurrent (Jeffrey, 1999, Jeffrey and Troman, 2004) – ensured that we took into account the broad experience of teaching and learning and obtained a complex, rich analysis of how the creativity and performativity discourses interacted with the lives of those in primary schools.

We based the research in six primary schools across five Local Education Authorities from 2005 to 2008. We judged this the maximum possible given the depth of fine detail we sought, but large enough to offer some limited reliability of the research schools (inner city, rural) in terms of size and socio-economic status. We ensured a balance of learner age range and teacher experience in terms of career status, positions, and roles. We have used this methodology in major ESRC projects in the past (Woods and Jeffrey 1996, Jeffrey and Woods 1998, Jeffrey 2007) in order to validate, to a limited extent, our qualitative approach. The ethnographic priority was to highlight the perspectives of the institutional inhabitants and their daily practices.

Four researchers carried out this ESRC (RES-000-23-1281) research, to a greater or lesser extent. The researchers in all of the schools, except City (see Table 1), carried out interview/conversations in the main, with observational fieldnotes accounting for just over 50% of their total data. We then began progressive focusing in City school where the rest of the observational fieldnotes were carried out and in particular the bulk of conversations with young learners.

This focus also included the largest group of teacher interview/conversations. This progressive focusing bears the weight of the ethnographic data and the analysis for this article, in line with a grounded theory approach (Glaser and Strauss 1967). The whole database included fifty two days observational fieldnotes, fifty four recorded conversations with teachers and other significant adults and thirty two recorded conversations with learners. We transcribed all recorded conversations with management, teachers, pupils and parents that we saw as being of theoretical significance (See Table 1 opposite).

Table 1 - Sample details

Schools/Data	City(C) Suburban Estate Two form	Istead(I) Rural One form	Hampstead(H) Rural One form	Morden(M) Suburban 3 form	Victoria(V) Urban 2 form	Westside(W) Urban 2 form
Researcher	BJ	EZP	EZP	EZP	GT	Consultant
Teacher Transcribed Conversations 54	19	3	4	1	11	16
Typed Fieldnotes – Days 46*	20	6	9	3	7	1
Transcribed children's conversations in groups 19	13	0	0	0	6	0

BJ = PI, GT = Collaborator, EZP = Researcher

Each researcher also had fieldnotes that were not transcribed and entered into the digital software.

Each school in the paper is identified in the text by the initial letter of its pseudonym; the Yr. refers to the year group taught by the teacher; each teacher's name begins with the school identification letter; DH and HT indicate deputy head or Headteacher; FN = fieldnotes; learner's names are not identified in full.

The conversations probed areas such as:

- Perceived tensions between creativity and performativity policies and the dilemmas and opportunities this creates for teachers, pupils and parents.
- Coping strategies used to ameliorate these tensions and dilemmas
- The educational identities being constructed in the context of the two policy imperatives.

Our analysis proceeded in the sequence: data collection – analysis – data collection – analysis. The process provided 'spiralling insights' (Lacey, 1976) as it sought to generate theory from the data using the method of 'constant comparisons' (Glaser and Strauss, 1967). Data storage, retrieval and analysis was supported by the use of the qualitative data analysis computer package Atlas Ti.

The Governance Turn

Four sets of related changes characterise Ball's (Ball, 2009) 'governance turn': forms of government (structures and agencies); the form and nature of the participants in the processes of governance; the prevailing discourses within governance and a change in the governing of and production of new kinds of 'willing' subjects, 'panoptic performativity (Perryman, 2006). Our research found examples of all four:

1. the change to a market approach for schools
2. the change to institutional professional identities
3. the institutionalisation of a performative discourse
4. the development of new willing aspirational subjects

Marketisation

The first of Ball's characteristics of the governance turn – changes in the form of structures and agencies – encapsulated the way in which schools have had to respond to the market approach of government policy.

The six primary schools, in our study, had an openness to the local community through their websites, publication of test results, community interests and willingness to engage;

'You just wander around, the teachers are used to people coming in and out, they won't mind' (Assistant Head – repeated on several occasions) 'Yes, the children don't mind adults coming in, they are used to it. There's always someone walking around the school, they are happy with that.'

(Head). On each of my visits, there were parents being shown around. (FN-I-2 February 2007)

The performance of the teacher was a daily public affair, unlike the closed classrooms of the professional autonomous phase of the 1980s (Hargreaves, 2000) and its qualitative nature had changed.

> Yeah it's more open door. We don't have our door shut and we don't teach like that so much. We're a bigger team than we used to be when we were on our own in the classroom from 9-3. It's not like that anymore is it? It's much more open and we encourage teachers to show us what they can do. (Carolyn-C-Yr.2).

The school invited parents and the community in more often and visitors, including parents, saw more of the school's work and the way teachers teach as the classrooms were more open.

> Some parents come in and look at the work in progress. This was announced this morning in assembly. Some Yr.6 pupils are in charge of welcoming the parents, meeting them at the entrance and taking them to the room where their child is working. The parents have not been met by or talked to a teacher yet, it's all been led by the Y.6 pupils (FN-H-23 February 2007)

Teaching had become a public affair. Even the private reports to parents were now virtually open with every parent knowing the school statistics on its SATs performance and OfSTED inspections and children and parents talked openly with each other about the child's 'level' (see Glossary), both in and outside the staffroom, the classroom and the school grounds;

> We had an afternoon where we invited parents to look at SATs papers to encourage them to help their children. (Carole-C-Yr.5).

Meetings often took place in public, not in the head's office but, for example, in the school café where we noted one with a government DfES person and another with six local headteachers. Schools were not just willing to share information, but positively eager to share it.

> On my second and third visits, I am left alone in the Head's office so that I can browse the curriculum and school policy folders. The Head welcomes

the policy aspect of our research project. They have many visits from other schools, who are sceptical that this school's curriculum flow approach could work for them. She hopes that our project will serve to convince other schools of the viability of the curriculum flow approach, eg: Beacon Role – Leading Practice, and sharing of good practice. (FN-H-8 January 2007)

Members of the community, often parents, assisted in classrooms voluntarily helping with maths or science in groups and reading. The openness was part of the market reconstitution of the school, for each local school knew details of each other's performance.

I get a lot of emphasis from the head saying we must get 88% at the relevant level and there should be no possibility that we get less. However, I think my cohort this year is not going to get 80%. We'll be lucky to get 50-60% but there's no option below 88% and it starts affecting us because the other school on the estate has raised its SATs results and now we're in competition with them and they're actually getting as many people applying to go to them as we are and so there is competition. We've been seen as the best school on the estate, but now we've got competition from the other school on the estate, so there's pressure from the performance of other schools. (Calvin-C-DH)

Internally professional psychologists, welfare workers and inspectors, advisors and even researchers often sat at the back of a class making notes about what was going on. There has been a sharp rise in the number of teaching assistants working in schools, many of whom were parents, who carry out supervised teaching roles and work in the classroom all day, another adult in the classroom (Garland and Garland, 2009). Senior staff regularly observed some aspect of the teacher's work and in some schools teachers observed each other in a form of professional reciprocity.

As Key Stage 1 Coordinator my job is to check on teachers, I say to my Key Stage 1 staff 'let's have a chat about how people are reaching their targets, how we are getting on and how many people in your class are meeting expectations, where they should be'. We'll discuss that and one may say 'no I'm really struggling with my middle group. We are constantly looking to see how people are getting on with our 'flying high' group – those who are near the class level and need extra help to get to it. I target them as soon as they came in and decide on my overall list as to where they should be by the end of the term. (Carolyn-C-Yr.2).

There was more collaboration between teachers who often worked together planning a term's work for the same age group and joint activities often took place with two teachers working in the same room or the whole school worked on one project for anything from one week to six in which teaching ideas and strategies were shared and displayed. This open culture made hierarchical power less visible and appeared to show how horizontal power (Bernstein, 1996) operated by focusing on the institution and less on hierarchical positions, a major aspect of this form of governmentalisation.

Institutional membership

The development of institutional identities rather than the broader teaching and learning theories upon which professional identities of the pre-1990s were based (Woods and Jeffrey, 1996) exemplified Ball's (2009) second characteristic of the governance turn – changes to the form and nature of the participants in the processes of governance. Resentment, in the 1990s of centralisation and deprofessionalism (Jeffrey and Woods, 1998) had turned towards ensuring the success and fate of the marketised institution and impacted more heavily on professional status, well being and self interests.

The result was an emergent team impression (Goffman, 1959) of conformity: actors sustaining a collective belief in both the institutional rhetoric and their voluntary adherence to it, making resistance seem unnecessary. A Reinventive Institution (RI), (Scott, 2010) which aims to provide a space for reinventing identities, applied to these schools. The RI inmate is both an actor who performs and a subject position defined by the sum of these performances. S/he is both agentically performative and constrained by the discipline of interaction (ibid.) and the development of a team approach was crucial to the operation of governmentalism.

Belonging to a team, the opposite of the lone professional of Lortie's 1975 study or those in Jennifer Nias's 1990 study (1989), is the major way in which a primary teacher's identity is now constructed (Jeffrey, 2002). Today's primary school teacher is a team player belonging to a team that is in open competition with other local school teams but also part of a team that needs to present itself as a unified, creative, inclusive and effective managerial organisation, 'doing member' (Garfinkel, 1967).

Also being part of a team, getting to know adults as well is rewarding. It was very lonely when previously I was with just children all the time. I've got a bit of a responsibility now for myself as an individual as well. I've got my own job. I like that. I like my own responsibility. I also like the people that I've met and I'm getting to know even more. It's like a community here. I know, as you are aware, that it is in the middle of an estate, but you know that is actually quite good. It is part of the community and that's what I've enjoyed. (Wanda-W-Yr.6)

Teachers in our research involved having more of a team role in the organisation of the school and using their creativity to develop the institution. In dealing with technologies of the self Foucault talks about how the self is governed, how we seek to to 'transform' ourselves (Foucault, 2000). Professional cohesion and good professional relations were essential to the development of the team approach.

I find, in the staffroom, a display board entitled 'Staff Achievement Board', with some displayed certificates on which some members of staff have been commended for certain actions or for just starting a new role. All staff are encouraged to download a copy and to fill it in for someone they think worthy. It's all part of the team approach used in the school. The head has indicated that this is crucial and that staff are encouraged to do kind things for one another, such as get them a cup of tea, and not to make it that obvious. Written in large letters above the main notice board, and outside at least one classroom is the TEAM approach 'Together Everyone Achieves More'. (FN-C-26 February 2007)

The team approach develops cohesiveness, bringing all staff into a closer embrace (Jeffrey 2010) of the institution's policies and values, including the performative ones;

Everything, children, background, curriculum, the way it's taught, the sort of input from teachers here, there's much more of a cohesive team in this school than in any I've known. That's a big part, that's what we're all striving for, the same thing in this school, for the welfare and the education of the children, everybody from the people who serve the dinners, to the cleaners who sweep the floors and sort out the leaks in the boilers to the office staff, to the teachers. It doesn't seem that there is a big hierarchy here of being a superior because you're the Head teacher or inferiority because you're a dinner-lady. (Christopher-C-Yr.3)

The team approach was manifest in the usual portrayal of photographs of all the school staff including support staff, kitchen and cleaning staff. These corporate teams reflect the modern commercial organisation in which everyone plays a part in the development and promotion of the cultural institution (Peters and Waterman, 1982). The team approach enabled class teachers to assist other teacher's professional practice, specifically in performative practices;

> I sit with the Yr. 5 teacher and we look at areas where there is a dip and we look at different strategies, with writing for example, looking at how the children can set their own manageable writing targets so that they understand in 'children speak', So we are constantly looking at how you can help those children and giving them more support in those areas. (Harriet-H-Yr.6)

Performative regulation (Scott, 2010) occurs where groups of people submit themselves to the authority of an institution, internalise its values and enact through them mutual surveillance in an inmate culture. Power operates horizontally as well as vertically, as members monitor each other's conduct, sanction deviance and evaluate their own progress in relative terms. The disciplinary gaze is not merely transmitted but reticulated: dispersed and refracted through an agentic network. Power is not only discursively constitutive but also interactively productive of new identities. The rituals of peer group interaction are central to this process and can be as important as the formal instruction they receive in motivating people to commit to an institution (ibid.) instead of going it alone.

Performativity and creative discourses

The third of Ball's (2009) characteristics of the 'governance turn' focuses on the change to the prevailing discourses, which in the case of schools initially involved the introduction of performativity in the 1990s and marginalising creative teaching and learning (Pollard *et.al.*, 1994, Woods *et.al.*, 1997). The constraints we identified in the mid-1990s were concerned with central imposition of a National Curriculum, specific pedagogies examined by OfSTED, a prescriptive literacy and numeracy programme and the beginning of the influence of SATs. The current research shows a continuation of some of those constraints, for example, tightly focused curriculum guidelines with detailed assessment criteria attached, the continuation of OfSTED inspections, albeit more frequent but less exacting and the extension of the influence on teaching and learning of SATs testing. We have noted a loosening of the constraints on the literacy and numeracy programmes, a more welcoming or tolerance of OfSTED inspections as a useful check on a school's accountability and progress, an acceptance by teachers of a progression narrative for assessment contained in the curriculum guidelines which assisted teachers in knowing what to do and where to go next (Jeffrey and Troman, 2009). The annual or twice annual testing, as a form of check on learner progress and indicating priorities for school and teacher targeting, is now generally accepted,

> There was external pressure to test the whole school every year to ensure they got higher in the league tables, it's not something that the head or I, or anyone particularly wants, but unfortunately it's the way it has to be. (Stephanie-W-DH),

...constructing organisational professionals (professionalism from above) as opposed to occupational professionals (from within the profession) (Evetts, 2005). Teachers internalised failures, marginalising the more public expression of heavy duty accountability (Jeffrey and Woods 1998) of the 1990s;

> The 75% target for us is a measure of how much progression the children in my class have made this year and I'm not going to get that. 75% of them haven't got the national average, so I haven't got them there. It's not that we look at it in the staff meetings and say 'Oh these teachers didn't get them to this target so you must be a rubbish teacher'. But I do feel personally responsible for it. However, I think it helps to feel personally responsible for the progression, and it focuses you more on the children that could do with a lot of help. (Celina-C-Yr2).

The internalisation of responsibility for achievement is exactly how governmentalism works, to transfer responsibility from central government to institutions and individuals. Perversely, the support of the team culture appeared to protect them from this personal criticism but the responsibility was nevertheless felt acutely. They accepted the situation and sought to manage the tension;

> Obviously we have targets for all children in the school that's how it is, not that I always agree with these things but you do have targets and children are assessed to a certain level of a target and at the start of the year you have the previous year's targets and you are expected to move them up. I have to bear in mind that you are not going to get every single child up to

those targets and I have to know that as a teacher that that's not a failing. I have to accept that because I'm quite hard on myself. I have to accept that I'm not going to move every single child to that level and you have to know their limitations as well as your own. I think you need to know that performance is being assessed because we have performance and appraisals and we have to reflect it in our practice and we need to know that what we are doing is working. (Harriet-H-Yr.6)

They embraced (Jeffrey, 2010) the imperatives of the performativity culture to ensure the continuing success of their institution in the local market place. We saw how testing and targets alongside external auditing was accepted by teachers as part of their role, more of a craft role ensuring everything was effective and striving for improvement.

People seem to find a way to deal with things, you've just got to find a way haven't you? Because you have to work with the system, there are certain things that are in a system. You work with government, you've got power within a system, you have to work the system or you have to make the system work for you too, otherwise you end up banging your head against a brick wall. (Wei-W-Yr.2).

However, the discourse of performativity also contained satisfiers (Herzberg, 1971) for testing and targeted teaching and learning sometimes brought instantaneous satisfaction;

I go from thinking I don't think I want to do Year Six again, for it is too much like hard work and too much stress and you have got too much responsibility on your shoulders, to thinking 'I like this, I like this responsibility'. It sounds a bit selfish really, but people look up to you if you are in Year Six, you are at the top of the school. The children respect you because you are at the top of the school, you are a Year Six teacher and the staff see you as a bit of unknown territory. I quite like that feeling it gives me, which, is a daft reason to want to stay in Year Six but that is a genuine feeling that I have. But then when days are really hard you feel you are not getting anywhere and you think 'do I really need this and let's get back to Year Five and have a nice creative year. (Carole-C-Yr.6)

Performative satisfaction is a powerful reward for maintaining and developing progress and has always played a part in primary school policies to a greater or lesser extent, for example the regular testing of reading proficiency. However, governmentalism is the process of ensuring that schools and teachers prioritise government policy rather than professional values and policies.

> I went through my results yesterday and although on the face of it they don't look great when you compare with October, they've all achieved, they've all moved up and that's made me happy because although the results aren't fantastic when you compare with other schools, everybody has gone up and that was good, so we must be making a difference. When you go through it with a tooth comb, you can see something positive and that's good. (Wheatley-W-Yr.3).

Performative satisfaction is both a product of its constitution and agency (Foucault, 1979a) for it is a possibility at the point that disciplinary power is being enacted that gives members the chance to shrug off the description of being a 'docile member' (Olssen, 2006: 14) and bringing their commitment to engage with the situation.

Our research also identified how government support for a creativity discourse, after a period of marginalisation in the 1990s (Woods and Jeffrey 1996), benefited teachers as well, although not to the detriment of performativity (Troman *et.al.*, 2007). Part of the global marketisation discourse included the realisation that new industries needed the creativity of the worker as a new resource of labour power to be tapped for increased performance and prosperity (Buckingham and Jones, 2001, Jones, 2001) and combined with the influence of a report on culture and creativity the English government funded a Creative Partnerships Programme (CP), of over a £100m during the 2000s. In recent times primary schools have been trying to manage the twin discourses of performativity and creativity resulting in what was termed 'smart' teaching by one of sample.

Smart teaching developed in some of our schools through a creative merging of both performativity and creativity discourses (Jeffrey and Troman, 2009) for the benefit of their learners, their school policies and teacher professionality. This situation opened up, to the teacher and the school, the opportunity to engage agency and the development of the capacity for freedom and decision making (Olssen, 2006). These 'smart' teachers became quite sophisticated at integrating subjects and assessment, acting as a policy creator, creative mediator and creative teacher (Brain and Comerford-Boyes, 2006);

> The topic was Vikings and we did everything through Vikings. There was an inter-active website on the BBC where they had to choose a long

boat and basically they were attacking Lindisfarne. So we did a bit of map work for geography and we did tacking, drawing zig-zag lines across to Lindisfarne. I do quite a bit of sailing so I could show them the principles of sailing, tacking against the wind and so forth and we actually worked out the bearings, the angles. We were doing angles that week so I introduced them to what angles were for and the purpose of them finding out the angles to see how their ship would sail. The more able ones could work out the bigger angles so they crossed from Norway to England and the ones who could only work on smaller numbers worked back the other way so it was differentiated. (Imogen-I-Yr.5).

The schools embraced the creativity discourse as a way of developing their own cherished values and pedagogies and ensuring teacher satisfaction but nevertheless we can see a powerful form of governmentalism in operation in the way government based global creative priorities have been incorporated into a discourse of creative performance supported by schools and teachers. Without the recent support of government for this discourse it would probably have remained marginal to the main performative discourse but nevertheless that support has opened up possibilities for agency for teachers.

Aspiring cultures

The fourth vital element of Ball's 'governance turn' (2009) is the development of new willing subjects and in this case it was characterised by the development of an aspirational culture.

The schools demonstrated an aspiring culture in which members held personal aspirations for career, for learners, for their school and community and the values underpinning these aspirations were at the same time meritocratic, egalitarian and humanist. Cultural and educational homilies littered our schools, exhorting members to think and act positively, to see learning as a comfortable but challenging journey made easier through self assessment and through co-operation with others, identifying mistakes as learning points and generally celebrating the joy of learning and education and downplaying authoritative power relations. These homilies targeted adults as well, some of them placed in staff toilets. An aspirational culture was prominent throughout with a celebration of continual improvement as each member arrived at a station on the never ending journey through professional and personal life. (FN-C-14 March 2007).

Professional life was hard but the new aspirational culture had its satisfiers (Herzberg 1970);

I don't want to paint a false picture and say we're always happy because that's not true. There are days when I'm quite tired, especially towards the end of the term and you think 'oh goodness' but the majority of the time I think we are very positive and I think we're always willing to try new things and I think that's the key. We are a fairly young staff who have that energy and we feel comfortable with change. If you haven't been teaching as long then maybe you're willing to change. (Carolyn-C-Yr.2)

Promotion and challenges were daunting but welcome in this new 'can do' culture.

It is a big job and it is a responsible thing to do. There are downsides to it but I think quite positive. Perhaps it's my innocence or my ignorance, I don't know. It's a big responsibility but I think it's one that I'm quite happy to take on. And I think I would do it very well. (Vicky-V-DH).

Challenges were a central part of the aspiring school cultures;

I think targets for the school give people a bit of ambition, it does for me anyway, just to say you need to achieve this in this time, it's a bit more of business psychology I think. The moment it feels like you're on a treadmill it's time to change and to set yourself some targets to know where you want to get to and if you're ambitious enough, targets for head-teacher or advanced skills teacher or a SENCO. (Christopher-C-Yr.3)

Continuous improvement and a belief in the possibility of success was an example of how performativity (Gillies 2008) pervaded the school culture.

The fact that OfSTED could drop in anytime means you have to always have it in place and always have to be motivated and keep things going and if you started some new initiative you need them to know that you can continue with it and if you've said on your school development plan and your school improvement plan that you're going to do it then it needs to be monitored and needs to be checked that we are doing it. I think those things are all good really. I think it's good to have the thought that OfSTED could be round the corner or could be checking up on you. I don't particularly like it when they're in (laughs) but no it doesn't worry me. I don't think it worries the school either personally because I think we know what we're doing and I think we know where we want to get to, we know what we want to achieve and we've got our school improvement plan and we know what's on it, so I think it's fine. (Cloe-C-Yr.2)

Working in schools in deprived areas was also portrayed as a challenge;

I think there's a real buzz working in these schools, you know you're up against the edge, much more than if I worked in more affluent areas where I live, because it makes them quite a lot more interesting. (Camile-C-HT)

A commitment to social justice strengthened the power of the institution and those individuals who embraced these principles. Their commitment was not just to maintain their league table position but to improve children's opportunities;

Actually I want the test results improved as well so a child going on to secondary school can read and write. Actually we're genuinely worried about test results not because I care about where I am on the league table. If I can get my kids reading and writing, fantastic so I do all the old stuff. If I want to break this cycle of deprivation, one of the ways is to teach them to read and write so they can engage with other kids, so I worry about that. (Victor-V-HT).

Added this we identified an educational entrepreneurialism (Woods, 2007), an energy to be innovative, to drive along new initiatives and to develop original strategies and activities particularly in areas of deprivation. Acting as commissioners of services schools focused on a variety of funding streams to develop their institutions, to engage in local partnerships, to raise the quality of training for everyone to develop skills and enterprise.

I prepared a programme that was short and hard hitting, but it was about our chance to seize education to re-look at what is education, why do we have schools, to start looking at that. It worked through modelling in the Excellence in Cities programme. It's given us the freedom now, we've got much more freedom around workforce than when I first became a Head. Now we've got much more freedom, we can do anything now with funding or I believe we can, or I choose to believe I can. I was saying to our governors the other day, if we want an Educational Social Worker then we buy one in, you don't have to be given your staffing or told what it is. If I feel I want a blacksmith in my school I can have one. (Camille-C-HT).

A culture of openness underpinned by a market discourse of aspiration and a discourse that promoted the possibility of universal improvement and success through aspiration forged governmentality in these primary schools.

Conclusion

Governmentality works at the micro level through examining local discourses, the kinds of power relations established and the emergence of agency through the strategic practices that Foucault (1979a) maintains dominate local situations. In this sense our research shows clearly how governmentality tied to performativity and a market context worked. Institutions and their members needed to be seen as successful in the market place but they also wanted to be successful in terms of their professional practices and they worked to ensure that this was so, both for the school to whom they were now more closely bound, and for their own psychic rewards (Lortie, 1975, Troman, 2008). Schools and teachers reproduce government policies and at the same time attempt to gain satisfaction from ensuring their success while attempting to assert their own values and creativity as in 'smart teaching'. There is clearly a strong affinity between market approaches, performativity and governmentalism which ensures greater success for the latter in the way schools and teachers incorporate the process and technologies into their professional competencies.

Nevertheless there have been some resistances as well as accommodations. The nationwide boycotting of SATs annual exams by roughly a third of schools in 2010 has led to a review of SATs, which appears to be recommending more inclusion of teacher assessment in the Year 6, end of primary school assessment, but it does not seem to indicate any reduction in the SATs exercise itself particularly since the new Coalition government has indicated clearly its continued support for SATs and the boycott has fizzled out. Indeed, the development of free schools announced by the coalition government in the UK in 2010 and the dramatic increase in the rise of Academies (see Glossary) in England is another structural change in the development of a governmentality in which schools take responsibility for educational progress tied to performative guidelines. Up to 200 failing primary schools will be turned into academies and taken outside of Local Authority supervision to improve performance through greater exposure to a market discourse and process (Shepherd, 2011).

At the same time a narrower basic curriculum is to be introduced in 2013 in England apparently allowing schools more freedom to prioritise and organise the rest of the curriculum including opportunities to specialise and compete in an educational market. In order to maintain success schools, their teachers and pupils will need to strive to construct a climate and culture that meet these basic requirements and then to compete in the market place for new recruits. The marketised school with its institutionalised teachers, government led performative dominant discourses contributes significantly to the development of willing subjects so completing the governmental turn.

Glossary

SATs – Standard Assessment Tasks given to all primary pupils, but the Yr.6 tests are externally marked and taken in one designated week in May each year across England. The government Department of Education publishes LA results.

OfSTED – The Office for Standards in Education, which inspects all schools and related educational establishments and provides regular reports on them.

LA – Local Authority – Responsible for overseeing and supporting most of the schools and educational establishments in each local authority.

SIPs – School Improvement Partners are usually private companies or LA groups purchased by schools to assist the improvement of school performance.

Academies – Privately managed schools, often charitable trusts, funded directly from government taken out of LA control and gaining more financial and curriculum freedom than LA schools.

Level – Achievement Level – A level descriptor that designates the level a pupil has reached in each subject and at the same time indicates the next level to attain according to the average standard for their Key Stage.

Table 2

	Key Stage 1	Key Stage 2
Level 1		
Level 2 a-c	Years 1+2 Aged 5-7	
Level 3 a-c		Years 3+4 Ages 7-9
Level 4 a-c		Years 5+6 Ages 9-11
Level 5 a-c		Years 7-9 Ages 11-13

Teacher Agency, Performativity and Curriculum Change: Reinventing the Teacher in the Scottish Curriculum for Excellence?

Mark Priestley, Sarah Robinson and Gert Biesta

In a year group assembly, our headteacher described to us what he called our moral obligation to the school. We are not, he said, to do well in our exams for our own individual achievement. That, he told us, would be selfish, and no employer would employ someone like that. Instead, the work we do for our Highers should be for the school. We are, and I quote, 'morally obliged to achieve the best possible attainment we can for our school'. (Scottish secondary school pupil, 2011)

Introduction

The anecdote reproduced above provides a telling example of Michael Apple's argument that there has been a 'subtle shift in emphasis ... from student needs to student performance, and from what the school does for the student to what the student does for the school' (Apple, 2001: 413). The latter reversal is a key dimension of the culture of performativity that has increasingly been shaping the everyday lives of teachers in schools, colleges and universities (see, e.g. Gleeson and Shain; 1999; Ball, 2003; Biesta, 2004; James and Biesta 2007; Sahlberg, 2010; Keddie *et.al.*,2011). Performativity is not simply the demand for teachers to 'perform' but more a pressure to perform in particular ways, most notably in terms of externally defined performance indicators. Teachers are therefore not simply asked to teach, but instead must ensure that their students achieve the kind of grades that give their school the desired position in league tables. Such requirements stand in sharp contrast with a professional discourse on education, as they position the teacher as a curriculum deliverer and producer of performance statistics, rather than as a curriculum developer, a responsible professional and an agent of change.

More recently, however, there has been an emerging tendency in curriculum policy in the UK and elsewhere to construct teachers more explicitly as agents of change (e.g. Goodson, 2003; Priestley, 2011a; Nieveen, 2011). This is a significant shift given several decades of policies that worked to de-professionalise teachers by taking agency away from them and replacing it with prescriptive curricula and oppressive regimes of testing and inspection. The [re]turn to teacher agency gives explicit permission to teachers to exert high[er] degrees of professional agency within the contexts in which they work. The important question this raises, therefore, is what happens when a drive towards teacher agency 'meets' a culture of performativity – and it is this question upon which we wish to focus in this chapter. Our chapter draws upon the *Teacher Agency and Curriculum Change* project, which comprises a number of in-depth ethnographic case studies in Scottish schools (primary and secondary)[1]. The immediate context for the research is the implementation of Scotland's new Curriculum for Excellence (Scottish Executive, 2004), a policy that aims to change the structure, content and method of Scottish education, and which is an example of modern curricular reform in which teachers are explicitly positioned as agents of change. The project focuses on the ways in which and the extent to which experienced teachers achieve agency in their day to day working contexts, against the background of the introduction of the new curriculum, and on the factors that promote or inhibit such agency.

Our chapter is structured as follows. We commence with an overview of the key features of performativity, both in Scotland and further afield, and describe the recent re-emergence of a discourse of teacher agency. We then outline the ideas about agency that have informed our research. Against this background we then present a number of vignettes from our research that provide in insight in the ways in which teachers are responding to curriculum change and, through this, shed some light on the factors that promote and inhibit teacher agency in the context of curriculum change. In the concluding section we reflect on the ways in which the encounter between a culture of performativity and a policy discourse focusing on teachers as agents of change is impacting upon teachers' ways of doing and being.

The Culture of Performativity and the Scottish Context

Performativity has been widely discussed and critiqued in the academic literature, and it is not our intention here to revisit this ground. However, it is useful, in framing our analysis of teacher agency to outline some of its key dimensions, and especially to show how Scotland, where our research is based, exhibits both features in common with the rest of the UK, as well as important differences. Wilkins (2011) identifies three main strands of performativity:

1) The *audit/target culture*, as improvement and quality are measured through statistical data (for example examinations statistics).

---

1. The project has been funded by the UK Economic and Social Research Council (project reference RES-000-22-4208).

2) *Interventionist regulatory mechanisms*, particularly school inspections. This includes the use of self-evaluation using external defined performance indicators or outcomes steering.

3) A *market environment*, where parental choice is facilitated by publicly available data from and attainment statistics.

While to a large extent these strands are part of a wider culture of accountability (see Biesta, 2004), what is particular for performativity is the fact that *indicators* of performance become performance *targets* in themselves. Under a culture of performativity, to put it differently, the performance of the system becomes self-referential. 'Quality' – 'the most empty and abused word of the last decade' (Biesta, 2010: 69); 'an aerosol word', a deodorant to 'cover up the slightly offensive odour surrounding the decay of the public provision of education' (Smyth and Shacklock, 1998: 51) – thus ceases to be defined in substantive terms and becomes entirely formal, something we can see in the strategic ambition of many organisations to achieve a certain position in a league table.

Performativity has been widely claimed to have a number of serious consequences. Smyth and Shacklock are 'distressed by the expunging and depletion of educative values and purposes out of schooling by mean spirited politicians and their technocratically-minded advisors' (Smyth and Shacklock, 1998: 27). Similar sentiments are clearly evident in the writings of Biesta, who has particularly highlighted how a culture of measurement drives out a concern for what constitutes good education (see, e.g., Biesta, 2006; 2010), and Robinson (2011), who cautions against an erosion of fundamental pedagogies and detrimental effects on education. An emphasis on short term instrumental goals driven by performativity thus encourages a detachment from big picture ideas, as teachers distance themselves from their personal values in order to 'play the game' (Gleeson and Gunter, 2001). This game can take the form of fabrication of the school's image – careful impression management and discourses of excellence (Keddie *et.al.*, 2011) and the concealing of 'dirty laundry' (Cowie *et.al.*, 2007), as well as more serious corruption and cheating (Ball, 2003; Sahlberg, 2010). According to these writers, ethical practices lose out to performative pressures, as survival strategies lead to tactical and even cynical compliance.

Such 'reforms that deform' (Smyth and Shacklock, 1998: 8) distort practices leading to what Cowie, Taylor and Croxford (2007) have termed perverse incentives. These include inflation of grades for internally assessed coursework, preventing poorly performing subjects from running examination courses, and not entering pupils for examinations (or entering them at a lower level than merited)[2]. Further 'collateral damage' (Sahlberg, 2010) lies in the effects on teachers. The time spent on 'maintaining and achieving a public image of a good school [means that] less time and energy is spent on pedagogic and curricular substance' (Apple, 2001: 416). According to Sahlberg (2010), educational quality depends on teachers working within a favourable and collegial social environment. However the intensification of teachers' work associated with performativity militates against this, and even leads to desocialisation (Keddie *et.al.*, 2011), low morale (Troman *et.al.*, 2007; van Zanten, 2005), stress (Troman, 2000) and diminished confidence (Helsby, 1999).

Scotland is extremely similar in many respects to England in terms of the first two dimensions of performativity identified by Wilkins (2011). Successive guidance and statutory regulation from 1997, known as the Quality Improvement initiative, has established an edifice of control and performativity that has similar effects to its English counterpart (see Cowie *et.al.*, 2007; Boyd and Norris, 2004). There is a strong attainment agenda, driven by statistical use of data derived from external examination results. This evaluative use of assessment is based around the production of what are known as Standard Tables and Charts (STACS). Such data are used extensively in secondary schools to manage teachers, enabling, for example, subject departments to be compared with each other, the performance of individual pupils to be compared across subjects, and the performance of schools and departments to be set against equivalent schools on comparator league tables (Cowie *et.al.*, 2007).

Poorly performing teachers are quickly identified and pressure is applied by school management teams to remedy such performance. In primary schools, data collected in relation to the attainment of pupils against curricular levels are collated by local authorities, and pressure is applied to headteachers of schools where performance is deemed to be unsatisfactory[3].

---

2. Statistical evidence supplied by the Scottish Qualifications Authority for examinations held in 2009 showed that 14,035 pupils were entered for level 5 Intermediate 2 examinations when they had previously achieved passes in the equivalent Standard Grade Credit course for the same subject. This practice is widespread in Scotland, and prevents so-called 'high-risk pupils' (i.e. those deemed to be at risk of failing) from taking level 6 Higher qualifications) from affecting the school's placing on comparator league tables (although schools often justify the practice as being in the pupil's best interests). Numbers were especially high in English (5,756, representing nearly one quarter of the total cohort). (SQA, 2009)

3. The use of such tests was said to 'voluntary' under Scotland's former 5-14 curriculum, but in practice schools were 'encouraged' to use a national bank of assessments rather than teacher designed assessments. Attainment information was routinely collected by local authorities and used for quality improvement purposes. Within the new Curriculum for Excellence, it is currently unclear whether such testing will take place, although it is clear that schools will continue to record data of pupil attainment in respect of curricular levels, and thus the potential for similar evaluative assessment will continue.

Inspections by Her Majesty's Inspectorate of education (HMIe) constitute part of an external quality control mechanism[4]. Attainment is taken seriously by HMIe as an indicator of quality, and in turn drives teacher perceptions of the inspection process. Inspections are framed around a set of performance indicators known as *How Good Is Our School?* – commonly referred to by the acronym HGIOS (HMIe, 2002). HGIOS is ostensibly a self-evaluation tool, but is also used by inspectors to judge the quality of schools. Following changes to the curriculum, in particular the advent of Curriculum for Excellence, HGIOS was revamped in 2006-7 (HMIe, 2006, 2007). This signalled a supposed shift from a hard to a softer managerialism, to accommodate changes to schooling resulting from the new curriculum. However, according to Reeves (2008: 13), revisions to HGIOS are 'cosmetic, since the basic instruments and methodology remain the same'. In parallel to the operation of HMIe as a quality improvement mechanism, Scotland's schools are also subject to local authority controls, which are more pervasive and extensive than in England. Several writers have documented a shift in emphasis from a supportive advisory role for local authorities to a quality improvement role characterised by audits that mirror the external inspection process, and indeed are seen as little more than a process of getting schools ready for inspection (e.g. Cowie *et.al.*, 2007; Boyd and Norris, 2004).

The third dimension, the role of markets, is less evident in Scotland, where there is a stronger tradition of comprehensive schooling and a slightly less prominent role of non state-funded schools[5]. Quality improvement mechanisms tend to be kept in place through bureaucracies, notably the local authorities. The effects of such central control were noted by an OECD report (2007), which suggested that centralised control over the curriculum and organisational structures has a detrimental effect on responsiveness and relevance to the needs of many pupils. Nevertheless, there are three features of quality improvement in Scotland that will be familiar to those working in England: compliance; a top-down approach; and a linear approach to change (see Reeves, 2008). In particular, 'improvement with pre-specified level descriptors' (MacKinnon, 2011: 91) requires schools to provide evidence of 'quality,' with the attendant dangers of fabrication, as mentioned above.

---

4. In 2011, HMIe merged with Learning and Teaching Scotland, a quasi independent, but government funded curriculum development agency, to form a new arm of the government. This is called Education Scotland, and is now a part of the civil service (http://www.educationscotland.gov.uk/).

5. The so-called independent sector educates around 6.5% of the total number of schoolchildren in the UK and over 7% of the total number of schoolchildren in England. See http://www.isc.co.uk/TeachingZone_SectorStatistics.htm . The Scottish Government no longer collates figures for Scotland. However, the latest available statistics (2009) provide a lower figure than England, showing a gradual increase from 3.9% in 2000 to 4.3% in 2009. See http://www.scotland.gov.uk/Topics/Statistics/Browse/School-Education/TrendInSchools .

Teacher Agency: New Directions

In apparent contradistinction to the managerialism described in the previous section, there has been a shift in emphasis in the degree of curricular prescription faced by teachers. While the last two decades have been characterised by highly prescriptive curricula, recent curricular policy across the Anglophone world has explicitly eschewed such prescription, drawing, for instance, upon theories of transformational change (for example, Senge and Scharmer, 2006). Intrinsic to such policy is a renewed vision of teachers as developers of curriculum at a school level, and more widely as agents of change (Fullan, 2003). This is explicitly the case in Scotland's Curriculum for Excellence, which

> aims to engage teachers in thinking from first principles about their educational aims and values and their classroom practice. The process is based upon evidence of how change can be brought about successfully – through a climate in which reflective practitioners share and develop ideas. (Scottish Executive, 2006)

As well as advocating an enhanced professional role for teachers in developing the curriculum, such curricula exhibit a number of common pedagogic features which sit uneasily with more performative cultures of schooling – 'a fundamental tension that rests underneath any attempt to apply the logic of schooling to many [new] forms of curriculum and pedagogy' (Ladwig, 2010: 129). Thus, there is, for example, a curricular focus on dialogic pedagogies, active learning, individualisation in learning, and learner autonomy (or pupils taking responsibility for their own learning), all advocated for their putative potential in producing modern citizens, well-equipped to thrive in a knowledge society and as members of a globalised workforce. While these ideas in themselves are definitely not unproblematic, and while the language of 'learning' and 'learners' can be said to have contributed to the erosion of a focus on educational purpose, they do suggest forms of pedagogy and wider educational practice that are in tension with a top-down culture of schooling driven by the performativity described above. Here, the intrinsic logics of policy collide with the institutional logics of the contexts within which the policy is supposed to be enacted (Young, 1998). This situation is further exacerbated by incoherence within and between policies (Reeves, 2008; Priestley and Humes, 2010). Policies demanding performativity are a prominent part of this inherent and fundamental tension in teachers' work. Thus, teachers are faced with 'an educational dilemma: how to deal with external productivity demands on the one hand, while simultaneously teaching for the knowledge society with moral purpose' (Sahlberg, 2010: 48). They are caught between a 'rock and hard place' (Reeves, 2008).

We note that some writers have witnessed the ways in which some teachers are able to mediate, mitigate or circumvent some of the more damaging aspects of external demands on their work. For example, Bowe, Ball and Gold (1992) noted the ways in which high capacity departments were able to work around the National Curriculum to maintain what they viewed as their core mission in education. Helsby (1999) suggested that teachers with high confidence in their own capacity and authority were able to act with a high degree of agency in the face of performativity, noting also that collegiality boosted such capacity, but that performativity eroded it. A related theme emerged in the writings of Osborn *et.al.* (1997) and Gleeson and Shain (1999). These authors noted the varied responses of teachers to performative demands; not merely a simple binary of resistance/ compliance but more nuanced forms of mediation of policy to reflect differing perspectives and positioning (see also Gewirtz, 2002).

The renewed emphasis on teachers as agents of change is not without problems. Firstly, policy can tend to construe agency as solely a positive capacity – as a factor in 'successful' implementation – whereas one might legitimately take the view that agency could equally well be exercised for 'non-beneficial' purposes (Priestley, 2011b), or for decisions and actions that go against the grain of official policy. Thus, there are legitimate questions of the sorts of agency achieved by teachers, and attendant dangers of seeing agency in narrow and solely positive ways (Leander and Osborne, 2008). Second, there is the question of the extent to which teachers can actually achieve agency, which is a question about capacity, resources and opportunities. Here it could well be argued that the combined influence of at least two decades of prescriptive national curricula and increasing levels of managerialism and performativity may well have to a large extent eroded teachers' capacity for agency and have taken away important resources and opportunities for the achievement of agency from their practice. It is this aspect of agency that interests us in writing this chapter – the interplay between performativity, new curriculum policy and teacher experience that has the potential to both open up and close down agency, and shape different forms of agency.

Theorising Agency

Teacher agency – in other words, agency that is theorised specifically in respect of the activities of teachers in schools – has been subject to little explicit research or theory development (Vongalis-Macrow, 2007). While there is some literature that locates the concept in relation to wider theoretical discussions of agency (e.g.

Pignatelli, 1993; Priestley *et.al.*, in press; Pyhältö, *et.al.*, 2012), existing change models tend to both underplay and misconstrue the role of teacher agency in educational innovation (Leander and Osborne, 2008), and it is often utilised as a slogan to support school-based reform. Unlike *teacher* agency, agency *per se* been extensively theorised, particularly in the sociological literature. Fuchs (2001) has argued that there is a tendency in social theory and research to either focus on an over-socialised, macro view of agency – thus ignoring the local and specific – or to concentrate on overly individualised notions of agency – thus ignoring questions of structure, context and resources. In recent years, systematic attempts have been made to find a middle ground on this position, or indeed to reframe the debate altogether. These include Bourdieu's (1977) notion of 'habitus', Giddens's (1984) theory of 'structuration', and Archer's (1995) realist social theory. While such work has done a great deal in refining our understanding of the factors that pertain on social action, it is important to acknowledge that this discussion is predominantly located within a sociological problematic where the main ambition is the explanation of social action (see Hollis, 1994). In the so-called 'structure-agency' debate 'agency' thus tends to appear as an independent variable in the explanation of social actor, rather than as a phenomenon in its own right.

Our interest, however, is in the phenomenon of agency itself and on how agency is 'achieved' in concrete settings and under particular 'ecological' conditions and circumstances (see Biesta and Tedder, 2006). Our perspective on agency, to put it differently, is not sociological but has its roots in the theory of action, particularly as it has been developed in pragmatist philosophy (Dewey, Mead). Agency is viewed here as the capacity of actors to 'critically shape their responses to problematic situations' (Biesta and Tedder, 2006: 11), as autonomy and causal efficacy (Archer, 2000). But rather than seeing agency as residing in individuals as a property or capacity, the ecological view of agency sees agency as an emergent phenomenon of the ecological conditions through which it is enacted.

> [T]his concept of agency highlights that actors always act *by means of* their environment rather than simply in their environment [so that] the achievement of agency will always result from the interplay of individual efforts, available resources and contextual and structural factors as they come together in particular and, in a sense, always unique situations. (Biesta and Tedder, 2007: 137; emphasis added)

Agency, in other words, is not something that people can *have*; it is something that people *do*. It denotes a 'quality' of the *engagement* of actors with temporal-relational contexts-for-action, not a quality of the actors themselves. Viewing agency in such terms helps us to understand how humans are able to be reflexive and creative, acting counter to societal constraints, but also how individuals are enabled and constrained by their social and material environments.

Building on pragmatism, Emirbayer and Mische (1998) have argued for a conception of agency that aims to overcome the one-sidedness of existing theories of agency which, in their view, tend to focus on either routine, purpose or judgement. They make a case for a conception of agency which encompasses the dynamic interplay between these three dimensions and which takes into consideration 'how this interplay varies within different structural contexts of action' (ibid.,: 963). For this reason they suggest that agency should be understood as a configuration of influences from the *past*, orientations towards the *future* and engagement with the *present*. They refer to these three dimensions as the *iterational*, the *projective* and the *practical-evaluative* dimension respectively. In concrete actions all three dimensions play a role, but the degree to which they contribute varies. This is why Emirbayer and Mische speak of a '*chordal triad* of agency within which all three orientations resonate as separate but not always harmonious tones' (ibid.,: 972; emphasis in original). Thus they suggest that agency should be understood as a 'temporally embedded process of social engagement, informed by the past (in its habitual aspect), oriented toward the future (as a capacity to imagine alternative possibilities) and 'acted out' in the present (as a capacity to contextualize past habits and future projects with the contingencies of the moment)' (ibid.,: 963). This, in turn, leads them to define agency as '*the temporally constructed engagement by actors of different structural environments – the temporal-relational contexts of action – which, through the interplay of habit, imagination, and judgement, both reproduces and transforms those structures in interactive response to the problems posed by changing historical situations*' (ibid.,: 970; emph. in original).

Emirbayer's and Mische's ideas are helpful because they first of all show that agency does not materialise from nothing, but builds upon past achievements, understandings and patterns of action. This is expressed in the *iterational* element of agency which has to do with '*the selective reactivation by actors of past patterns of thought and action, routinely incorporated in practical activity, thereby giving stability and order to social universes and helping to sustain identities, interactions, and institutions over time*' (ibid.,: p.971; emph. in original). Their approach also acknowledges, however, that agency is in some way 'motivated,' i.e., that it is linked to the intention to bring about a future that is different from the present and the past. This is encapsulated in the *projective* element of agency which encompasses '*the imaginative generation by actors of possible future trajectories of action, in which received structures of thought and action may be creatively reconfigured in relation to actors' hopes, fears, and desires for the future'* (ibid., emph. in original). Although agency is involved with the past and the future it can only ever be 'acted out' in the present, which is precisely what is expressed in the *practical-evaluative*dimension, which entails *'the capacity of actors to make practical and normative judgements among alternative possible trajectories of action, in response to the emerging demands, dilemmas, and ambiguities of presently evolving situations'* (ibid., emph. in original).

Emirbayer's and Mische's analysis emphasises the importance of context and structure in that agency is seen as the 'temporally constructed *engagement* with different structural environments' (ibid.,: 970; emph. added). The combination of context and time highlights that it is not only important to understand agency in terms of the individual's lifecourse. It is at the very same time important to understand transformations of contexts-for-action over time. According to Emirbayer and Mische such contexts are primarily to be understood as *social* contexts in that agency is 'always a dialogical process by and through which actors immersed in temporal passage engage with others within collectively organized contexts of action' (ibid.,: 974).

Unlike a voluntaristic and deterministic approach, this three-dimensional perspective on agency makes it possible to generate rich understandings of how agency is achieved by concrete individuals in concrete situations and of the different factors that promote or inhibit the achievement of agency. Based on these ideas we have used the following model in our research, both to guide data-collection and to assist data-analysis.

Figure 1. Agency

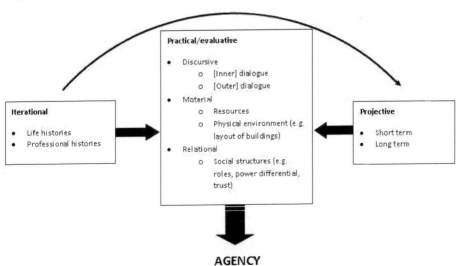

The model highlights that the achievement of agency is always informed by past experience – and in the particular case of teacher agency this concerns both professional and personal experience. The model also highlights that the achievement of agency is always orientated towards the future in some combination of short[er] term and long[er] term objectives and values. Moreover, it emphasises that agency is always enacted in a concrete situation, therefore both being constrained and supported by discursive, material and relational resources available to actors.

Research Design

This paper draws upon ethnographic research undertaken within a single education authority in Scotland in one primary school and two secondary schools, focusing primarily on two experienced teachers in each setting. We also interviewed senior managers in each school. In this chapter, we have drawn upon the stories of six of the teachers to illustrate themes that have emerged from the data: two from primary school (including the head teacher); and four from the two secondary schools. This focus on both primary and secondary schools has enabled a limited comparative dimension, allowing us to provisionally identify agentic trends and issues that might be particular to each sector. However, we emphasise that the often idiosyncratic nature of agency precludes generalisation in such a small number of cases, and it was never our intention to make large scale comparative claims.

Case studies highlight the biographies of teachers, the nature of the culture in each setting, social relationships which impact on the decision making of each teacher and the incidence of significant events. The construction of these case studies has allowed us to infer how the ecology of each setting (existing cultural forms, social structures and personal capacity) impacts on the subsequent teacher practices. The research extends to consideration of how connections with key personnel and policies within each school and the relevant sections of the education authority and other agencies impact on the work of each teacher.

The project covers a full year, with data-collection undertaken over three distinct phases following an iterative design, where each phase is partially determined by the findings of the previous phase. Data-collection involves observation; semi-structured individual and group interviews (including, at the start of the project, a personal and professional history interview); analysis of key policy texts; and event mapping. The vignettes that follow are based on data from the first phase of the project (which consisted of participant observation during three to four day field visits in each school; record keeping by each teacher of significant events over a two week period; individual life history interviews with each participant; group interviews focusing on the teachers' records of significant events; and individual follow-up interviews which explored tensions within their working lives as they grapple with professional dilemmas that arise from completing demands upon them. Data-analysis comprised open code of all data to identify key themes for each case. Detailed case studies constructed for each setting were then subjected to a comparative analysis to generate concepts, themes and meanings inductively from each setting. Instances of the achievement of agency – or lack thereof – were analysed in light of the distinction between the iterational, practical-evaluative and projective dimensions of agency, and with a focus on discursive, relational and material resources. All participants have been given pseudonyms and where testimony might be seen as especially sensitive, we have further anonymised the data by making only generic reference to the teacher in question. The research adheres to the guidelines for the ethical conduct of research of the British Educational Research Association.

Changing Discourse, Changing Practice

The introduction of Curriculum for Excellence (CfE) in Scottish schools occurs in a number of different ways. On the one hand CfE introduces new practices and way of working into Scottish schools and the school system more generally. On the other hand CfE also introduces a new discourse into the existing situation, that is, new ways of speaking and new ways of reasoning. Such changes provide teachers both with a new set of demands and with a new set of opportunities. The question this raises, from the angle of agency, is how teachers respond to and engage with such changes, both with regard to the demands for changing their practice and with regard to the new ways of speaking and reasoning that come with the new curriculum. In the following sections we look at a number of aspects of the impact of the introduction of CfE, particularly focusing on the ways in which teachers engaged with these changes and what this tells us about their achievement of agency.

In the space available it is not possible to elaborate on the biographical details of each participant. While we acknowledge the importance of teachers' unique and often idiosyncratic professional and personal biographies in the shaping of their agency, we cannot do justice to this dimension in this short chapter. Instead we focus in more general terms on the issues that emerge as teachers grapple with tensions and dilemmas resulting from the collision of policy that permits or even mandates teachers' agency with the cultures of performativity that simultaneously pull them in a different direction. In brief we present six of the participants from this study, whose stories form the basis of this chapter. These are illustrative of themes that have emerged more generally from the data. All of these teachers expressed their engagement with pupils as being their priority. They were enthusiastic about teaching and about their pupils achieving their potential. All of them admitted to working in the evenings and sometimes at weekends; preparing lessons, marking and assessing as well as reporting. Each teacher noted the reduction in time for individual professional development and that time was instead allocated to meetings on the implementation of CfE. In both secondary schools, working groups were formed to organise and plan integrated subjects and to work on a new reporting format. In one of the secondary schools, we discuss the cases of Charlotte, a teacher of Religion, Moral and Philosophical Studies (RMPS), and Lauren, a Modern Studies teacher. Both are experienced mid-career teachers, with around ten or more years of teaching experience. Charlotte and Lauren are in the same faculty. At the other secondary school the research focussed on Helen, an English teacher with an acting management role, and Abigail, a Maths teacher. Both teachers have similar levels of experience to Charlotte and Lauren. In the primary school, the focus in this chapter rests with Judith, a classroom teacher with six years experience and her head teacher Rachel, who has been at the school for over twenty years.

Understanding CfE: changing practices in primary school

In one of the interviews, Judith explained that in her situation the introduction of CfE had not changed the content or teaching practices, but had rather initiated major changes in the framework around what she termed as the delivery and assessment of learning. Instead of carrying out summative assessment at the end of a topic, Judith explained that, although they were still allowed to do this 'if we wish', she now tried to involve her pupils in formative evaluation by asking them to write a comment about their understanding of the topic. Allowing pupils to take part in their own assessment was a new practice for Judith and one which she admitted she still found difficult. Judith was aware that there was a need to develop assessment techniques that were related to 'using knowledge in context' and had found that she was relying on 'her judgement' more extensively than she had previously. She explained her understanding of the changes made to assessing pupils in the following way:

> ...for some children, they could have been doing level C work and done the test, passed the test and then went on to level D work but weren't secure enough in level C to progress. But because, well, they have been on that level for eighteen months they really get pushed on because this looks bad on the attainment, so they have to get pushed on. Then you feel like they have got gaps, whereas with CfE when they are secure they are then able to apply knowledge in other contexts.

'It's assessment within learning' she explained, telling us that she experienced 'less pressure' and was aware of 'working through it at my own pace, it is more active and practical.' Judith felt able to experiment with and was enthusiastic about using other media, such as video and drama, for what she referred to as the assessment of the development of learning. Some pupils may find it hard, she explained, to understand a question out of context (in the test), or find it difficult to formulate the answer. She was certain that the use of a range of formative assessment practices was more accurate. 'If they get it wrong there (in the test) you think they can't do it.'

Judith comes from a culture where performance measures provided information about attainment, and we wondered how comfortable she felt about devising her own methods of assessment. Judith articulated uncertainty about assessment practices of CfE being rigorous enough. She reflected on the types of evidence she was gathering and commented:

> ...the assessment part is very new. Are we doing it right? Is it OK to use a lot of teacher judgement or, are they still wanting to see the evidence? What kind of evidence have we got? There has not really been a thing on 'this is how you do it'. Every authority and even every school has been left to devise their own method of assessment.

She explained that she would have liked to have had something that 'all schools use or all schools can adapt and at least have a starting point. But we have not really been given anything.' She did however state that the local council had already produced assessment for level one and level two Maths, which it expects primary schools to complete. This information would then be used by secondary schools about the 'on entry' level of the individual pupils. The primary school had also started to devise internal summative assessment forms, and alongside collaboration with her colleagues and with working parties outside of the school, this made her feel more confident about the new assessment practices that were initiated. However, Judith expressed a concern about how the whole school would be measured in future, and generally seemed uncertain and under-confident in respect of assessment. In the past she had shaped her teaching to fit the performativity agenda and now she was unsure about the requirements that would replace the old national assessment. We discuss in a later section how the use of data and information systems at local and national level conflict with the discourses that underlie CfE.

This example already raises a number of important issues about agency and curriculum change. Perhaps the most remarkable aspect is the tension – if not clash – between Judith's professional 'habits' – or with Bourdieu's (1977) term 'habitus' – and the demands from the new curriculum to take more responsibility. While she expressed enthusiasm about the opportunities for experimentation, she seems to be lacking the expertise to do this in a confident manner. A reliance on external prescription and central quality assurance seems to have been internalised and seems to have become part of her professional 'habitus', and the new demands of CfE seem to be at odds with this. This is not something that Judith in any way should be blamed for. It rather illustrates something about the irony of the fact that CfE demands that teachers become agentic – and the irony lies in the suggestion that agency is something that can be demanded. This example demonstrates that simply to say that teachers should become more agentic, and simply presenting them with a situation in which they need to be more agentic, but without providing resources that would allow teachers to make such a shift, is not a very effective way to promote teacher agency. That a strong professional 'habitus' is not in itself a barrier for agency, but that this also depends on the kind of 'habits', becomes clear when we go to the second vignette.

Understanding CfE: changing practices in secondary school

In contrast with Judith's statement about assessment taking place within learning, Helen, the English teacher at one of the secondary schools, commented that in her case 'assessment drives the curriculum.' Her statement resonated with similar comments made by the other secondary teachers. But on closer examination all the teachers expressed strong commitment to educational values that were centred on what they described as developing and encouraging the individual pupil's learning. So while attainment was the goal for the secondary teachers, each of them articulated their professional agency in the enactment of their practices towards the goal. Helen and Abigail, the Maths teacher were both positive about what could be achieved by CfE. They felt that communication had improved within their respective faculties and that throughout the school there was more awareness of how other people worked.

Charlotte, a secondary teacher of Religion, Moral and Philosophical Studies (RMPS) at the other secondary school, agreed that assessment was carried out through different agendas at national, local and school level, but she had always worked hard to 'make them fit together.' Charlotte had made a conscious decision early on to get involved with CfE and felt empowered by her involvement. A picture of a faculty that was supportive, sharing of practices and open was presented by both Charlotte and Lauren, a Modern Studies teacher in the same faculty. Both teachers had a strong sense of their agency and professionalism based on a commitment to strong ideals and educational values. Learning was central to their work and while assessment was a crucial end point, what pupils achieved, and their experiences in getting there were clearly important to these teachers.

An example was the use of 'traffic-lighting'. As pupils progressed through a topic they were asked to decide whether they understood and were able to apply what they knew in other contexts (green), understood but were not yet able to apply to other contexts (orange) or still were unsure of the strategy or area of knowledge (red). While this is usually used as formative assessment, Charlotte, like many other teachers, tended to use this strategy in summative ways. This reflects the strong culture of summative assessment amongst the teachers in our study. However, Charlotte commented on her use of a range of assessment strategies and the involvement of her pupils in their own evaluation. Her teaching practices included pupil self-assessment, peer assessment, as well as collaborative assessment by grading via consultation between the individual pupil and the teacher. Charlotte asserted a belief that the range of strategies provided a 'very fair and balanced view' giving the pupils a realistic understanding of evaluation. She believed that it was important for the pupils to understand how assessment was done and the criteria used. Moreover, she also exhibited what has been termed 'protective mediation' (Osborn *et.al.,*1997). She mentioned that she sometimes gave tests without telling pupils that they were being tested. Upon being questioned about this practice, she stated that she believed that excessive testing placed harmful demands upon students; thus, while she felt obliged (by the system) to administer tests, she sought to protect students from their worst excesses.

Both Lauren and Charlotte talked about the 'minimal changes' that had been made to their classroom practices, due to the congruence between existing ways of working and what was perceived to be required by CfE. For example, they already used cooperative learning throughout the faculty and in all year groups. In their school there seemed to be a stronger culture of sharing ideas and practices and of collaborative learning within this faculty as well as across faculties, than was evident in Helen's and Abigail's school.

What is significant about this vignette is that we see a similar strength of professional habits as in the case of Judith, but whereas in Judith's case this seemed to have been formed mainly in terms of the culture of performativity, Helen, Abigail and Charlotte's professional habitus seems to have been formed as a more agentic response to the culture of performativity which, in turn, seems to allow them to be more effective in adopting the agentic opportunities with which CfE provides them. In terms of the distinction between the iterational, the practical-evaluative and the projective dimension of agency, we can say that the iterational dimension that these teachers brought to the introduction of CfE led to a stronger projective quality – that is, they had more explicit ideas about what they deem as desirable for their students – which allowed them to respond more purposefully to the changes of CfE. This is not to suggest, however, that their response can be characterised as entirely agentic as part of what allowed these teachers to operate in the way they did seems to lie in the fact that their educational values resonated to some extent with CfE. In this regard it was relatively easy for them to adopt new ways of doing and incorporate them in their practice and thus comply with the new demands and the new discourse of CfE.

Change and continuity: the audit and target culture

Although, as mentioned, CfE comes with a *discourse* of the teacher as an active agent of change, the teachers we interviewed did make it clear that at the level of *practice* – at least where it concerns questions of audit, targets and the measurement of performance – there has been far less change. Rachel, the head teacher at Judith's school talked about the shame linked to seeing the performance of the school in league tables. Rachel particularly commented on the use of STACS (explained earlier in this chapter).

> What happened was every year you were expected to do better regardless of the cohort, and that is madness, because you can't possibly, you know, make children Einstein if they haven't got the calibre to do that. I felt under enormous pressure at the end under the scrutiny of 5-14[6].It wasn't helpful and it had lost what I thought it had been put in place to do. It became too intense and not a tool. It became a whip.

She was concerned about how the introduction of CfE, with a focus on 'active learning' and 'transferable skills', would fit with what she saw as a continued focus on accountability. Recounting a recent head teachers' meeting she explained that:

> ...it was made clear that standardised testing was the way forward. So there is likely to be training for standardised testing of pupils in P3, 5, 7 and S1, I believe. So that is the authority stepping in and doing base lines[7]. So we are not too far away from National Test Mark 2 and Big Brother!

At both secondary schools the school year starts typically with a staff meeting at which the data from STACs are used as evidence of the schools performance.

---

6. Prior to the introduction of Curriculum for Excellence, Scotland's schools had been guided by a non-statutory curriculum known as 5-14.
7. In Scotland primary school cohorts are referred to as P1-7 (Primary) and S1-6 (Secondary).

Abigail, the Maths teacher, told us that the league tables are based on the results from senior pupils and 'are very much what the school is measured on'. She explained that her school's performance was similar to the previous year, 'which is quite disappointing in some ways, it is quite hard when you are hearing the whole school statistics. It is difficult to relate that to your individual classes'. She continued:

> There are things we have learned from. I think we have put people in for exams that we shouldn't have put them in for, which then looks bad on the statistics, and that has certainly happened before.

When we asked if they had expected those pupils to pass she admitted that they probably had not. She thought that it was just a hope that they might be able to, 'to give them the chance'. However she understood that from the school statistics point of view it would be better not to put them in for the exam. There were often discussions between her colleagues on the effectiveness of their internal assessment systems. In fact the school was performing no better or worse than in previous years and she felt this was disheartening. She commented:

> ...if you just saw the results published in the paper it makes the school sound like a not very good school but it doesn't feel like that to me when I come here everyday. I think we are a good school and that the pupils are well behaved and that there is a lot more to it than the exam results. But the exam results are what we are ultimately judged on.

What we see here, therefore, is a dimension of the introduction and implementation of CfE where old patterns of the culture of performativity seem to continue. While the teachers do note a change in some aspects of the discourse – for example the idea of 'active learning' – they also note that the changed discourse is not followed by a change in practice, in relation to the apparent need to produce comparative statistical indicators of performance. From our conversations with the teachers we gained the impression that they mostly accepted this as an inevitable reality – something that is simply happening and being decided elsewhere – and therefore not as something that triggered an agentic response from them, despite their doubts about such systems of performativity. This vignette, therefore, not only shows that the discourse of teacher agency that comes with CfE is in practice limited to some but not all aspects – which reinforces the point made earlier that CfE is and remains a central policy issued from the top down, and not just a possible option that schools or teachers can either decide to adopt or decide not to adopt. It also demonstrates that, even when teachers have strong professional values, the dynamics of the here and now – the practical-evaluative dimension of agency – to a large extent determine whether such values and the professional habitus through which they are expressed will result in an agentic response or not.

Regulatory mechanisms

As we have mentioned before, in Scottish school regulatory mechanisms operate at three levels: nationally by HMIe, locally by education officers called Quality Improvement Officers and internally by the school. Within the schools the inspections were called 'observations' and were carried out by the management teams, head teachers and senior managers. In the secondary schools an additional level of 'observation' was carried out by the Head of Faculty. At all schools the teachers spoke about initiatives that had been introduced to allow for peer observation by the teachers.

Several teachers remarked upon their responses to inspections and audits. Judith talked about external inspections and said 'some people think, oh gosh, what am I going to do, but at the end of the day you just have to do what you normally do, because (otherwise) it is not a true reflection of what you actually do.' Charlotte commented that preparing for an inspection was 'false' and that 'teachers should always be teaching as if an inspector could walk into your class.' Abigail talked about some teachers 'putting on a show.' Judith said 'we do get observations within the school so it is not like it is anything different.' Inspections for these teachers were part of their environment, and the traditional image of teachers teaching behind a closed door was not recognised by these teachers, who were proud of their 'open door' policy.

Lauren said:

> I feel you should see a school 'warts and all'. Some people talk about inspections where they appear unannounced and I kind of think, yeah, it is not to put on a show because that is not fair and it is not right. If there are issues they should be aired and if you are doing it right you should be doing that all the time anyway.

However Lauren was critical of the inspections that were carried out at the local level where there had been a shift from support to quality control. She felt frustrated at the lack of either informal or formal feedback at that level. She felt the silence weighed heavily from the 'judge in the corner.'

> What annoyed me about them that it was conducted by people who were supposed to help and support schools but I never saw these people. They were never a common face in the school or name on your email. What I

did feel was that they were people who had not taught in years, coming in and observing and in one case I got feedback and in the other the lady sat at the back and she wrote and she highlighted and said thank you very much and left my room!

Peer observation was also undertaken in all the schools, where the individual teacher was allocated time to observe particular classroom practices or shadow a pupil. Personally, Judith found peer observations more rewarding than the observation of her own practices by school management or the external inspectors. CfE articulates that teacher engagement with curriculum development returns to principles of educational aims and values in an environment 'in which reflective practitioners share and develop ideas' (Scottish Government, 2006: 4). Sharing practices with colleagues has become embedded in the culture of each of the schools. However the teachers complained that time for observation, sharing, reflection, along with time for staff development, have increasingly become under prioritised.

The manner in which teachers commented on inspection and observation shows that, to a large extent, they seem to accept this as a normal – and even desirable – aspect of their practice. They find little reasons to 'resist' except, that is, when what presents itself as an opportunity for professional learning transforms into surveillance and control. On the one hand this confirms what we have seen earlier: that the professional values that have informed the habits of these teachers allow them to make a judgement about which aspects they find desirable and which aspects they find troubling. While they do express views about the desirable and undesirable aspects of observation and inspection, they do seem to accept the changes, so their professional doubt does not turn into action – at least not within the examples we discussed with the teachers in the interviews. This confirms another point made earlier, which is that there is a gap between what we might call agentic judgement and agentic action. This gap can perhaps partly be explained by the ways in which the teachers have internalised aspects of the culture of performativity so that they appear to them as either inevitable or as impossible to resist.

Conclusions: Teacher Agency, Performativity and Curriculum Change
Our research presents a messy and often conflicting picture in respect of teacher agency. The data illustrate the conscientiousness of the teachers, and the very real difficulties they often face in enacting their practice, as they seek to reconcile the often irreconcilable. Such decisions and subsequent actions are often consequently fraught with risk. The pragmatic issues framed around the

practical/evaluative dimensions of agency are thus clearly significant in shaping agency, and it is clear to us that policy formulation needs to take greater account of these issues. Conversely there are issues of capacity, which are more firmly rooted in the iterational and projective dimensions of agency. Of particular note is the socialisation of teachers into the discourses of performativity, so that such discourses are largely accepted uncritically. As such, it would appear that teachers' agentic responses to the challenges posed by CfE are necessarily circumscribed – the teachers in our sample often lacked a sufficiently broad repertoire for manoeuvre to be able to respond in a flexible, agentic manner to the situations in which they found themselves. This presents a contrast with earlier studies, for example the Jeffrey and Woods (1998) study of school inspections and primary schools in England, which suggested generally more sceptical views towards performativity mechanisms. In this sense, while we should be cautious in comparing England with Scotland, the 'profound change' to teacher culture predicted by Jeffrey and Woods (ibid: 75) seems to have come to pass.

Our research suggests that teachers achieve agency within their current performative environment in the following ways. First, there is agency formed by perceptions of risk. There is significant evidence in our data of anxiety, lack of confidence and even ontological insecurity, as CfE disrupts established patterns of assessment, for instance. Such agency manifests itself in the form of strategies to play safe (for example teaching to the test). There is a strong practical/evaluative slant to such agency – strong perceptions (whether justified or not) about the likely outcome of inspections, or the reactions of senior management to new ways of working. However, such agency is also rooted in the iterational dimension (memories of previous negative experiences) as well as the projective (an inhibition of aspiration). It is highly likely that such agency inhibits innovation.

Second, there is agency where teachers are applying the existing logics of schooling (into which they are well socialised) to new situations. Charlotte's development of traffic lighting as a summative rather than formative strategy is a good example of this. It is also evident in the views of several of the teachers that struggling pupils should not be allowed to sit exams, as this would damage the school's performance. A third example lies in the internalisation of performative language by all of the teachers in our study. The ubiquitous use of the word delivery (previously noted in Judith's dialogue) provides a powerful illustration of how education is viewed by many teachers – as a product to be delivered and potentially measured, rather than as a developmental process for students. Such agency is strongly iterational, which in turn seems to delineate and limit the projective, rendering agentic responses to professional dilemmas problematic.

Conversely, we also saw significant evidence that many teachers continue to grapple with, and are made uncomfortable by such dilemmas, where they are faced with demands to perform in certain ways while their values are leading them differently. This was most clearly evident in Charlotte's protective mediation in testing. It is significant that those teachers, who were able to strongly express their educational values, were also able to articulate a clear vision for CfE. This was especially the case where strong collegial relationships existed, and where teachers were not working in isolation. The nature of professional relationships clearly forms part of the practical/evaluative dimension, from which agency emerges, helping to shape both the confidence and capacity of teachers to respond agentically to problematic situations, such as those described in this chapter.

Our study thus raises important and uncomfortable questions about how policy makers might frame policy to facilitate the emergence of particular types of agency, rather than seeking to control implementation processes or outcomes. Specifically, these relate to how teachers might be enabled to become active, critical and creative agents of change, rather than drones implementing policy uncritically. It raises important questions about how school leaders might shape their schools to be places where agency can emerge in ways which contribute to the development of a good education (Biesta, 2010) focussed on the needs of students rather than upon the performance of the school. This, in conclusion, suggests that it is one thing to reinvent the teacher at the level of policy discourse but still quite another to promote the actual emergence of teachers as agents of change in the practices that make up their everyday lives.

Acknowledgement

We wish to acknowledge our gratitude towards the teachers and school managers who have participated in our research project. Without their input, and freely offered time and support, this project would not be possible.

Who do I listen to?

6 Performing health: an ethnographic investigation of Emotional Health and Wellbeing (EHWB) in a high performance school

Vanessa Hayward and Pat Thomson

Introduction

Schools in England are now held accountable for outcomes which range from test and exam results to the Emotional Health and Well Being (EHWB) of children and young people. Since the launch of the Healthy Schools programme in October 1999, schools in England have been required to work towards achieving National Healthy School Status (NHSS). To gain NHSS schools need to meet a minimum of 41 outlined criteria in four theme areas – Personal Social Health Education (PSHE), Healthy Eating, Physical Activity and Emotional Health and Well-being[1]. By 2009, more than 97 per cent of schools nationally were participating in the programme, and over 70 per cent of schools had achieved NHSS.

It is against this backdrop that we report doctoral ethnographic research which investigated how EHWB policy was constructed and mobilised in a designated 'outstanding' secondary school in the East Midlands. In this chapter we first of all explain the ethnographic project that was undertaken and then how Healthy Schools policy was organised. We show how the external audit and accountability policy regimes framed what happened inside the school to produce a climate of fear and corrupted relationships. We argue that this performative regime constituted a paradoxical situation in which the health of most of the school seemed to be undermined by the standardised approach to healthy schooling.

The ethnographic research into Healthy Schools

Lowbridge School[2] was, at the time the research was conducted, an over-subscribed 11-18 Foundation School and Specialist College located in a regional town in the Midlands. Twice judged outstanding by OfSTED since 2006, and with a string of local and national awards (including NHSS), staff and pupils at Lowbridge were under intense pressure not only to sustain these achievements but also to demonstrate improvement each year.

---

1. Although the Coalition Government has brought about changes to NHSS, Healthy Schools is still an active project, maintaining schools' accountability for planning, monitoring and evaluating health and wellbeing outcomes.

2. Renamed to preserve a level of anonymity – we recognise that individuals in the site at the time the research was conducted may be able to identify the school through association with the first author. With this in mind we have used pseudonyms for focus group and interview participants and, with the exception of the headteacher, have clustered identifiable roles under broad headings to protect the identity of individuals within the research site. We have also changed some details about the school which might allow it to be found through search engines.

An ethnographic approach was taken because it seemed the only way to get at the story behind the school website, prospectus and inspection reports (the public face of Lowbridge). It seemed likely that the school had a coherent narrative which it presented to visitors and inspectors. Getting past this to explore the detail of how and why the school performed in the way it did required an intense engagement.

The study was informed by ethnographic principles of participation, observation, conversation, contextualism, interpretation, reflexivity, and flexible research design. The researcher Hayward volunteered as a teaching assistant in exchange for permission to undertake ethnographic research. This role made it possible for her to participate in and closely observe routines, practices and interactions, and to access school resources and other documentation.

The corpus of ethnographic data was generated over a period of 5 months between January and May 2009 and includes participant observations, school documentation, interviews with teaching and support staff, and focus groups with pupils. Participant observations included:

- lessons in subjects across the curriculum (years 7-11) – with a particular focus on tutor period (TP) where tutors covered Personal, Social, Health and Education (PSHE) topics, and Personal, Learning and Thinking Skills (PLTS)
- registration (in tutor groups)
- assemblies
- after school activities
- lessons/activities taking place in the Student Development Department – with the school's Behaviour and Guidance and Teaching a Learning teams
- the pastoral office (Pastoral Support Assistants)
- student council meetings
- staffroom interactions – including weekly staff briefings
- staff forums
- union meetings

The selection of lessons and activities for observation was guided by school policies and staff and pupils' suggestions that demarcated what activities were considered to relate to EHWB. School documentation included policies and guidance (e.g. behaviour policy, management of stress policy, staff handbook and student planner), OfSTED reports, the evidence file submitted for NHSS, promotional materials such as the school's prospectus, schemes of work, lesson plans, classroom resources, and posters and school displays (including examples of pupils' work). Interview and focus group participants are summarised in table 1.

Table 1: Interview and focus group data

Interview participants (12 in total)	Focus group participants (46 in total)
Headteacher (1)	Yr7 (6 pupils)
Student Development team (6)	Yr7 (6 pupils)
Health professionals working in school (2)	Yr8 (6 pupils)
Health practice/curriculum coordinators (2)	Yr8 (6 pupils)
Other pastoral (1)	Yr9 (4 pupils)
	Yr9 (6 pupils)
	Yr10 (6 pupils)
	Yr11 (6 pupils)

As the list of interviewees begins to illustrate, responsibility for the EHWB of children and young people was largely assigned to the student development team and those in a 'health' or 'pastoral' role. Although only one tutor was formally interviewed, conversations with 8 additional tutors about their role were recorded as fieldnotes. Focus groups were carried out during TP with pupils selected by their tutors. Participants were chosen from a group of volunteers on the basis that they were likely to offer a range of perspectives (i.e. groups generally included a mix of girls and boys, high and low achievers, and well behaved and 'naughty' pupils).

The organisation of Healthy Schools policy at Lowbridge

The first task of the research was to understand the complex ways in which Healthy Schools policy was organised. Unlike many comparable schools,

Lowbridge had not adopted the officially recommended Social and Emotional Aspects of Learning (SEAL) syllabus. Nevertheless, the school did offer health related curriculum through its PSHE and PLTS programmes.

Pupils in all year groups had one fifty minute PSHE TP per week, and those in year 7 and 8 had an additional fifty minute PLTS TP each week. These lessons were standardised across the school, with all tutors using the same set of lesson plans and teaching resources provided by the school's Skills for Life and PLTS coordinators.

PSHE lessons covered topics such as bullying, negotiating friendships, puberty, hygiene, sex and relationships, personal safety, smoking, drugs and alcohol. In PLTS lessons pupils were taught to reflect on their experiences using the PLTS framework which sets out six groups of skills that are regarded as 'essential to success in learning, life and work' (QCA, n.d.) – independent enquirers, creative thinkers, reflective learners, team workers, self-managers and effective participants. For each group of skills a focus statement and a set of outcome statements were provided to sum up the desired skills, behaviours and personal qualities. For example, in order to be effective self-managers pupils were expected to be able to manage their emotions and build and maintain relationships.

Throughout these lessons, as well as establishing the skills and qualities believed to be necessary for success, pupils were also taught (explicitly and implicitly) what were considered to be 'normal' and indeed 'healthy' emotional responses to a variety of situations, as well as appropriate expressions of emotions (emotional conduct). For example, in a PSHE lesson on bullying it was stated that the desired learning outcomes were that students would be able to empathise with victims of bullying behaviour, and develop confidence and assertiveness in supporting each other.

Registration activities were also highlighted as playing an important role in promoting the EHWB of pupils, with daily contact intended to enable tutors to build relationships with their tutees. The registration period began at 8.25am every morning and lasted twenty minutes. During this time tutors were expected to complete administrative duties such as recording the attendance of pupils using an online computer system (this was frequently hindered by slow running computers and internet problems), reading out school messages and distributing forms and letters. Administrative activities regularly took up the majority of the registration period, with any remaining time spent following a weekly activities rota – checking/signing student planners, silent reading, a weekly quiz, and a weekly theme. As we will discuss later many tutors found it frustrating how prescriptive the school was about how their time with their tutees should be used.

A timetable of weekly themes was created to comply with the statutory requirements of a daily act of collective worship, but was championed by the Senior Leadership Team (SLT) for its contribution to pupils' EHWB.

(Headteacher) By its nature it [weekly themes] supports EHWB because of what those themes are. They're not religious and they are not really to do with acts of worship at all, it's more about sort of moral messages and having time to reflect. (Interview)

The themes, generally matching the school's programme for Citizenship, were fairly broad and designed to stimulate discussion and encourage reflection. Listed in the school diary these themes included: rights and responsibilities, social justice, tolerance, healthy lifestyles, human rights, discrimination, conflict resolution, fair trade, the human condition, temptation, worry, courage, cultural diversity, sustainable development, identity, and enterprise.

Tutors were required to explore the themes using standardised guidance materials that were distributed to tutors via a tray in the staff room every Monday morning. Laminated sheets were to be displayed on tutor notice boards in tutor rooms and pupils were instructed to write the theme in their planners. Before leaving registration pupils were also required to complete a standardised 'personal reflection' sheet.

The same themes also provided the focus for assemblies, with each year group participating in two assemblies per week in accordance with an established rota. One assembly was led by a member of the SLT (during the lunch break), the other by the Achievement Leader for the year group (during the twenty minute registration period). Again there was evidence of standardisation of approach, with the same PowerPoint presentations observed in assemblies across the year groups.

Lowbridge had also developed a highly structured pastoral support system whereby tutors, Achievement Leaders and Pastoral Support Assistants provided guidance and support to all pupils involved in incidents or experiencing problems that might impact on their EHWB. Here, EHWB involved listening and empathy by adults supporting pupils. In turn children and young people were expected to learn to talk appropriately (calmly and rationally) about problems and incidents, at an appropriate time and place, to the appropriate people. Pupils with on-going problems were routinely referred to the Student Development Department and added to the school's intervention register. Here the Behaviour and Guidance team worked closely with children and young people exhibiting emotional and behavioural problems to develop their social, emotional and behavioural skills. The team also ran termly group intervention programmes, including a self esteem/drama therapy group and an anger management course. These sessions followed set programmes and again established a set of skills deemed necessary for health.

The performatisation of policy at Lowbridge

The organisation of Healthy Schools policy described in the previous section represents the instantiation of national policy at school level. As Ball notes:

> ...policies are made and remade in many sites, and there are many little-p policies that are formed and enacted within localities and institutions... (Ball, 2008: 7).

In other words, policies are never simply implemented, they enter a specific site and are read and re-read and aligned with ongoing practices and taken-for-granted ways of doing things. This was precisely the case at Lowbridge where the senior leadership saw its task as recontextualising national priorities. Here, the organisation of Healthy Schools policy was shaped and framed by the requirements of performativity, defined as:

> ...a technology, a culture and a mode of regulation that employs judgements, comparisons and displays as means of incentive, control, attrition and change – based on rewards and sanctions (both material and symbolic). The performances (of individual subjects or organisations) serve as measures of productivity or output, or displays of 'quality', or 'moments' of promotion or inspection. As such they stand for, encapsulate or represent the worth, quality or value of an individual or organisation within a field of judgement (Ball, 2003: 216).

Indeed, our analysis suggests that this particular local enactment of national health policy, as illustrated above, can be understood through three key performative systems.

External framing and pressures

Educational reforms in England have brought about an increasingly target-driven culture. Bearing in mind the threat of sanctions (including school closure) if schools fail to meet national targets, it is not hard to understand how particular outcomes become prioritised in schools. For example, where GCSE performance is one of the few indicators used to demonstrate school success, the current five good GCSE model provides a powerful incentive for schools to focus their efforts on attainment to secure league table positioning (Gillborn and Youdell, 2000; Thomson, Hall and Jones, 2010).

Within this system of accountability staff and pupils' experiences and relationships were profoundly affected by externally imposed targets and pressures. As the following example illustrates, the experiences of staff at Lowbridge were constructed through an intensive workload resulting from the national requirements for outstanding status and ensuing competition between schools:

> (Amanda) We have to be first. It's not just being an outstanding school because we are outstanding teachers. We have to initiate everything. I mean that's a classic what happened in the corridor. As if bing I fly down the corridor, bing I can instantly think of what John's going to do in the next lesson. And most of the time I do somehow manage it. And then I wonder why I'm so knackered. I'm pulled from pillar to post. (Interview).

The pressure to perform produced particular kinds of paradoxical consequences, as we will show later. External pressures also limited the scope for valuing activities not linked with targets. The following discussion, typical of many observed throughout the research, is illustrative of widespread recognition amongst teachers and support staff that exam targets dominate the school's agenda.

> (Alex) I don't know if it's just the inference that, well I start to feel that everything important is examined here.

> (General agreement)

> (Alex) I think here if something is outside examination it isn't recognised. I don't think it's valued. The kids seem to value it, but other people don't seem to give it any thought. That's not healthy. (Curriculum team meeting, 27 April 2009).

Furthermore this clearly demonstrates concern expressed about performativity in relation to health. This was a connection frequently made within the school as we will illustrate.

Internal standardisation
External framing and pressures resulted in the curriculum and school routines

becoming increasingly codified and standardised so they could be easily evidenced. In response to external requirements Lowbridge standardised what counted as outcomes, measurements and procedures *viz*:

outcomes in health were tightly defined as skills such as pupils talking about how they felt, showing reflection and empathy, and learning how to control emotions and in turn behaviour.

measurements were standardised in the forms of work and lesson plans with levels of attainment demonstrated by indicators of behaviour. Standardised evaluation forms, personal reflection sheets and classroom observations were also used as measures, and an intervention register maintained data about problems/referrals, interventions put in place, and outcomes.

procedures constituted a standardised response to emotional and behavioural problems. The school's behaviour policy, presented as a flow chart, set out a highly structured process of referral and intervention. At each stage in the process members of staff were required to carry out directives and complete reports to demonstrate that procedure had been followed, e.g. incident report forms.

This auditing process reduced health to a set of easily observable and immediate behaviours which were taken to equate to the knowledge, values and dispositions that would allow students to make 'good' decisions in the present and future. That these behaviours might not constitute deep and sustained learnings was not at issue; what could be counted was what mattered.

Internal monitoring and inspection (self regulation)
The requirements of audit and inspection were significant in the Lowbridge construction of EHWB policy and practices as the performance of standardised activities and skills. These provided the basis for particular routinised procedures.

A central record was kept of all year assemblies, and the SLT and Achievement Leaders were required to complete a weekly proforma as evidence of the themes covered. Achievement Leaders also had the responsibility for monitoring all tutor based activities within their year, including the use of registration time when the weekly theme was explored. Here, the list of themes, copies of the resources used and personal reflection sheets completed by pupils acted as evidence. PSHE and PLTS activities were monitored by Achievement Leaders and the Skills for

Life and PLTS co-ordinators through a programme of team meetings, student evaluations, classroom observations and Student Development Team meetings. During the fieldwork an audit of registration and tutor period practices was also carried out for the purpose of self-evaluation (SEF).

With the school required to provide such evidence of the EHWB criteria for NHSS, Every Child Matters outcomes, and OfSTED's criteria for outstanding personal development and wellbeing/guidance and support, activities were inevitably shaped to fit the requirements of evidence. Arguably, through processes of monitoring and evaluation these requirements functioned as a surveillance technology.

Evidence requirements meant tutors did not have the choice not to carry out these activities or to deviate from the script. Indeed, once these activities had been completed tutors had very little time to invest in other activities such as informal conversations with tutees. It is not altogether surprising that tutors, who already felt overburdened by an intensive workload and accountability for multiple outcomes in their role as a teacher, found it difficult to embrace highly prescriptive activities they saw little value in.

Throughout the research staff at Lowbridge problematised the extent to which everything from pupil attainment to EHWB outcomes were scrutinised and judged through the processes of audit and inspection. For many staff this was perceived as a major source of stress.

Performativity and health

We have already illustrated some of the ways in which EHWB policy and practices at Lowbridge were taken up and constructed within the discourse of performativity. Here we continue by showing the specificities of how performativity affected staff and pupil experiences, and health.

Instrumentalisation of relationships

Although many staff talked about the importance of EHWB and relationships it was clear that their value was instrumental rather than intrinsic. The notion that relationships were a means of producing learning rather than being a worthwhile end in themselves was echoed by many staff at Lowbridge, with behaviour and attainment outcomes most frequently cited as their purpose. The headteacher, for example, described the value of relationships in terms of their instrumental role in improving grades:

(Headteacher) There are some good examples of individual teachers who have very good relationships with students as well. We've got a lad in year 11 called X, I don't know if you've come across X? Huge, huge lad who has had all sorts of issues with violence and all sorts of things. His relationship with his English teacher has been so strong that she has got him ... he's going to get a grade in English and it's all to do with the fact that she's built this relationship. (Interview).

Paradoxically, school policies and the pressures of accountability for outcomes (particularly attainment) could run counter to the relationship-learning connection:

(Jane) There is so much pressure and it's all built up with threats, you know, if you don't do this then you can't go to prom, you know. And we are told that's what we have to do. I mean it could ruin a whole relationship with a student that you've spent a long time building, when you deal them a blow like that. (Interview).

This kind of disruption was problematised by and deeply problematic for teachers and support staff and led to ongoing concerns for staff and pupil wellbeing. The apparent clash between building and sustaining relationships and enacting performative policy was reoccurringly expressed as a cause of stress.

In the head's view attainment targets dominated the school agenda and shaped practice because all else depended on this outcome. His view demonstrates the ways in which external pressures and their internal management combined to make a difficult, shifting ecology in which what is certain is the fear of external reprisal and its knock-on effects if attainment data should falter:

(Headteacher) ...from a school perspective [high attainment] unlocks the door for us to access all sorts of other resources. Part of the reason school is the way it is in terms of the provision you sort of mapped is because we've been allowed to access these things because of high attainment. And if you take your eye off the high attainment ball and concentrate on something else then suddenly a lot of those avenues close down and then that has... it's amazing how that snowballs because then you start to lose your best staff, you can't recruit such good staff umm and then suddenly all of the things you are trying to achieve can implode. It really is a very difficult tension. (Interview).

Under these conditions it is not difficult to undertand how relationships (and in turn health) emerge as instruments for achieving outcomes rather than as outcomes in themselves. It is however important to problematise this instrumental representation as an over simplified understanding – in the data generated it certainly seems that relationships, behaviour, learning and health were much more complexly interrelated.

Culture of fear for staff

Staff at Lowbridge were largely reluctant to voice in public their disdain for school policies and practices for fear of reprisal. Although some staff spoke out at the staff forum and in their curriculum team meetings, there seemed to be an unspoken rule that staff would be in trouble if they spoke critically about the school or leadership. they often wanted to talk to the researcher about the difficulties they experienced. As was frequently recorded in fieldnotes, whenever staff talked about issues relating to their personal EHWB they appeared to take precautions to ensure no-one overheard, such as getting up to close doors and checking corridors to see who was around. The following data excerpt exemplifies the sense of threat in school:

> (Rachel) I mean this is me being very bold, but I can be because I'm going to be moving on in the next two or three years. So I don't care. I mean if I was a younger member of staff I perhaps wouldn't say anything, but it shouldn't be like that. One of the things I can say now is that I don't care what goes on because what will they do to me? They won't do anything to me because I'm near retiring. But if I was a younger member of staff the pressures are immense. (Interview).

Staff widely believed they would face punishment or competency procedures should they complain or reveal they were not coping. During the research period the question of staff stress and external pressure was discussed at a union meeting. In this discussion staff depicted a futile situation in which admitting difficulties "would be like giving them [leadership] the rope to hang you" (Fieldnotes, 12 February 2009). This was further evidence that at least some staff experienced their work at the school as being under continued scrutiny and pressure.

This was borne out later when a Curriculum Team Leader (CTL) told the researcher how he and his team were reprimanded following their team meeting on staff EHWB:

> (Vanessa) How did your team meeting about staff EHWB go?

> (David) I got pasted. Absolutely pasted … they [SLT] all basically came and said they are dreadful minutes and I shouldn't be doing that. They said basically my team had moaned … they didn't want me to minute it

because it was negative on them and they said that OfSTED could come and look at my minutes of meetings and these minutes indicate that all is not well ... So obviously I gave the others [other CTLs] the heads up not to include whatever it is you've talked about because obviously they quite honestly don't want to know ... I think given my experience people might be giving a rosier picture in these proformas now which is wrong. It sounds quite Stalin-esque. (Interview).

This particular example is again illustrative of the ways in which external framing and pressures came to bear on practices and relationships at Lowbridge. Not surprisingly, word about the reprimand spread in the school and appeared to have a direct effect on other teams who became apprehensive about raising issues in open forum. Interestingly, staff depicted a more favourable picture of the school in the proforma they were later asked to complete by senior leadership, and we can only speculate that this may well be a further indication of the repressive culture that had developed in the school. Moreover, this example illustrates the general dismissal by leadership of issues relating to staff EHWB, a sentiment that was echoed by staff throughout the interview and observational data.

Staff needs were at odds with professional duties

Strikingly, within this climate many staff responsible for promoting the EHWB of children and young people (especially tutors) saw this as an additional pressure and source of stress. Even though staff members valued various activities aimed at promoting the EHWB of children and young people, the actual responsibility was a cause of stress because, due to competing pressures, they felt they could not dedicate enough time to it. Rachel's words help to summarise what many tutors expressed in conversation:

(Rachel) The work involved in being a tutor can actually be incredibly stressful. The problem is there are too many aspects that they want us to cover. And with the amount of work we have it's [EHWB] the last thing that tutors can concentrate on ... And I know that what I do with them isn't enough but it's the only thing I can do. (Interview).

Some tutors also felt they did not have the expertise to make a good enough job of promoting health and warned the researcher in advance of her observing their PSHE and PLTS lessons that they had very little time to prepare properly and knew very little about some of the topics they were expected to cover. There was a widespread sense of dread when it came to these lessons – many of the tutors I observed made it clear that these lessons were a cause of much stress. Staff thus often reported that they felt their own health was pitted against that of students.

In addition, many tutors and pastoral staff felt forced to perform activities they did not believe would help students, and felt that their professional opinion meant very little to school leadership. Here, a sense of powerlessness and deprofessionalisation amongst staff emerged in direct relation to the task of promoting the EHWB of children and young people. There was much consensus amongst staff that "even if you don't believe it works you have to do it" (Jane, interview). External framing and pressures, in the form of Government and Local Authority (LA) performative requirements for provision and resources, were identified as dictating practice with little or no regard for their professional views.

For tutors, the role of promoting the EHWB of children and young people in school seemed to create 'role conflict'. According to Travers and Cooper, role conflict occurs when "an individual is torn between conflicting demands placed on them by others in the organisation ... or when conflict exists between their job and personal beliefs" (1996: 47). Indeed, Emma's concern about the school's performative approach to promoting the EHWB of children and young people, shown in the extract below, was typical amongst tutors:

> After the meeting Emma talks about her form group. Tutor time consists of the kids having to do loads of written activities to demonstrate they have covered each topic. She says it is all about evidence. Even in the mornings during registration she says there is rubbish like theme of the week. Emma says she loves teaching and wants to be able to talk to her group and help them with problems and relationships rather than doing pointless activities. She explains that they are a really lovely bunch of kids but they have their heads slumped on the desks because they think it is rubbish. She says she finds it very hard to encourage them because she thinks it's a waste of time. She says it is really sad because all these box ticking activities take away from the time you can spend with them properly. She doesn't think she will stay in this school much longer because she hates how it is all about getting the grades and making sure the school looks good. (Fieldnotes, 12 February 2009).

This is a significant paradox. In order to be a good professional, school staff members must support the health of students and must model healthy behaviour. Yet the task of supporting students' health education produces ill health which is poor modelling since it demonstrates poor self-management, something which good professionals are meant to do well.

What is alarming here is that the promotion of children and young people's EHWB at Lowbridge, far from ameliorating the damaging effects of performative culture, provided another example of the way in which "teachers, as ethical subjects, find their values challenged or displaced by the terrors of performativity" (Ball, 2003: 216). But this is not Lowbridge's fault alone. Government policy which frames the work that is done in the school also fails to consider how responsibility for managing the EHWB of children and young people can affect staff.

Divisions created between staff

Reinforcing a long-standing pastoral/curriculum binary (Slee, 1988; Hunter, 1994; Thomson, 2002) which separates the affective from the cognitive, there was a resounding acceptance that in response to the current policy climate and classroom conditions the teachers' role was primarily to do with the curriculum, and pastoral support staff were responsible for pupils' emotional development. Health education clearly straddles the two, but the school found ways to manage the potential overlaps. This tension is best illustrated in the following data extract:

> (Paul) It's always difficult with the teaching staff because the aim of teaching is to teach the students. And you are governed solely on your results in the classroom. So there are different expectations. I also have far more time which gives me the flexibility. So I would say there is a divide but I wouldn't say it's an uncaring divide. I'd say it's due to Government commitments and the implementation of lots of Government strategies, school strategies. When you're continuingly developing something sometimes the students get lost. So I think pastorally and the teaching assistants and student support centre they have a far more child focused approach. Teachers will say they do, but at the end of the day they have to produce results in the classroom. That's not gonna change until we get rid of league tables. Because that's what schools are measured on. (Interview).

In much of the data we see an understanding about the importance of relationships which hold out some criticism of a strongly results driven culture. While the purpose of relationships is still primarily instrumental, students are not held entirely responsible for their own learning difficulties. Some of the problems are attributed to school organisation – class size, timetabling and the press for curriculum coverage and attainment data.

Arguably, this curriculum/pastoral divide also created tensions between teachers and support staff. Indeed, the study found evidence that the competing agendas of attainment and EHWB placed strain on relationships. This was most clearly articulated by one of the student development team working in the school's behaviour and guidance unit:

> (Jason) But quite a lot of the time we are the enemy of the teachers, you know. Well it's down to inclusion isn't it. We are encouraged to include as many students as possible but if you're teaching that's the last thing you want. You don't want me turning up with someone saying you know I've brought him back. It's like oh thanks a lot (sarcastic tone). You know, there goes my lesson. So we are the enemy of lots of the teachers … The problem is not everyone has got the time, you know, to invest in it [EHWB]. Umm, and not everybody else recognises what it is you're trying to do and they've got their own agenda and they've got their own deadlines to meet. (Interview).

This conflict too has its roots partially in external framings: OfSTED inspection reports require schools to be both inclusive while producing good test scores at the same time. The mediation of these two imposts happens within classrooms and also, as can be seen above, between staff with different roles and responsibilities. Such conflict is further indication of the kinds of pressures that existed for different staff within the school.

Student cynicism about purposes and practices

The objects of attention, the pupils, regarded the school's concern for their EHWB as a fabrication, working in institutional interests rather than theirs. As the following excerpt illustrates, during discussions about the school's role in managing EHWB, a number of children and young people expressed cynicism about the intentions of the school and doubts that the school cared about their EHWB for reasons other than self-promotion:

> I just think they want to compete against other schools so they can say this school's the best. They aren't doing it for us, they are doing it for them. They're just trying to be the best school to get more people (Heather, Yr8 focus group).

For many students, rather than feeling valued as individuals and as part of the school community for their own worth, it seemed their felt significance in school rested primarily on their contribution to the public performance of the organisation. Students from all year groups believed that over everything else (including EHWB) the school valued attainment results. This view was expressed in focus group discussions and informal conversations, and was most apparent in the accounts of those in Year 10 and 11 (GCSE years). For example, students in the Year 11 focus group described how they felt their individual needs and aspirations were disregarded by the school in the drive for grade targets:

(Sofia) It's like with the grades, it's like the [school's] target is to get this many A grades, but it's like don't they think we are all trying our hardest? It shouldn't be about our grades as a whole, but about what grades we get as a person and what <u>we</u> are proud of.

(Oliver) And it's like sometimes, like in music, we'll be doing something and then when we've finished, even if someone's got an A*, they are like 'but how can you improve it'? It's like how can you improve an A*?

(Sofia) I got told because my target was an A*, and I got a high A, that I wasn't working hard enough. I was happy with an A but they were like 'but you're not achieving your target grade so you can stay back after school'. I was like 'forget that, I'm not staying back after school for getting an A'. Well I went home and Miss X called me and said if I didn't come in I'd get a detention (Yr. 11 focus group, original emphasis).

Students also described feeling dehumanised by their teachers, treated impersonally as if they were not individuals but rather, we surmise, as performing outcomes. Although there were some exceptions, teachers were largely described as 'too busy to get to know you' (Yr9 focus group). Where this was the case their teachers' focus on the work rather than relationships also led them to describe their teachers in deindividualised and dehumanised terms. The following extract exemplifies this:

(Malcolm) Yeah like most teachers will talk to you like you're a lump of wood. Like 'you, do this', or whatever, and you get treated like crap. But with some of the TAs they treat you like people and they get to know you. They're quite friendly.

(Oliver) Cos like if you've got a question they [teaching assistants] come and help you because the teacher ignores you. And like, if they don't know they can ask the teacher and the teacher doesn't ignore them. Most teachers are focused on their job so they are like robots whereas the assistants are more like down to earth (Yr11 focus group).

It certainly seemed to the researcher that the teacher's 'deflected gaze' led many students to conclude that 'the teachers just do not care' (c.f. Devine 1996: 131-2).

The teachers who pupils saw as 'caring' were those who were able to resist or ameliorate the depersonalising and dehumanising effects of disciplinary systems of judgements, classifications and targets. They were the ones who were able to find enough time to regularly ask about students' lives, and they were the ones who were able to manage their own stress well enough that they could create and maintain a positive atmosphere in the classroom and resist taking things out on their students. Students often described these individuals as those who were *prepared* to go above and beyond the role of the teacher. This is a clear illustration of how children and young people at Lowbridge tended to see poor relationships as a matter of individual choice on the part of the teacher, rather than recognising the impact of performative culture on the teacher's role.

Conclusion: ethnography and performing health

In this chapter we have illustrated the influence and power of performativity to develop absurd practices. We have suggested that the performatisation of EHWB at Lowbridge plays out in the everyday lives of staff and students. The school has developed a set of standardised measures and procedures which meet external demands and which create a culture of coercion and technologies of surveillance in the school. Staff and students are variously able to mediate and resist this architecture. Overall, a paradoxical situation is constructed, where, in the name of producing better health outcomes, the intense pressures schools, teachers, children and young people already face are in fact extended with unhealthy consequences.

The school has nevertheless been able to produce evidence of EHWB sufficient to garner inspection approval and numerous awards. Decals on its website, letterhead and prospectus are testimony to the regard which others have accorded their implementation of health education. Indeed the school was selected for study in part because of its apparent good track record in the implementation of EHWB. This ethnographic study suggests that these signs of good performance are more a fabrication, covering up the consequences of a thorough and thoroughly performative approach.

It is arguable whether such a finding could have been produced through other methods, such as surveys and interviews. Because the researcher was in situ for five months she was available for staff to confide in her in private, something that they did at the outset and continued to do throughout the study. She was also able to observe the way in which, when staff did begin to discuss their own health and concerns they were subject to top-down pressure to stop; she was also able to observe the effects of this disciplinary activity – public compliance and private concern and stress. It was this public-private healthy/not healthy binary which was the most significant finding of the study and which ought to be of most concern.

This is of course only one school. It is clearly desirable for other schools to be similarly investigated to see whether the analysis presented here is much more widespread. However, given the difficulties of accessing the 'private' through quicker and less detailed methods, this will clearly not be an easy task.

Acknowledgements
This paper is written with thanks to the staff and students who shared their experiences, thoughts and feelings.

7

Embedding citizenship education: An ethnographic tale of Trojan horses and conflicting performativities
Michalis Kakos

Introduction

The research which is discussed here is a case study of the interaction between students and teachers in citizenship education in a comprehensive secondary school in North England. In terms of its conceptual framework, the study places itself within the wider context of modern interactionism and more particular within the interactionist ethnography paradigm (Castanheira *et.al.*, 2001) without, however, developing an exclusive interest in the linguistic phenomena of social interaction. The project was conceptualised as a response to Vanderstraeten's call for *'the school class to be understood as an interaction order'* (Vanderstraeten, 2001: 275) and its aim was to study the negotiation by the school community of the educational practices, of policies and of the curriculum which was brought in the school with the introduction of Citizenship as statutory subject in the secondary English education in 2002.

The study was largely instigated by early discussions foreseeing some challenges for the successful implementation of the subject and particularly those discussions which had located these challenges within the social roles being performed by the school community as well as within the broad social function (historical and modern) of English schools (Davies, 1999; Frazer, 1999; White, 1999). In one such discussion, Pring (1999) had described the introduction of a 'quality circle' in education leading to the development of a 'business-like' modern educational discourse, and he raised the issue of the compatibility of this discourse to the one of a (democratic) political education.

The report of the Advisory Group for Citizenship (The 'Crick report'; QCA, 1998) which provided the framework for the new subject with its calls for active participation and active learning, for relevance of the curriculum to students' experiences and for the development among students of a sense of ownership of the learning processes and indeed of the school itself seemed to be the carrier of this new, political in its essence, discourse.

Indeed, the establishment of a new discourse was a central aim of the Advisory Group which saw the new subject as the vehicle which would bring 'no less than a change in the political culture of this country both nationally and locally'

(QCA, 1998: 7). Evidently the Advisory Group's expectations from Citizenship education suggested that the new subject would be more than just an addition to the curriculum. The change that its implementation was expected to bring made its introduction effectively resembling to a Trojan horse entering the walls of comprehensive secondary education with the potential to open its gates to the opportunity for a form of education for democratic citizenship.

During the ten years that followed the introduction of the subject it is still debatable whether Crick's Ulyssean trick has delivered its purpose. The reports of agencies which have monitored the implementation of the subject such as the NFER (through the citizenship education Longitudinal study) and OfSTED seem to suggest that the effectiveness of its implementation has slowly been improving. Most importantly, the reports seem to verify both Crick's ambitions but also Pring's concerns in that they have located the difficulties for the effective implementation of the subject in the very heart of the question about schooling and educational discourse: 'The introduction of citizenship challenges some assumptions about the status quo because it is intended to empower pupils. The trick is to harness that power in a democratic school where the pupils recognise their ownership and the opportunities presented to them. For some schools, this is a long journey. They need to go back to their aims and values and ask what education is about' (David Bell, Her Majesty's Chief Inspector of Schools (HMCI) quoted in OfSTED, 2006: 10).

Most recent reports from both OfSTED and NFER seem to suggest that many schools have managed to overcome some of the major difficulties and frictions. Indicative of this is the title of the latest OfSTED report on citizenship which indicated that the question is not any more whether there is a consensus about citizenship and its place in the curriculum, but whether its implementation can now be considered as effectively established within secondary education (OfSTED, 2010). The fact that it is taking more than a decade for the subject to be established should not necessarily be considered as indicative of an underachievement since it can be suggestive of the subject's democratic and revolutionary nature. In such case however, it should also be indicative of the validity of Pring's (1999) claims about at least a degree of incompatibility of democratic political education to modern schooling.

The aim of the study was to examine this incompatibility and consequently the resistance and the friction that the implementation of the subject has generated within the school community. Following the suggestions which point to the educational discourse as the source of this friction, the study focused on this discourse as it is being constructed by and as it frames the educative process (i.e. the process which manifests itself within the relationship between those who are considered as 'learners' and those who are officially assigned with the responsibility to teach). In a sense, a tentative ambition of the study has been the validation or rejection of the assumption generated by Pring's (ibid.) claims. By doing so, the study's contribution is not limited to the discussion about the place of citizenship education in the English curriculum but concerns also the development of a better understanding of the modern schooling experience.

The conceptual framework: performativity and intersubjectivity

Referring to the still emerging in late 1990s educational reality Pring (ibid.) described a change in 'the language of education' which has paved the way for the introduction of an educational 'quality circle'. Pring had pointed out that 'The shift in the language of education [...] brings with it a shift in how we see the relationships between teacher and learner, and between teachers and those who organise the education system – indeed, how we perceive the political framework within which teachers are asked to relate to their pupils and to what are now referred to as stakeholders' (ibid.,: 73-74).

Pring has not been alone in detecting the 'shift in the language of education' and in the relationships between teachers and pupils. Apple has effectively described the processes of 'conservative modernization' and the effects of marketisation of education (Apple, 2000; 2001). Ball (2003) has also discussed the role of the market and has identified marketisation, managerialism and performativity as the three policy technologies driving the modern education reform. Quoting Rose (1989), and effectively echoing Pring's views, Ball points out that 'education reform brings about change in our subjective existence and our relations one with another' (Ball, 2003: 217). Ball is concerned about how this reform affects 'one's social identity' and focuses on the role of performativity to study 'the subjectivities of change and changing subjectivities which are threatened or required or brought about by it' (ibid.,: 217). His definition of performativity is apocalyptic of the processes behind this shift of subjectivities: 'Performativity is a technology, a culture and a mode of regulation that employs judgements, comparisons and displays as means of incentive, control, attrition and change – based on rewards and sanctions (both material and symbolic). The performances (of individual subjects and organisations) serve as measures of productivity or output, or displays of 'quality', or 'moments' of promotion and inspection. As such they stand for, encapsulate or represent the worth, quality and value of an individual or organisation within a field of judgement' (ibid.,: 216).

Ball's definition of performativity operates as a useful conceptual tool for the description of the turn of educationalists to 'enterprising subjects' (Rose, 1989; in Ball, 2003: 217) living in conditions of constant surveillance through evaluation and in that way it explains the paradox of the construction of inflexible performances within an apparently flexible and 'devolved environment' in education. Ball points out that such conditions and the profound change on teachers' subjectivity lead to the development of an 'ontological insecurity'. In this context, 'both the interactions and relations between colleagues and those between teachers and students are affected' (ibid.,: 224). Ball points out that performativity causes 'inauthenticity' in teachers' practice and in their relationships with students and that this is the result of their own alienation from the role which they perform (ibid.,: 222-3). Acting within such role they develop a 'socially empty identity' which is the direct response to others' expectations and one that is 'hailed and rewarded by educational reform and 'school improvement' (ibid.,: 222). Although those who hold these expectations are not present when teachers perform their roles, they are able to direct these roles through the constant surveillance and evaluation of the performances.

Surveillance is often associated to OfSTED's inspection teams. OfSTED holds the authority to define a period during which they visit a school, to observe the interaction of teachers and students and to evaluate the extent to which their performances (together with other aspects of the school life) address the priorities and support the attainment of a set of pre-defined outcomes. With the authority to define the time of the inspection, OfSTED seems to operate in a way that resembles the function of the Panopticon (Bentham, 1787): the cells (classrooms) are the spaces occupied by inmates (teachers and students) who have no knowledge of (or the power to define) the time in which they shall be observed by the supervisor (inspector). 'Thus', as Perryman (2007) notes, 'institutional authority is invisible, but the objects of power, which in school are the teachers and pupils, are visible and supervised' (Perryman, 2007). However, OfSTED is not alone in this role.

The act of surveillance is operated also by the headteacher 'the new hero of educational reform' (Ball, 2003: 219) and is also achieved through the constant collection and public exposure of information related to 'myriad of judgements, measures, comparisons and targets' (ibid.,: 220). Of course, the effectiveness of the surveillance which is achieved through the public exposure of such information could not be sustained unless the public adopts and values it. Indeed, as Holden's study suggests (Holden, 2004), parents do share the priorities leading to such outcomes. In that respect, teachers can feel that the members of the public perform the role of the OfSTED inspectors by their constant (and outcomes-based) interest, which is fed by the uninterrupted flow of relevant information (results). Furthermore, the antagonistic form of the presentation of these results (as in League tables) leads to the adoption of the role of the inspectors by members of the schools, including of course teachers themselves.

Through such processes 'panoptic performativity' is manifested, 'a regime in which frequency of inspection and the sense of being perpetually under surveillance leads to teachers performing in ways dictated by the discourse of inspection in order to escape the regime' (Perryman, 2006: 14). The final goal of panoptic performativity is the 'normalisation' of the school through the construction of a discourse which is compatible to that of the inspection regime. In such a sense, panoptic performativity is 'the regime within which teachers and schools can successfully demonstrate their acceptance of the OfSTED and school effectiveness discourse and successfully normalise' (ibid: 152). Therefore surveillance has no end, but several manifestations leading to the internalisation by teachers of standards that are imposed upon them and which seem to be produced outside the educational community. Ball recognises that this is a common source of frustration for teachers who recognise in this the alienation of teachers from the very meaning of education. In the words of a teacher quoted in Ball's (2003) article: 'Education has traditionally been about freedom. But there is no freedom any more. It's gone.' (ibid.,: 222).

An assumption which offered some early guidance in this study was that some of the friction of the implementation of citizenship education could be generated within this loss of freedom and the alienation of teachers from their own role. Indeed, freedom and teachers' ownership of their role seem to have been considered by the Advisory Group for Citizenship as prerequisites for the effective implementation of the subject: '… we are strongly against any single source of authoritative guidance. However permissively worded, this could in practice take back the greater freedom and flexibility which is the very object of the learning outcomes; and could also raise proper public worries about imposing a single way of teaching about political and social issues and values' (QCA, 1998: 32). It is not however, only the 'loss of freedom' which should be of concern here. What is often missing from the discussion about surveillance and performativity in education is a consideration of students' role. And although the relevant literature seems to make worrying suggestions about the students who might be turned into mere voiceless 'products', (Pring 1999) it is likely that this same literature is guilty of a similar crime in that it rarely turns to them to explore their own understanding of this discourse and students' own contribution in its construction.

The acknowledgment of the intersubjective nature of discourse and the employment of an interactionist understanding of school classroom has allowed this study to pay attention to students' and teachers' role in a process of co-construction of the educational discourse. In that way neither students nor teachers were predetermined as the victims of performativity but the focus was on the way that performativity is being manifested in their interaction, allowing or restricting their freedom, allowing or preventing them from attaining their expectations from their engagement with school-based education.

Methodology
The methodological framework of this study is constructed upon a critical approach to Symbolic Interactionism and on the view of interaction as a process which depends on the mutual contribution of the participants, who are 'taking the role of the other, thinking about one's own communication, interpreting the acts of others, as well as considering both the expectations and the directions of others' (Charon, 1995: 150). The study sought to understand these expectations but also the perceptions of the interacting parts about each others' expectations. It also considered these expectations as the foundation of power in human interaction, an element which has often been overlooked in interactive studies, particularly the early ones (Hargreaves, 1972, Manke, 1997). Although some of the claims that are made in this paper echo some of the suggestions attributed to organisational role theory (particularly in relation to the phenomena of role transition (Allen and van de Vliert, 1984), the conceptualisation of 'self' in the context of this study does not coincide with those found in early symbolic interactionism and role theory. Therefore the use of the term 'interactionist' does not suggest that this research borrows its conceptual and methodological framework directly from symbolic interactionism but it is rather a suggestion for it to be placed tentatively within the long and broad tradition of social studies which embark from the claim about the central role of human interaction and attempt to explore the social reality that this interaction constructs.

An element which this study borrowed from symbolic interactionism is the process of 'role reversal' i.e. the interacting parts' continuous exchange of view points from which they examine themselves. Evidently (Kakos, 2008: 130) this is a process often excluded from the focus of interactionist studies, possibly because of the complicated methods which otherwise would need to employ. In order to avoid such inconsistency with its theoretical framework a two-step approach concerning role-reversal was developed in this study. The first step involved a re-conceptualisation of role reversal based on psychodrama and sociodrama (Landy, 1986) and on Goffman's dramaturgical approach (Goffman, 1971, 1991). Adopting Goffman's (1971) doubt over the need to assume the existence of a 'real self' and acknowledging the long-standing view in psychodrama that empathy is the key process laying at the heart of role reversal, this re-conceptualisation led to the development of the concept of 'egocentric empathy'. This concept refers to the intersubjective process which leads to the construction of the sense of self through its perception from the point of view of the 'other'. The second step was the development of methods (presented more analytically in the next section) that allow the study of the empathetic element in the interaction between students and teachers and more particularly of the perception of themselves which attribute to each other.

The conceptual framework of this study took also into account a set of institutional parameters ('rules and rituals' as in McLaren, 1986) which affect the definition of the situation of the interaction between students and teachers. It did so through the acknowledgement that this definition is not subjected directly to these parameters but to the participants' own perception about them which is informed by their views and expectations from their participation in the specific social or institutional setting (see Blumer, 1969; Hargreaves, 1972; Charon, 1995). Emerging for all the above, the conceptual framework of the study has been constructed on four pillars which guide the methodology and data analysis: 1) the notion of power; (2) egocentric empathy (3) participants' expectations from their involvement in the interaction process and from each other; and (4) participants' perspectives of the function of the institutional conditions which affect their interaction.

By acknowledging students' and teachers' active participation in the construction of the social situation in which they participate, and by investigating their (subjective) interpretations of this situation the study sought to enter into the social word constructed by this interactive, political in nature (Webb, 1979) process in order to experience 'at *first hand* what people do and say' (Hammersley, 2006: 4). A key principle which guided this enterprise was Charmaz' (1996) suggestion: 'We enter our research participants' worlds to understand their thoughts, feelings and actions. But we do so as genuine participants ourselves, not as distanced, unbiased observers who dispassionately record the doings of others' (Charmaz, 1996: xii). Therefore the employment of an intersubjective conceptual tool led naturally to the development of 'a methodology that both respects the intersubjective nature of human group life and maintains coherence with the researcher's hermeneutic viewpoint'. Such methodology cannot be but 'a variant of an ethnographic approach: an approach that opens the researcher to the life-world of the other through interpersonal exchange' (Prus, 1996: 21). Besides, the appropriateness of ethnographic methods in the study of participants' perspective of their interaction has been supported effectively in a number of cases (Prus, 1996, Cohen *et.al.*, 2000: 24; Hammersley, 2006, among others).

For reasons that lie very close to those suggesting an ethnographic approach a choice was made for this project to be a case study, a method which allows the researcher to 'recognise the complexity and "embeddedness" of social truths' while safeguards his/her ability to be actively involved in the analysis of this complexity as this is manifested through the different perspectives which construct it and 'to represent something of the discrepancies or conflicts between the viewpoints held by participants' (Bassey, 1999: 23). Cohen illuminates the relevant strengths of the case study in relation to the observations made above: 'Case studies strive to portray "what it is like" to be in a particular situation, to catch the close up reality and "thick description" of participants' lived experiences of, thoughts about and feelings for, a situation' (Cohen *et.al.*, 2000: 182).

Sources of evidence

The study employs whole school and classroom observations, interviews with students and teachers and field notes as sources of evidence collected from a 6 months engagement in the life of the school. A total of thirteen individual interviews with teaching staff, forty-three interviews with students and thirty-four observations of citizenship lessons were carried out. However, following the official guidelines for the implementation of the subject and the school's management team suggestions who pointed out that Citizenship is channelled also though the ethos of the school, whole school observations were carried out and extended field notes were kept describing the interaction between students and teachers during assemblies, school trips and break times. A total of four whole days activities and school outings and fourteen school days were systematically observed (break time, beginning and end of school days) which produced a 3.5 hours of field notes recordings.

The aim of the observations was to describe the roles that participants in this interaction perform, the way that power is applied and the models of empathy practised or experienced by the participants. Semi-structured interviews supplied evidence about participants' understanding of each others' expectations, their perspectives regarding each others' definitions of the situation and generally about their subjective experience of their interaction with each other (Blumer, 1969; Charon, 1995).

A final methodological tool that was successfully tried in this study was the observation of a set of role-plays followed by group interviews with students. These role plays required the construction by students of and their engagement in staged situations that are possible to occur in the school. These activities included: an interview for the appointment of a new teacher; a teachers' council meeting where a students' issue is discussed; another council meeting on teachers' potential participation in a strike is discussed; and finally a random encounter of a teacher and a student in a school corridor. These activities allowed students to vividly represent and then discuss their views on teachers' perspectives of the roles that both, students and teachers hold, their understanding of teachers' views regarding the application of power and of teachers' expectations from their interaction with students (Kakos, 2008).

The School

The study was carried out in a secondary comprehensive school in Northern England, here named 'Hillcliff High' (pseudonym). Hillcliff is an 11-18 mixed comprehensive school situated in a sub-urban area in North England and it accommodates a population of about 1200 students.

The selection of the site was suggested by the fact that the interaction between students and teachers appeared to be unproblematic as this was established through preliminary visits, discussions with students and staff. It was also supported by the diversity of the students' population (in terms of social class and ethnic background) and the level of co-operation the school offered.

The school has a very good reputation in the local community based on the good results its students achieve in the national exams and its positive multicultural environment, something that has been considered as one of the main strengths of the school during a number of OfSTED inspections. Strong and effective leadership, students' positive behaviour, and good teaching are also referred to as being the strengths of the school as well as the excellent standards of personal and social education teaching, the good relationships between the members of the school community and the high standards of pastoral support to students. A small-scale survey that was also conducted by OfSTED indicated parents' positive views about most aspects of the school's educational provision.

Discussion

The embarking point for the analysis of the evidence of the study concerns the dominance in the interaction between students and teachers of a depersonalised, conformist perception of each others' identity which is based on the institutional role that they hold. The stepping stones for the development of this part of the argument are: (a) The phenomenon of out-of-role interaction avoidance; (b) the development of 'functional empathy' (Cooper, 2002) as dominant model of empathy in the interaction between teachers and students; and (c) the shared perception among teachers and students that their interaction is guided by the terms of an 'imposed contract'.

Interaction avoidance

During the time spent in the school it was observed that in many occasions students and teachers seemed to be reluctant to have what was named in this study as 'open interactions' i.e. interactions that are not directly related to the institutional roles that students and teachers hold within the school. Such observations were made for example during break times, when students are required to go out of the school building. Some students try to escape teacher's supervision and remain in the classrooms but the majority of them spend their break in the school's courtyard. Regardless of where they choose to spend their time they tend to avoid contact with teachers and all interactions with teachers observed were about school-related issues. During the long breaks a large number of students choose areas in the courtyard that are away from the building and which are rarely visited by teachers.

During the same time, teachers are split in four groups. The first is the group of teachers who stay in their rooms or in their offices to work. Students are not allowed to enter these rooms unless the teacher has asked to meet them. These students are provided with a green card with the word 'PASS' typed on it, the teacher's signature and the date. The second is the group of teachers who have their break in the two common rooms (the 'Staff room' and the 'Teachers' library'). Again, students are not allowed to enter these rooms and this is clearly stated on the rooms' doors. On the rare occasions that students have to speak to a member of staff they have to knock on the door and wait for the teacher outside. In the corridor outside the common rooms there are three desks that are available for students who are in 'break-time detention' to sit and work. These students are required to work in silence and it is usually only the teacher who has decided their punishment who interacts with them (for instructions or to assess their work). The third group is formed by teachers who are 'on duty' 'guarding' the school building and keeping students out of it. The fourth group is of teachers who are also 'on duty', but their task is to supervise (selectively to some extent) the outdoor spaces that students use for their break-time activities.

Students' preference for remote spaces and the rules applied and rituals followed lead to the formation of spaces that are exclusive of each other's presence. This was considered as one aspect of a phenomenon which is described in this study as 'interaction avoidance'. Evidence of 'interaction avoidance' also occurred during school outings. In these students and teachers were observed consistently occupying different spaces, something that was apparent especially in the bus, where there was always a gap of one or two rows with empty seats separating teachers (sitting in the front of the bus) and students (sitting at the back). The same observation was made in the field that was visited during a Geography outing with Y9 class.

> Every time we stop at a place Ms Hill and Mr Dyce (accompanying teachers) walk close to Mr Web (leading teacher, Head of Geography),

who gives information about the place. In the cataract there is no space for anyone to stand next to Mr Web so Mr Dyce sits near me although he had to go through the group of students in order to get where I was standing. We were waiting for the rest of the class and for Ms Hill to arrive and I was chatting with Mr Dyce about hiking. I turned to the group of students that I was chatting with (also about hiking) while we were walking there and tried to engage them in the discussion. I gave up – it was either me talking with them while Mr Dyce was observing or me discussing with Mr Dyce which made students chat with each other [......] Mr Web occasionally talks with students when we walk but he seems to prefer to talk to me or Ms Hills when one of us is around. [...] Mr Dyce seems to be uncomfortable when he walks next to the same group of students for some time. There is consistently a reason for him to stop and let the group overtake. (Field notes from Y9 Geography outing – Dales)

The above are indicative of the tendency of both teachers and students to minimise opportunities for interactions that can lead both towards the construction of situations that are not determined by their institutional roles. In that sense, they seem to prefer a model of interaction that is –to some extent at least- de-personalised. This de-personalisation is also apparent in the process of 'role exchange' and in the model of (egocentric) empathy in the interaction between students and teachers.

Functional empathy

The exploration of the empathetic aspect of the interaction showed that teachers systematically approach and interact with the class as a whole, while the personal interaction with individual students is exceptional or circumstantial. Teachers in the classrooms seem to rarely address individuals and when they do, this is usually in order to praise students for their participation or to warn or punish those who obstruct their teaching with their behaviour or in order to apply rules which protect the uniformity of the class (such as the request for students to remove their coats, a request that has been addressed numerous times in the lessons observed). Even in those cases, however, many teachers prefer not to address the individuals who break these rules but, instead, the whole class:

Y9 listen! There are two important questions to answer! DO YOU LISTEN? Listen to what I say because I will say it only once. Some of you may think that this is not for them. Well, the exams are for all of you Y9! (Observation of Y9 Geography lesson)

In this respect, the interaction between students and teachers seems to be more accurately described as interaction between teachers and 'the class'. This supports the claim about the development of a 'functional' model of empathy (Cooper, 2002) in which the students are considered as forming a unified group and this group being 'the other' in the interaction (Hammersley, 1990:16).

Cooper observes that 'functional empathy is the teacher's response to having to interact with large numbers and their attempt to engage with and support a whole group' (ibid.,: 316). As Cooper states: 'This model of behaviour functions at a much shallower, lower moral level because children are not treated as unique individuals for sufficient amounts of time' (ibid.,: 316). Inevitably, functional empathy supports an interaction which keeps students and teachers at a virtual distance from each other, operating in a way similar to the distance observed in the field trips and break-times:

> [my interaction with students]...tends to be, hmm ... very, very rigid – you know, you are the teacher, *they are the class*. It's hard to ... get close to them. (Interview with Mr Tess, Head of History)

The rigidness and distance between students and teachers do not only strip students of their individuality, but it affects also the way that students perceive teachers' individuality. Aaron's view of the kind of attitude he wishes his teachers to have in order for him to have a good relationship with them is indicative of this:

> ... hmm ... Not to shout a lot; if they don't shout a lot then I am all right with them; just being normal, not like a teacher.

> Being normal – not like a teacher? (Interviewer)

> Yes, like ... be a normal person, just ... don't have the relationship as a teacher and a student ... have a relationship ... like ... a friendly relationship. (Interview with Aaron, Y9 student)

The quote does not only point out Aaron's inability to think of his teacher as a person; it shows also that for Aaron the expected (although not ideal) relationship between teachers and students is one that does not allow teachers to present themselves as real people. Indicative of this is Ashid's inability to imagine his teachers out of their role:

> ... the teachers are teachers; I cannot think of what they do after school, I

cannot imagine how teachers are when they are leaving school. (Interview with Ashid, Y9 student)

The lack of interest (or the inability for such interest to be expressed due to lack of time, pressure applied by the class-size etc.) reinforces the distance that Mr Tess referred to. Even in cases that students attempt to show understanding about teachers' behaviours choices and actions, this happens in a way that shows empathy with the teachers' role rather than with the persons who perform this role. By doing so, they show that they –similarly to teachers- demonstrate 'functional empathy', empathy towards a unified and de-personalised group:

[Teachers] have to be like that; otherwise they would not be able to teach and we would not learn'. [...] 'It is not up to them ... – they have to teach classes of 30. (Notes from group discussion, Drama exercise 1, Y9)

An interactionist understanding of the above which takes into account the egocentric empathy as essential element in human interaction should suggest that functional empathy does not only affect the way that the interacting parts perceive each other but that it provides the base for the development of a similarly 'functional' self-perception. In the context of the interaction between students and teachers the view of each other as representatives of a de-personalised institutional role cannot but penetrate the understanding of the self as such. The *rigidness* in the interaction that Mr Tess referred to, the discomfort that teachers and students experience when they meet in out-of-role situations and indeed the 'interaction avoidance' seem to verify this.

Role interaction and the contractual agreement

Functional empathy together with the out-of-role interaction avoidance as indications of the de-personalised 'role interaction' in which students and teachers engage themselves do not seem to be inappropriate or dysfunctional in the context of the school life. On the contrary, the maintenance of such interaction would be impossible to explain if we fail to recognise the support that it receives from the participants in it.

Indeed, the note from group discussion quoted above is indicative of students' view that the formation of teachers' roles is a response to conditions which are beyond their control. In other parts of this study students seem not only to appreciate these conditions, but they also actively support such roles as they consider that they are mostly effective in fulfilling their expectations from schools. In the context of these expectations active participation and personalised interaction are considered as exceptions in school life and are closely linked with the rigour of subjects and the status of teachers. Commenting on styles of teaching of teachers with whom they have a more personalised interaction, Lilah, a Y10 student states:

Which lessons are like this?

PSE. PSE is like that. … And in Art, [it] is a bit like that.

You said that you would like to have more lessons like PSE. Do you mean that you would like other lessons to be taught like this?

No, I meant … to have more PSE lessons, not the other lessons to become like PSE… You cannot have like … History like that. You don't learn the same things. (Interview with Lilah, Y10 student)

The relationship between content and significance of learning, expectations from the schools and styles of interaction is also evident in a quote from another interview. Commenting on the implementation of a new, rather rigid and strict behavioural policy which requires the consistent among staff application of specific measures for the punishment or reward of students' behaviour Alex gives a glimpse of his expectations and how these are linked with an 'imposed' form of learning leaving little room for personalised exploration and interaction:

It seems that this system helps parents and teachers to have better control.

Yes.

Is this a good thing?

I think so, yes.

Why?

Because, hmm… students can't do what they want, and if they do *what they want*, they don't learn, so… . I want a good job, where I can get money, and, so… I have to learn. (Interview with Alex, Y8 student)

Such views seem to be shared particularly among high achieving students in Hillcliff High and are indicative of students' view that their interaction with teachers is purpose-led, supporting the chain that links schools with Higher Education and employment. This effectively indicates that the interaction between students and teachers is developed in the context of a mutual, concealed agreement allowing access to specific 'goods'. Mr Web graphically describes the interactive aspect of this agreement:

> …We've got certain … work / we've got *work* to complete, we've got *specifications* to follow, and I'd expect … students to make every effort to get to do that; and that's one of the most important ones; the other one I would think is that … to me … [……] I say 'Well, you know, I'll make a pact with you, that I make the lessons interesting and I'll try to make the lessons fun, when I can, and if we are doing any assessments or tests you'll know in good time, and if possible I'll actually make sure that you are aware of what we have to cover for those, and I'll give you the support that you need, and what I'm asking for is co-operation and … to be co-operative.' (Interview with Mr Web, Head of Geography)

Evidently, this contract is not one which supports participation or personalised interaction but co-operation, mutual support for the performance of each other's operational role.

Normalisation, surveillance and performativity

In the extract from the interview quoted above, Mr Web points out that the contractual agreement which guides his interaction with students is determined by 'specifications' which do not seem to be in his or his students' control. In line with the argumentation about a de-personalised 'role interaction' between students and teachers which implicitly promoted the view of this interaction as a theatrical performance, it can be argued that his quote suggests the operation of a 'pre-written script' which guides the interaction. What is left to be defined then is the 'audience' of this performance. It appears that for the school community and particularly for the teachers the role of the audience is occupied by three groups: the school's management team (and more specifically the headteacher), the Government (and the OfSTED inspection teams) and the students' parents. Teachers acknowledge that their interaction with students is monitored and affected by the priorities, directions and expectations of these three groups which operate at a distance from the actual settings in which students and teachers interact. This distance is evident not only from the physical absence of members of these groups from the classrooms, but also from the lack of any reference in the evidence supplied by teachers regarding the influence that they can have in these groups' actions and decisions. This is evidenced particularly when teachers discuss the role of the management team:

> I think the management is more ... hmmm ... I am trying to find a nice way of putting it ... but, it's not ... it's not as democratic ... ; we find things are imposing upon us more ... we find that ... / I think they are more concerned about results, ... than the / as they are on paper / than they actually are in producing ... students(?). (Interview with Ms Wales, Head of PSE)

The government seems also to hold a similar role:

> You said about being effective and ... getting students through their exams. How important do you think that this is for the school to accomplish its role?

> Personally, I think it's not; it isn't important I mean; but it seems to be the priority that the establishment did place on us now, these days. (Interview with Mr Web, Head of Geography)

The 'invisible audience' does not only hold the authority to evaluate teachers' performance but by doing so, it effectively provides them with the script of their performance. This process however, supports the de-personalisation of their interaction with students, who turn, as Ms Wales, similarly to Pring (1999), remarks from participants to 'clients' and then to mere 'products'.

What needs to be noted is that although teachers are sceptical of the decisions, actions and expectations of the 'invisible audience' their criticism does not enter into their interaction with students. Indicatively, Mr Web associates this with his understanding of 'professionalism':

> Would you support the students if they bring up a demand about changing the behavioural policy? Would you say clearly what you think about the policy to them?

> No, I wouldn't do that ... I think you would be most unprofessional really... (Interview with Mr Web, Head of Geography)

It seems that in the context of teachers' performance, the rules of professionalism coincide with the expectations of the 'invisible audience' (as teachers understand them). These rules become then integral aspects of the professional roles performed by teachers. This internalisation of the expectations and priorities defined by the Government, adopted by the public and promoted by the management of the school echoes Perryman's (2006) description of 'normalisation' of teachers' performance. Teachers' criticism though of these expectations indicates that on a personal level they denounce the subject that is established through this 'normalisation' process. This change on teachers' subjectivity (Perryman, 2006: 219) and its denouncement by teachers on a personal level might be the greatest price that needs to be paid for the introduction of the 'performativity' culture in English schools because it leads to their 'ontological insecurity' (Ball, 2003), their bipolar relationship with their own role. Performativity, however, takes an additional dimension when it is projected into the context of citizenship education. This dimension is the topic of the discussion that follows.

Citizenship Education in times of performativity

The discussion so far showed how students and teachers tend to consider each other as unified expressions of specific institutional roles rather than as individuals who actively construct these roles. In such context, Pring's (1999) claims about the incompatibility of a democratic political education to modern schooling discourse seem to be tentatively verified. The introduction of Citizenship, a subject at the roots of which there lies the need for interaction between individuals who expose (and construct), through their interaction, their views, beliefs, and their political stands, can be seen as intrusion of a new, ill-assorted discourse. Indeed, even the simple examination of the essential elements of Citizenship as these are suggested in the Crick report can easily demonstrate the need for personalised interaction in the context of the subject. The 'disposition to work with and for others with sympathetic understanding', the 'courage to defend a point of view', the 'willingness to be open to changing one's opinions in the light of discussion and evidence', the 'ability to tolerate other view points' (QCA, 1998: 44) are indications of how Citizenship invites and expects the establishment of forms of interaction and roles that do not suppress or hide the personality of the ones performing them and to create a model of teaching and learning as an 'internal relation', as 'constitutive –like authority – of the very fabric of human moral and civic association'. (Carr, 2005).

However, the introduction of Citizenship in Hillcliff High, through and because of the incompatibility of the subject to the operational discourse, has another significant effect which offers further support to Pring's (1999) scepticism. Evidently, it is experienced by teachers as a request for a performance that satisfies two conflicting forms of expectations and consequently as a new role strain for teachers involved in the implementation of the subject.

> I mean they talk about ...citizenship [...] but [...] they are expecting us to do more and more, but at the same time they are expecting us to get the results; [...] Where do we get the balance between producing well adapted students who can contribute ... socially ... and sort of ... and actually getting the kids with the result that the Government want to have? (Interview with Mr Web, Head of Geography)

The way that the tension caused by these conflicting expectations described by Mr Web is resolved is the question about the kind of citizenship education currently offered in English secondary schools.

A way to view the nature of this conflict and of the choices for its resolution can be borrowed from Lyotard's two models of knowledge (Lyotard, 1984): the narrative and the scientific-technical model (Sarup, 1993: 135). Knowledge in a scientific-technical sense 'involves questions of competence extending to both the determination and application of criteria of efficiency (efficient/inefficient)' (Fazzaro *et.al.*, 2002: 18). Performativity is driven by this model of knowledge and requires a technical use of language in order to 'optimise the relationship between inputs and outputs'. Narrative knowledge, in contrast, 'concerns abstract notions including, but not limited to, justice, freedom, liberty, morals, beauty, ethics, happiness, virtue, and, of course, access, equity, and fairness ... which are not reducible to mere objectively defined scientific true/false or technical efficient/inefficient descriptions. They have no absolute meaning. They represent values; thus, they are subjective prescriptions' (ibid.,: 19). Knowledge in scientific/technical terms does not allow the development of such subjectivities, but it presupposes a consensus which, however, is easily achieved because of the descriptive nature of this model of knowledge. The nature of the scientific-technical knowledge and its dependency on a consensus which is not the product of a dialogue and which excludes any possibility for such dialogue to take place led Lyotard, as Fazzaro points out, to 'disqualify scientific-technical knowledge as the knowledge necessary for good citizenship' (ibid.,: 23).

Freire (2005) has convincingly argued for the importance of such dialogue. He writes: 'Dialogue is the encounter between men, mediated by the world, in order to name the world' (Freire, 2005: 88). In the context of an interactionist approach, Freirean dialogue allows interacting parties to participate freely in a process of defining the situation which is constructed through, and because of, their interaction. Dialogue, in that sense, is a deeply humanistic and humanising process or, as Freire puts it, 'an existential necessity' (ibid.,: 88). 'And since dialogue is the encounter in which the united reflection and action of the dialoguers are addressed to the world in which is to be transformed and humanised, this dialogue cannot be reduced to the act of one person's "depositing" ideas on another, nor can it become a simple exchange as ideas to be "consumed" by the discussants' (ibid.,: 88-89). But as the discussion in this section showed, this depository/consumerist interaction is what appears to be happening in Hillcliff High. Teachers indeed report this product-based view of education and of their students, while the 'naming of the world' is based on a vocabulary which is the product of a consensus achieved outside of the interaction of students and teachers and as such is viewed as a vocabulary imposed rather than constructed. Under such conditions the expectations from teachers and students to participate in open dialogues and to construct conditions of 'active learning' as Citizenship suggests, is nothing more than a demand to operate contrary to the modern educational discourse promoted by and constructed in performativity. The imposition of such requirements upon schools can be nothing more than an attempt to integrate such requirements in the discourse of performativity, altering the very nature of the knowledge that such requirements advocate and leading to the promotion of a technical-scientific approach to narrative knowledge which reduces Citizenship to skill training. As a quote from the History teacher indicates, teachers at Hillcliff High may be exactly at the stage where they need to decide whether they will create the space for a dissensus model of Citizenship or proceed with the above reduction:

> [...] certainly in Citizenship I don't see how you can teach *meaningfully* without becoming involved in a 'two-way flow'; I really don't. Otherwise, you are doing some sort of civics or constitution where you are simply *teaching* some basic rules – this is the Constitution, this is the name of this, this is the name of that, this is how our laws are passed and that's it. (Interview with Mr Tess, Head of History)

Conclusions

The seventh report of the citizenship education Longitudinal Study (2009) seems to suggest that what it monitored during the six years after the introduction of citizenship is the process of embedment of the subject in secondary education ('Embedding citizenship'; Keating *et.al.*, 2009). In previous reports the same study had described a number of what the researchers recognised as obstacles in this process. The lack of specialised teachers, of time and of familiarity of staff with the content and methods of Citizenship (Kerr *et.al.*, 2004; Ireland *et.al.*, 2006; Keating *et.al.*, 2009) do explain to a large extent the struggle of the new subject for successful implementation. Equally importantly the same study (particularly in its second report) (Cleaver *et.al.*, 2005) offers support to and seeks support from a very rich literature on students' participation and relates this struggle to the way that schools are organised and the role of the students.

The study that is discussed in this chapter neither doubts nor challenges the value of any suggestions justified by the above findings. Having a different focus and following a different methodological pathway it attempted an ethnographic insight into the micro-political setting of human interaction and through this the struggle of citizenship as experienced by those who are assigned with the task of implementing it. Its contribution therefore is not so much in adding any further 'successes and challenges' to those reported in the longitudinal study (Keating *et.al.*, 2009: 70-73) but in offering a deeper understanding of the processes that generate some of these challenges. The picture that emerges from the analysis suggests that citizenship in Hillcliff High has been considered as a carrier of a new discourse which for many participants is very near to 'what education should be about'.

Importantly however, the introduction of the subject is viewed by the school staff not as a liberating force but as yet another expectation of the 'invisible audience' which represents and promotes the performativity discourse which alienates the teaching role from that of the 'true educator'. From such a point of view, the subject is considered as a manifestation of 'conflicting performativities' and its effective implementation an impossibility. Autonomy, personalised interaction and human relationships, which the teachers themselves consider as necessary elements of the new subject, are at the same time those which performativity-driven secondary schooling seems to lack. Therefore the embedment of citizenship which many of us are aspired to, might not require more resources, time or training but a different approach to schooling. As it appears, the debatably revolutionary nature of the subject may currently being constricted (in some schools as least) into a performativity-compatible, safe technical form.

Ten years after the introduction of the subject such discussion is more important than ever. The language and the educational policies of the Government which came to power in 2010 have already signalled that we may already be in the beginning of the end of citizenship as a statutory subject. This might be a strong enough indication that the embedment of the subject has not happened yet and might never do. Of course there is no doubt that after the ten years of siege, secondary education has now accepted (albeit somewhat forcefully) the gift offered by Crick and other proponents of citizenship education. It is apparent, however, that unlike Trojans, the school community remains still reluctant to fully open this gift which is still left in the periphery of the school life, too large and odd-shaped to enter the purposefully narrow streets of Troy's centre.

8 Performative cultures: changing professional roles, responsibilities and relationships of teachers and teaching assistants

Irene and Paul Garland

Introduction

This chapter explores the extent to which teacher and teaching assistant (TA) roles and identities have been 'formed' through performativity discourse and practices with reference to an ethnographic study of two primary schools in the North of England. Against the backdrop of school workforce reform policy in England, we attempt to explain both accommodation and resistance to performativity cultures in relation to externally imposed restructuring of professional roles.

Empirical data is drawn from a study (Garland, 2008) of the roles of teachers and TAs in primary school settings with observed practices analysed in relation to policy discourse. Our view is that a Foucauldian analysis of policy discourse is metaphorically powerful but can mask the *varied and chaotic nature of the actual experience and outcomes'* (Dwyer, 1995: 475). Ball (1994) distinguishes between policy as text (drawing attention to the agency of individuals to contest, change, negotiate policy) and policy as discourse (emphasising structural, external influences or determinants). Similarly, Hollstein and Gubrium (2005) distinguish between 'discourse-in-practice' (Foucault's 'regimes of truth' – 1979a) and discursive practice (with its emphasis on the interactive processes in real time that produce the 'structures'). Likewise we are interested in the tension between structuring forces (policy interventions, discourses, performativity regimes) and local practices indicating space for agency (local solutions, accommodations, compromises). We also draw upon Bourdieu's notion of habitus and his discussion of the structuring force of social constructions such as the family (Bourdieu, 1990) to consider how actors can both absorb performativity but also be a source of resistance to such externally imposed discursive practices when these conflict with other practices that seem more 'natural' to those actors.

Ball (2003) sees performativity in terms of a Foucauldian disciplinary technology:

> ...a technology, a culture and a mode of regulation that employs judgements, comparisons and displays as means of incentive, control, attrition and change – based on rewards and sanctions (both material and symbolic).

The performances (of individual subjects or organizations) serve as measures of productivity or output, or displays of 'quality', or 'moments' of promotion or inspection. As such they stand for, encapsulate or represent the worth, quality or value of an individual or organization within a field of judgement. (Ball, 2003: 216)

Troman outlines the specific practices in schooling which illustrate performativity cultures in English primary schools:

...systems and relationships of: target setting; OfSTED inspections; school league tables constructed from pupil test scores; performance management; performance related pay; threshold assessment; and advanced skills teachers – systems which demand that teachers 'perform' and in which individuals are made accountable. (Troman, 2008: 620)

Much of the work relevant to providing the context for this paper has focused on the role of the teacher (as the frontline role in schools) and the effects of performativity regimes on teacher identities (Troman, 2008; Ball, 2003; Jeffrey, 2002), and on the juxtaposition of discourses of performativity and creativity in policies relating to schooling (Burnard and White, 2008; Troman *et.al.*, 2007; Turner-Bisset, 2007). This chapter has school workforce reforms under New Labour (1997-2010) as its central focus and the tensions arising from the mix of these reforms and performativity practices in primary schools. During this period teachers ceased to be the only 'frontline' staff in primary schools.

Looking at performativity from the perspective of a wider school workforce, we see new challenges for teacher professionalism, specifically on the border between teacher and assistant roles. Workforce reform has led to an expanded TA role and, potentially, to an overlap between teacher and assistant roles (for example, in the taking of whole class groups). In the context of performativity culture we explore the way that the reforms 'played out' in the two primary schools.

Lyotard's discussion of performativity in relation to teacher and teaching assistant roles

In *The Postmodern Condition* (1984) Lyotard describes performativity as part of the larger language game of technology, itself serving the logic of capitalism, where the distinction of efficient/inefficient is the ruling criterion and where truth and rightness are brought together in the 'performativity of procedures', their objective being 'the best possible input/output equation' (Lyotard, 1984: 46). The backdrop to performativity is a commodification of knowledge ('knowledge in the form of an informational commodity indispensable to productive power' 1984:5) made possible through technologies of data collection, storage and management. Lyotard refers to 'simple' and 'extended' reproduction, the former being earmarked for institutions, programmes and professional groupings for the reproduction of professional skills and the latter being for 'the promotion and "stimulation" of "imaginative" minds' (1984: 53).

Supporting this commodification process are the technocrats whom he sees as subscribing to positivist-functionalist and systems perspectives akin to those of Parsons and Luhmann, through which society is conceived as a unified totality and where the key concerns are functionality/dysfunctionality. Identifying two main narratives in the legitimation of knowledge (the second being the speculative search for unification of knowledge) Lyotard observes how the first tends to appeal to 'the narrative of freedom every time it assumes direct control of the training of the "people", under the name of the "nation", in order to point them down the path of progress' (1984: 32). Here we are reminded of the practice of recent years of setting targets (for pupils and teachers) using norms derived from national standards. Recalling Foucault's 'regime of truth' (Foucault, 1979a) we find the 'obviousness' and incontestability of National Standards at their most general level: each statement almost impossible to object to, appealing to sentiments of inclusion, equality of respect and treatment. Lyotard argues that the legitimation of such modes of knowledge (here, the Standards) is made in terms of 'context control' (1984: 46-7) and system functionality.

For Lyotard (1984: 48-9), Higher Education makes an 'optimal contribution' to the performativity of the system by playing a 'professionalist function' in system performance improvement through retraining and continual education. The incorporation of national standards for teachers and TAs is the classic example of this in relation to the present discussion, though standard attainment tasks (SATs), league tables and performance management are also key emblems of the performativity culture in schooling. The role of the university in 'improving the system's performance' is reflected in the use of Standards for TAs and HLTAs, the higher levels of which were incorporated into Foundation degrees. In his distinction between 'simple' and 'extended' reproduction of knowledge, the former would seem to fit the requirements of initial teacher training (ITT) and TA standards; the latter being reserved for more elite groupings and taking the form of 'pure' and 'abstract' domains of knowledge. The knowledge forms prescribed for teachers and TAs in the National Standards are essentially the same (many statements being identical for QTS, TA and HLTA Standards) in that they become perlocutions of 'obviousness' in their combination of facts and norms and their exemplification in guidance commonly calls upon the candidate to learn and follow institutional policies and procedures. There is little in these exemplifications that hints at the possibility of problematising the statements of competence to which they refer.

However, the empirical evidence informing this paper indicates a more chaotic picture in practice, where the contexts to be controlled (in this case primary schools and their classrooms) both follow and escape the prescription of the standards (some of the principal means of realisation of the performativity regime). This occurs through the elision of school and outside contexts and the different discourses of education, care, learning and discipline that are evident in the practices of individuals whose identities have different anchorings, some of which are much stronger in structuring practice than the discourses supporting an obedient adherence to standards. This argument will be developed in a theoretical section following a a brief outline of the workforce reforms and our view of the impact of these on the continuum of teaching assistant to teacher roles.

Workforce reform and the teaching assistant-teacher continuum

There was a rapid increase in numbers of school support workers (including TAs) following New Labour's election to power in 1997. In 1997 there were 133,500 full-time equivalent (FTE) support staff in schools. By 2007 this had risen to 305,600: the number of support workers rose by 172,100 in this period whereas teacher numbers rose only 36,000 (DCSF, 2007). In this period, the number of TAs increased from 60,000 in 1997 to 163,000 in 2007, the majority of these being employed in the primary sector. By November 2010 the number of TAs in local authority maintained and Academy schools had risen to 213,900 (Statistical First Release, 2011). Alongside this dramatic increase in numbers, TAs have taken on a greater 'pedagogical' role in schools (all figures in FTEs).

In recognition of the workload pressure on teachers the National Agreement (DfES, 2003) appeared to offer some respite by relieving them of a number of tasks which it was considered people not having qualified teacher status (QTS) could perform (the '24 tasks') and allowing teachers to concentrate on their 'core' role (this 'core' role being firmly linked to performativity agendas and the unceasing attempt to raise 'standards'). In addition, the National Agreement ensured that all teachers had the statutory right to 10% planning, preparation and assessment (PPA) time (a new departure, particularly in the primary sector), and was introduced with the overt intention of helping teachers achieve a better work/life balance by enabling them to carry out planning, preparation and assessment duties during school time rather than at home. The amount of cover by teachers for teacher absence was also to be addressed. TAs were key to such a plan and new Higher Level Teaching Assistant (HLTA) standards were introduced to allow support workers to take whole class groups (though the research reported here found TAs, as well as those with HLTA status, taking whole class groups). Thus the National Agreement threatened the coherence of the professional teacher role by allowing TAs to take whole class groups for PPA time and to cover for teacher absence. TAs were also drawn more overtly into the frame in terms of 'raising standards' and have, following the National Agreement, performed a higher profile role within schools.

The binding in of teachers and TAs to performativity regimes does not only rest at the level of daily practice in schools. These two groups have also been affected by changes in their professional training/education such that they can be viewed not as separate roles but on a continuum. Teacher preparation and CPD are now dominated by the 'practical': described variously as discourses of 'competency' (Edmond, 2003; Furlong, 2001; Carr and Hartnett, 1996), of 'performativity' (Jeffrey, 2002; Ball, 1999), of the 'technical rational' (McNamara *et.al.*, 2008; Whitty, 2000; Bottery and Wright, 2000). Teacher 'education' has come to be viewed as teacher 'training' (McNamara *et.al.*, 2008; Coffey, 2001; Carr and Hartnett, 1996) and the introduction of Standards for QTS were part of this move. The Standards for HLTA are based on the current Standards for QTS (that is, those produced under the New Labour government – see TDA 2007a and 2007b – though new Standards for QTS are due to take effect from September 2012, see DfE, 2011) and these Standards are said to be set within the same 'wider framework of standards for the whole school workforce' (TDA, 2007b: 2). The whole school workforce is now covered by the one training body (the TDA), the training provided and Standards to be achieved having been funnelled into a similar model, the two roles begin to lose their separate identities. This point is most clearly illustrated in an online text in which the QTS, HLTA and the TA roles were placed in order with the TA role on the left, the HLTA role in the centre, and the QTS role on the right in what was described as a 'progressive framework'. (TDA, 2007c).

Explaining compliance and resistance to performativity

Earlier we discussed ways in which we have conceptualised what Lyotard calls the 'clouds of sociality' (1984: xxiv) from which the actions of individuals emerge, and Hollstein and Gubrium's (2005) notion of 'discursive practices' was mentioned as a tool to help account for the variability and openness of actual practices. Bourdieu also stresses the contingency of practice, though agency is powerfully constrained through the operation of the habitus. For Bourdieu both resilience and openness are explained through the operation of a relational analysis in which actors are understood in terms of their position within a field, the relative worth of their different forms of capital and the operation of habitus within an open stream of interactions which, despite the high level of their predictability, always offer the possibility of change. The school plays a crucial role in contributing to the reproduction of the distribution of cultural capital: 'the reproduction of the structure of the distribution of cultural capital is achieved in the relation between familial strategies and the specific logic of the school institution' (2001: 19). Within the school setting different educational workers are positioned according to their possession of various forms of symbolic capital, amongst which we can include the range of qualifications, standards and statuses now available to them (degrees, QTS, HLTA, NVQs, etc.):

> ...institutionalisation sets up strictly established, legally guaranteed relations between recognised positions, defined by their rank in a relatively autonomous space, distinct from and independent of their actual and potential occupants, themselves defined by *entitlements* which, like titles of nobility, property titles or educational qualifications (*titres*), authorise them to occupy these positions. (Bourdieu, 1990: 131*)*.

In the educational field we now have a 'totalising' architecture of standards and levels as well as definitions of roles and workforce agreements that help us to position TAs in relation to teachers. Within this architecture the different ranks of educational workers would seem to be relatively clearly placed in relation to each other and it is evident in the fieldwork data that actors use such reference points. However, they seemed more likely to position themselves with reference to certain practices which they see as 'theirs' rather than to qualifications. Yet the focus on children and standards, coupled with Workforce Reform and the extended roles of TAs and HLTAs appears to have led to situations in practice where teachers are not necessarily acting in their own best interests as 'players' in the field.

Following Bourdieu, each individual brings a habitus to the field that has been shaped primarily through family within the broader context of that family's social position in relation to the different forms of capital. The habitus of individuals and collectivities is further formed and modified by key life experiences, including education, training and work experiences. Habitus also has a collective dimension in that actors positioned closely within a field are more likely to share perceptual schemes, norms, values and expectations. In this respect alone, TAs and teachers might well be positioned quite differently within the field of education, for example in terms of their previous educational and employment experiences, their past and current social milieu. The TAs were all found to be living in the school locality and many had come to their roles through firstly helping out as parent-helpers and then gradually moving on to take paid positions, though most had few or no formal qualifications. Generally, TAs will normally be in an inferior position when it comes to the key indicators of cultural and symbolic capital that hold value in the school (degrees, QTS, permanent positions), and although we are aware from our experience that some TAs are highly qualified, we would support, both experientially and theoretically, Bourdieu's theory of capital and field in this case. This means that we would expect roles and relations between TAs and teachers to be broadly reflective of the power dynamics of the field. We would also expect these dynamics to be reflected in the responses of agents to the demands of the performativity regime in primary schooling and this too is borne out to some extent by the empirical evidence, for example in the way TAs were deployed to deal with children having difficulties.

However, if we then consider their actual formation as individual teachers and TAs and relate these to roles within the field of educational practice, we can see that each individual, whether teacher or TA is slightly differently dispositioned in terms of social, cultural, economic and pedagogical capitals within their classroom and school, and so the arrangements made in actual contexts with their own particular urgencies understandably vary. Despite these contradictions, from a wider perspective the notional continuum represents opportunities for TAs to increase their capitals within the educational field (if they wish to do so) and in this respect they have much to gain. It is difficult to see what the teachers have to gain, however, except in terms of their daily work and the possibility of, in the symbiotic relationships between teacher and TA that were found in some cases at least, finding some relief from the intensity of the work. On the other hand, a shift in role towards 'people management', might be seen by some as evidence of a new status for qualified teachers, though managing others in their pedagogical practice might not be seen as quite what New Labour was seeking in its drive for a 'new professionalism'.

We can see the practices of individual educational workers as reflecting a logic that is consistent with their position within a field and the collective logic of different educational workers as reflecting the structure of relations within that field, a structure which has been to a great extent formed through the demands of performativity. We can agree that the roles of TAs and teachers reflect those structures, not inevitably but predictably, and that the structures in some ways are leading to the removal of demarcations. However, habituses are not only:

> ...systems of durable, transposable dispositions, structured structures predisposed to function as structuring structures, that is, as principles which generate and organise practices and representations that can be objectively adapted to their outcomes without presupposing a conscious

aiming at ends or an express mastery of the operations necessary in order to attain them (Bourdieu, 1990: 53)

They are also 'classificatory schemes, principles of classification, principles of vision and division, different tastes' (Bourdieu, 2001: 6) and thus we can account for the differences in compliance and resistance to the demands of the regime, the differences in 'feel for the game' that TAs and teachers held.

The empirical data revealed that teachers and TAs were not necessarily cowed or re-formed by the disciplinary technologies of standards, attainment tests, performance review and so on. However, the teachers in particular were struggling with the conflicts arising from this mix of performativity culture and workforce reform, and they were uneasy about ceding the closeness in relations with children to the TAs. Intervention schemes, coupled with workforce agreements had opened up space for TAs to develop their roles, whilst the teachers were not getting the relief that the agreements promised. We now discuss these findings in more detail.

Researching teacher/TA roles: performativity at the local level

The empirical research referred to in this paper was carried out in the first half of 2006 in two primary schools in different Local Authorities in the North of England. Time was spent in relatively unstructured observation (shadowing TAs, one at a time, as they went about their day-to-day work) and relatively open-ended interviewing of TAs and teachers (thirty-two recorded interviews of approximately one hour duration). The detailed fieldnotes, which those involved in the research agreed could be taken throughout the day, were drawn on as extensively as interview data during analysis. In terms of 'participation' as an observer in the context, the researcher role as 'fully visible shadow' seemed to describe this most appropriately: a role in which the researcher is 'available' to help out if required and does not sit back from ongoing events, but in which it is not necessarily assumed that the researcher has any useful role to play in the daily life of the school. Observation and interviews, the two key aspects of ethnographic work (e.g. Walford, 2007a; Hammersley, 2006; Atkinson *et.al.*, 2001), provided rich data concerning the research focus.

In this section, we discuss the dominance of performativity agendas in the schools within this study and the effects of that dominance on work intensification and the roles of TAs in intervention schemes and ability grouping within this agenda.

Work intensification

That performativity regimes have added to the intensification of teachers' work (Troman *et.al.*, 2007) was also evident in this research, not least in terms of teacher and TA roles and their relation to each other. Workforce reforms meant that despite the greater numbers of TAs in the schools, the TA role was expanding and no longer simply involved assisting in the classroom. Teachers indicated the pressure they were under, for example regarding SATs tests, yet the help they might have previously counted on for other aspects of their role (such as 'classroom maintenance' tasks) was not so forthcoming as before, leading, in some cases, to further feelings of stress and dissatisfaction.

Heather (teacher) talked of the pressure on teachers to gain the best scores possible in SATs (see Troman *et.al.*, 2007), observing that 'Year 6 is known for being pacey – with the SATs...'. She also noted that though the pressure was on both teachers and children during Year 6 she had less help than when teaching other years because TAs were so involved in intervention work:

> ...because there's displays to be done, things to be mounted and photocopying to do and...it just doesn't get done....Because I do...I've got a wall half finished and I like the walls complete and looking nice. And it's like as if we've got on a treadmill and we're rushing and trying to catch up with things – we can't get things done.

On the issue of work/life balance, as a former Y6 teacher, Tessa, observed:

> I can tell you now that if you're in Year 6 you have *no* work life balance, because I was going home when I was in Year 6 and marking till goodness knows what time every night of the week...

The pressure in schools to make maximum use of school time to press target areas was discussed by Pam (teacher), illustrated in her school by the practice of having TAs take groups of children for reading or spelling during assembly time. Pam also indicated that having more staff in the classroom had not necessarily always helped her with the pace of her work either:

> ...it's the management skills...of managing your own time and other people's time. And I know quite often – it sounds very ungrateful – but, I mean, at the moment I've got [a particular TA] working with me, sort of teacher training, and I've got [another TA] and I've got various people linked to [a particular child] who is a special needs ...and sometimes I just

feel *exhausted* and I feel that all *my* time is going into organising others, to make sure that everybody's time is best utilised. And it…takes a lot of organising.

Tessa (a teacher of many years experience) pointed to the intensity of the working life of the primary school teacher – 'we've never had time to turn around…' – and that although the increase in TA numbers might have been assumed to provide some relief from this intensity she (and several other teachers from the same school) pointed out that since workforce reforms they had become more likely to be involved in classroom 'maintenance tasks': 'I'm more likely to be washing my *own* paint pallets and getting my *own* newspaper on the tables because I've timetabled them [the TAs] in'. The following comments from Tessa suggest that TAs taking on a 'timetabled' role meant that she could not perform her already intensified teaching role to her own satisfaction:

> …ordinary things aren't in as good a state of repair. What I mean is the wall displays won't be as tidy because there's nobody watching for the bits dropping off. The art area isn't as organised because there isn't time to go and set about it.…in the past I've worked in Key Stage 1 a lot – this is my first year back in to Key stage 1 – so go back into the past and in those days when we did a topic I would always change my area into that topic. We did Australia so it became Captain Cook's ship…and the whole of the room turned into that. I had the help of a teaching assistant to do that.…Now the other…just before Christmas we were doing Narnia and I attempted to change my home base into Narnia. I did it all myself, I was here 'til seven o'clock at night cutting out and putting trees up with *no* help, and it lasted a very short time because there was nobody watching for it falling down.

On the issue of classroom maintenance tasks, Naomi declared:

> It's back to how it was in the beginning where I do most of my own displays, my own preparation, my own mixing paint, washing my paint pallets out and.…I've actually done more of them *since* they were supposed to have been taken away.

Naomi's ironic comment also indicates how, with a cocktail of work intensification, TAs working on intervention schemes and the drive to improve standards of achievement, teachers' and TAs' roles were in a state of confusion. Pam's emphasis on time and management of other workers suggests also that she was going through a period of transition in relation to her role, with management of other adults in her classroom now added to the list of responsibilities. Whilst such new responsibilities might be construed as indicative of an elevated status for some, the additional burdens were not compensated for.

Involvement in intervention schemes: harnessing both teachers and TAs to get the best test scores

In this research it was evident that both teachers and TAs had been harnessed into this aspect of the performativity agenda: the drive to achieve the best possible scores in SATs. TAs were bound in through their work on intervention schemes, with all TAs/HLTAs involved in some type of scheme. These schemes were aimed at raising children's levels in numeracy or literacy as part of the National Numeracy Strategy (NNS) or National Literacy Strategy (NLS) forming an important part of the TA/HLTA role.

Through these schemes TAs became (alongside teachers) charged with working towards 'raising standards' (see DfES, 2003). When TAs are harnessed into performative regimes through involvement in intervention schemes, costly teacher time is not drawn upon, but 'outputs' (Lyotard, 1984) might be increased in a cost-effective manner: if support workers are 'used in place of a teacher...such staff have the potential to save teacher time'. (PricewaterhouseCoopers, 2001: 44).

During observation and 'shadowing' of TAs it was evident that much of their work now consisted of taking individuals or groups of children for intervention work. According to one TA (Jo) 'every day's just so many different programmes... following different programmes, you know?' Children were usually taken out of the classroom in order to follow these schemes and 'spaces' were found in corridors, dining halls, assembly halls and small rooms which were probably originally cupboards. The schemes were to be delivered each day in twenty or thirty minute 'chunks' and it was not unusual to find the same children appearing on different schemes at different times of the day. An ambivalent attitude towards the schemes was evident in some interviews with teachers: they acknowledged the potential for the schemes to help children progress in their learning (and, importantly here) towards targets, though there was also evidence of irritation that the schemes affected their ability to plan numeracy/literacy time to their own satisfaction: 'you've got to work your whole timetable around it [the intervention scheme]' (Pam, teacher).

Such comments are ironical in relation to the thrust of this paper: a performativity culture requiring continual raising of standards is the structuring force behind such interventions, but some teachers suggested that though children might be seen to be progressing, in an overall sense they might be missing out on the teaching that was taking place simultaneously in the classroom. Indeed, a tension was emerging between the need to comply with government initiatives and their own professional judgements on the teaching of numeracy and literacy. Some quite tricky readjustments in lesson planning were described which aimed to overcome these problems with children being out of the class on intervention schemes. For example, Fiona explained that in order for the groups of children who were going out of her class (about eight or nine children at a time out of a class of thirty-two) not to miss out on the main class sessions, she had ensured that she planned these periods as 'reading time' when she would go round the children left with her and listen to them read. She would then make sure that she listened to the children who were out on an intervention scheme at another point. In this instance a policy external to the school provided a 'context of control' (Lyotard, 1984: 46) of the professional work of the teacher and she in turn was trying to find ways of compensating for the detrimental effects of the intervention scheme upon the children, thus increasing the stress involved in the planning of teaching, though perhaps constituting in itself a small act of 'resistance'.

'Ability' groupings and SATs scores

Teacher and TA roles also intersected in relation to performativity through the discourse of 'ability'. In order to 'perform', schools divide children into ability groups: in this research TAs were found to take the 'lower' ability children leaving the teacher free to take the 'higher' ability ones. All the work that TAs/HLTAs carried out with individuals or groups of children (apart from whole class work to cover for teacher absence or PPA time) was with children seen as being of 'lower' ability, as having SEN or as exhibiting challenging behaviour (see Blatchford *et.al.*, 2007).

Sandra (TA) commented that in 'normal numeracy and literacy...we move with the poorer abilities' and similarly Judy (TA) said that when she supported children with their numeracy she generally supported 'the lower ...ability group'. Fiona (teacher) said that she had two TAs helping with her 'lower ability numeracy set' and that one TA would take 'the really diabolical ones out of the classroom working on basics...', whilst the other was supporting a group working in class but perceived as in need of extra support. This arrangement then left Fiona free to work with and 'push' further her 'very, very good twelve – which are the high ability'.

The pressure of performativity regimes is evident here: the exigencies of the situation leading to arrangements that reinforced reproduction of inequalities. Similar processes operated with children seen as exhibiting challenging behaviour. One TA took two junior-aged boys, who were considered too disruptive to be placed with their class group, for three hours every morning (fifteen hours per week). The boys spent this time in a small workroom with the TA working on literacy and numeracy (timetabled in the morning in this school). This arrangement could be justified: the children remained in mainstream schooling, they engaged with their learning more effectively with the TA and so on. Yet it also illustrates the effects of pressure on schools to produce good test scores for league tables and related status issues.

Teachers, TAs and opportunities for close relations with children
With the new right to 10% PPA time for teachers, schools needed to find ways of covering classes. Schools addressed this issue in a number of different ways (as was illustrated in the many 'case studies' on the websites of the National Remodelling Team, 2005) but, because of the financial implications, many chose to use their support staff (and other non-teacher qualified 'specialists' in areas such as sport) to cover class groups. Both schools in the study used their support staff to cover PPA time, one school's policy being to use *all* the support staff to cover. This movement of TAs onto the territory of the qualified teachers (by taking whole class groups) is the clearest instance of the roles moving onto a notional continuum.

Furthermore, this seemingly clear infringement of the territory of the qualified teacher was linked to divisions of labour between core' and 'peripheral' curricula. TA/HLTAs had begun to 'colonise' areas of the curriculum such as arts and crafts, music, sports, leaving 'core' curriculum areas to the teachers so that a 'PPA time curriculum' had developed oriented towards 'peripheral' rather than 'core' curriculum areas. The 'core' curriculum, (mainly literacy and numeracy, though science might also be included here) was the focus of the performativity agenda and was frequently referred to during interviews with teachers as curriculum 'territory' which should not and would not be ceded to support workers. Thus, the teacher role was partly reformed by performativity priorities through pressure on teachers and schools to get the best possible SATs scores. Defining some areas as 'core', however, allows others to become 'non-core' within the discourse and it is here that support workers were found to be developing their curriculum interests. Support workers were taking classes for PE and sport and, often during 'golden time', were able to involve the children in areas such as art and music.

The intensification of teachers' work and their overall responsibility for the 'core' curriculum was affecting their relations with children. The areas which TAs had 'colonised' were also the areas in which the children were more likely to feel relaxed and not under pressure themselves to 'perform' (see also Troman *et.al.*, 2007). Such divisions of labour were affecting the relative abilities of the teachers and TAs to develop close relations with children. TAs/HLTAs were prone to develop closer relations with children and children felt able to relax in their presence, come to them with their troubles or insecurities regarding academic work, and to treat them as parent/grandparent substitutes. Not only is teachers' work constrained by performativity regimes and work intensification, but it is possible that their opportunities for developing and maintaining close relations with children outside the context of 'performing' are being reduced, with support workers stepping into the 'vacuum'. It is not uncommon, furthermore, for PPA time to be given on Friday afternoons (as it was in one of the schools in this study), a time when, it might be assumed, both teachers and children would have relished 'winding down' from the week's work. PPA time for teachers from these perspectives seems less positive and linked more to the intensification of teachers' work, especially as some teachers in the study felt unable to relinquish their class to the support worker and were seen to hover around the classroom door during PPA time.

Jeffrey (2002) suggests that the discourse of performativity has challenged the previous 'humanistic' discourse (see also Woods and Jeffrey, 2002) which characterised relations between teachers' and those they work with as professionals. In a similar vein, Troman argues that the 'old Plowden self-identity' has been 'challenged by a new, assigned social identity' (2008: 630). Although this research also found evidence amongst teachers of '"love" and commitment to "care"' (Troman, 2008: 631) several other aspects of the TA role would point to this potential for closer TA/child relations as opposed to teacher/child relations. One TA (Lucy) suggested that:

...teachers are so busy, they've got so much. They've got thirty other children in the class and we've got time to take them aside and listen.... And that's what children need....They need us to be able to sit and listen. If they've got a problem...they need to iron it out. They can't make it last until the end of the lesson. They need to talk about it right there and then. And that's what we...we're able to do.

In other instances, simply being with an assistant rather than a teacher seemed to allow children to do things differently. On one occasion, when Hannah (HLTA) was covering a junior class for the afternoon, the children asked if they could 'sing' the register as they had done with her when they were in Reception. Hannah was happy to do this and the children seemed to thoroughly enjoy this departure from the normal routine. Teachers also recognised that the TA role sometimes meant it was easier for them to become close to the children and have enjoyable interpersonal relations:

I think if you're a TA you've got a job which is a lovely job because you have all of the good bits of teaching, but then you don't have to have the… pressure of the responsibility and you don't have to have the discipline side with the children….Obviously you've got to enforce behaviour management, but you don't have to be quite as strict as the teacher…who's in charge of the class. (Sophie, teacher)

I'm the kind of person at the front doing all the…all singing all dancing… being the crowd control kind of person….Whereas erm…the teaching assistant is like the nice person in the room! …who the children like! And I'm like…I'm like the evil woman…because if I ever used to say, 'you're working with…' whoever it was in an…in an afternoon they always used to cheer and didn't want to be with me!… So, they…yeah, they do like to be with the teaching assistant. It's like a special treat. (Heather, teacher)

TAs did not have the full weight of responsibility for the learning and progress of whole classes of children and as a consequence could devote more time and energy to developing close, warm relations with children.

Tensions affecting professional roles

Work intensification and performativity agendas on the one hand and the expanded role of the TA on the other seemed to have caught the teacher role in a pincer movement. Not only were the teachers under a heavy workload driven by performativity demands but the 'maintenance' work that TAs might have performed had, in many cases in the schools, fallen back on teachers following workforce reforms. To compound this situation, TA/HLTA work was spreading onto the territory of teacher work most notably in the area of whole class work, but also in their direct 'pedagogical' work with children on intervention schemes. On this expansion of the TA role into teacher territory, Heather (teacher) explained:

Again, it kind of does niggle me a bit, because…I do think…in that role they're really a teacher aren't they?…And then it follows as if…well…what the Government are trying to do…what they're saying is that anyone can teach. Well, bring…bring the person off the street and let them, and let the cleaners now become teachers, and let's have everybody having a go.

Regarding TAs taking classes Tessa (teacher) said:

They're not trained to do it. Err...I don't think that HLTAs are trained to do it either, and I don't think HLTAs should be taking the teaching job... *or* should be delivering. That's the job of the teacher. I feel quite strongly about that...

The barriers/boundaries which might have existed between the roles are partially removed as a 'consequence' of policies driven by performativity concerns: teachers must work harder and harder in order to get the results for comparison in the education 'market' so they need the help of TAs, but at the same time TAs are no longer providing the same level of support within the classroom and are moving partially onto teacher territory and apparently undermining their status. Performativity regimes are key to this situation.

Performativity policies and discourses might dissolve boundaries between teacher and assistant roles and place them onto a notional continuum, but teachers sought ways of reasserting those boundaries and creating new distinct ground for the qualified teacher role. These 'role boundary reassertions' were evident in areas such as planning, the control of 'core' National Curriculum areas, the overall responsibility for whole class groups and the learning and progression of every individual within that class (the 'whole' child), as well as, more straightforwardly, control over the classroom: 'I'm the boss, I suppose, in the classroom...' (Jane, teacher). Thus, although there was evidence that TAs were involved in planning (particularly of intervention group work but also, in some cases of whole class work – in one school RE was planned and taught to some junior classes solely by a HLTA) teachers pointed out that they had overall responsibility for planning for the whole class group: 'the teacher should take the overall responsibility for the planning...we have been trained to do that' (Naomi, teacher).

These boundary reassertions of the teacher role against the TA role were very evident in relation to the control of 'core' National Curriculum areas such as literacy and numeracy. Whilst some teachers indicated that they were happy (or happier) to allow TAs to take classes in areas not within the 'core' curriculum, they drew a line at TAs taking classes in literacy or numeracy on a regular basis. With reference to TA cover for PPA time, Heather said:

...the lessons that I am not teaching are the lessons I least like teaching. So at least I get out of teaching!...I mean, I hate teaching PE. So, for me not to have to teach PE it's like wonderful!...I wouldn't be happy letting go of numeracy and literacy. But...PE's a different matter!

Both teachers and TAs drew a firm boundary between teacher and TA roles in terms of overall responsibility for whole classes and each individual 'whole' child within those classes. Sophie (teacher) summed up this overall responsibility of the teacher by saying that the main way in which she would distinguish between the teacher and the TA role was in terms of:

> ...responsibility really, because even though the teaching assistant...I mean there's been a big shift where they're actually teaching groups of children...but the responsibility if that child isn't learning something or isn't progressing as well as is expected, or...or if there's a behaviour problem it's not down to them it's down to the teacher. They've got the responsibility...

A 'symbiotic' working relationship

Given the above discussion of research findings, it might be expected that the expanded TA role would cause universal friction between qualified teachers and support workers. However, this was not found to be so in the schools in which this research was carried out. Where teachers and TAs had worked together as a team for any length of time (several years in some cases) TAs were valued for their capacity to take some of the pressure off classroom teaching and, indeed, TAs and teachers had, not infrequently, developed a sort of verbal 'shorthand' in order to cope with the pace of classroom life without allotted time outside the classroom for discussion. In these cases of 'symbiosis' teachers apparently perceived infringements of their professional territory in a less negative light for the sake of good working relations and for the ultimate good of the children in their care. In the day-to-day workings of the busy classroom, distinguishing hierarchically or in terms of status between teacher and TA did not seem to have the same significance as might have been expected. This situation may be in the process of changing, however, as a result of workforce reforms, in that TAs in the study were rarely simply placed with a teacher in a classroom for the whole school day where they could work as a team on the education of all the children.

In conclusion: resistance and compliance in performativity cultures

In discussing this research on workforce reforms and teacher/TA roles in relation to performativity a complex picture has emerged. Performativity regimes have led to teacher work intensification, a focus on SATs results and comparisons between schools within the education market, on targets, and pupil and teacher performance. Workforce reforms have led to increased TA numbers and an expanded role which threatens to blur boundaries between teacher and TA roles (thereby impinging on notions of teacher professionalism). However, on the ground, teachers and TAs are able to distinguish between the roles and work together (often harmoniously) as teams to try to overcome work intensification and overload. There was evidence from this research, though, that support workers might be moving into the vacuum created by teachers no longer having sufficient time to develop close relations with children, making this scenario potentially a rather bitter pill to swallow.

The empirical data referred to in this paper shows that at the levels of individual and collective agency, actors are not necessarily re-formed as the compliant subjects of a regime requiring submission and obedience to the demands of the system, as might be expected from a Foucauldian analysis of the discursive formation (1972) of perfomativity. The teachers especially drew upon different discourses when articulating views on their practice, reflecting the ambiguities and tensions in which actors stand in relation to their roles. Moreover, in their actual practices, they displayed a logic of practice that we have understood as a mix of (and therefore a tension between) action based on the exigencies of situations (what is 'best' for the children and who is 'best' at providing that) and a deeper logic regarding the maintenance or development of the individual and collective positions of agents in an educational field. Nevertheless, in dealing with the demands imposed upon them through performative regimes and in balancing their need to maintain status with the exigencies of concrete situations in which TAs, with their sanctioned expanded roles, were available as an important 'resource', it would seem that the logics of practice of the teachers in this study were leading them to cede important ground to TAs.

Bourdieu is at pains to remind us of the danger of producing the 'perfect' model that masks '... the uncertainties and ambiguities that these products of a practical logic owe to their functions and to the conditions in which they are used' (1990: 85) and we follow this warning in concluding that the settings investigated show high levels of ambiguity of roles and in the meanings of everyday practices. What is distinctive about practices is their ' ... uncertainty and "fuzziness" resulting from the fact that they have as their principle not a set of conscious, constant rules, but practical schemes, opaque to their possessors, varying according to the logic of the situation, the almost invariably partial viewpoint which it imposes, etc.' (1990: 12). Because habitus, as embodied history (1990: 56) shows elements of permanence and in practice shows tendencies to relative autonomy, so we can arrive at an understanding of both resistance and compliance to performativity regimes at the local level. This study, in exploring the differences in roles and practices between TAs and teachers in primary settings, demonstrates this paradox by contrasting the roles and practices of two 'types' of practitioner, each bringing their own unique and collective dispositions into play within a field that is structured by external demands of government agencies and is internally structured, though somewhat confusedly in practice, by different ranks of educational worker.

However, the research did seem to suggest that teachers are the ones most at risk of losing out in the ongoing restructuring of the educational field: the 'assigned teacher' has been relieved of one tenth of her contact time in order to meet the requirements for greater precision in planning, preparation and assessment so that she must also lose some of the 'non-core' aspects of the curriculum. In this and in other respects outlined elsewhere, the effects of the performativity regime, in the context of teacher and TA roles, are to progressively confine the teacher to pedagogical roles which are more to do with control and management and perhaps less to do with openness and creativity. The colonization of teacher roles by performativity leaves these latter aspects of learning increasingly associated with the work of TAs: to put it bluntly, the 'fun' is being taken out of the teacher's role.

The construction of performative identities
Bob Jeffrey and Geoff Troman

Introduction

The influence of policy texts upon learners depends largely on how much influence such texts wield. Policy discourses are one of the main means whereby policy texts, in the settings in which they operate, influence the value, the implementation and the inscribing of those texts on learners. The Economic and Social Research Council-based research project described in this article examines the ways in which Lyotard's performative practices affects the identities of primary school learners and how they are constructed by Key Stage exam process and on performative progression through a system of learning targets. It uses a Foucauldian approach to show how learners are influenced by performativity discourses and how they take part in constructing these performative identities. Employing an ethnographic approach we see how Foucault's social relations characteristic of extra/intra/inter dependencies are explicated through governmentality, the construction of knowledge and subjectivity which act as major relays through which learner's performative identities become embedded.

General Policy Context

A powerful policy of performativity now exists and is underpinned by a major policy to improve economic status and social well being; a market-based approach that encourages performance-based activity and the generation of a culture of performativity (Ball, 1998, Ball, 2000, Lyotard, 1979). It is a technology, a culture and mode of regulation that employs judgements and comparisons and displays the performances of individual subjects or organisations to serve as measures of productivity. Policy makers believe it raises standards in schools and the achievement of the mass of the population. In setting targets for Local/District Education Authorities (LEA) and schools government hopes to develop a highly skilled workforce that can compete in what it sees as a new global industry – the knowledge economy. It is argued that a higher skills base and higher levels of excellence in knowledge acquisition and the best use of that knowledge the higher the economic return will be for the UK (Jones, 2005).

Theoretical Framework

Our approach is a critical one based on the approaches of Michel Foucault. The genealogical approach of Foucault seeks to chart ruptures/changes between systems of thought and to identify coherences across discourses, in our research case the performativity and creativity discourses (although we only deal with the former in this paper). It seeks to discover rules of formation by which spoken and textual discourses operate within institutions.

Schools, in this framework are discursive arenas where discursive statements are monitored and controlled, vetoed or allowed by those with power, including the practitioners themselves. We follow Foucault's methodology in analysing discourse in relation to social structure and focus on the effects of power. We are interested in institutional analysis and how technologies of power – performative practices such as testing and targets – isolate the mechanisms by which power operates, and to document how polices and their cultural antecedents attempt to normalize individuals through increasingly rationalized means by constituting normality, turning them into meaningful subjects, and in some cases docile objects.

Foucault's description of the complex processes of governmentalisation, (Rabinow, 1984) which involves the effects of the emergence and development of new technologies of power on individuals and populations, accounts for the construction of different forms of social beliefs and values, and hence furthers our understanding of hegemony. Governmentality thus refers to the coordination of power at the level of the state. It refers to discourses concerned with the 'arts of government', the means by which the State politically coordinates power to effect particular constructions of the subject, the conduct of conduct (Bragg, 2010). For Foucault, the liberal art of government is not an ideology or philosophy but a prescription for rule.

Central to our research into governmentalism is the influence of performativity which according to Lyotard (1979) our pursuit of knowledge has altered in our current market economy to one in which its use value is paramount rather than a value in itself – a postmodern condition.

> The transmission of knowledge is no longer designed to train an elite capable of guiding the nation towards its emancipation but to supply the system with players capable of acceptably fulfilling their roles at the pragmatic posts required by its institutions (ibid.,:48).

A consequence of this change in our engagement with knowledge and the ends of learning becoming functional, is that the student changes. In the context of the

> mercantilisation of knowledge, more often than not this question is equivalent to 'Is it saleable?' and in the context of power growth 'It is

efficient?'...What no longer makes the grade is competence as defined by other criteria true/false, just/unjust, and of course low performativity in general. This creates the prospect for a vast market for competence in operational skills' (ibid.,: 51)

Performativity differs from modernist approaches to knowledge, not only in terms of enlightenment values, but also from other educational systems of assessment and grading in which the pupil was held responsible for 'performance' and systems which used 'performance' for stratification. In Lyotard's performative cultures the emphasis is on continual performativity by individual, institution, regional government and State, all striving to continually compete to improve 'performance' and to be assessed according not only to the outcomes, but to the increase in performativity. These assessments of the rate of improvement are again continual and create a neverending imperative to maintain improvement by individual, institution, regional government and the State.

Performativity therefore influences the identities of both individuals and organisations, who become committed to improvement in outputs measured against competing peers and institutions, a major characteristic of markets and one which encourages continual improvement to maintain market position.

Central government educational policy texts in England have dominated schools in recent times from the introduction of a National Curriculum in 1989, the publication of curriculum guidelines by the Qualifications and Curriculum Authority (QCA), annual national assessment through Standardised Assessment Tasks (SATs), regular inspection reports of schools by the Office for Standards in Education (OfSTED) and the publication of school standards by the government. These texts are written documents, but they also contain values perpetuated through specific discourses mediated by language and beliefs about the role of education in society and the economy. These discourses bring objects into being, they form the object of which they speak (Ball, 1993) such as policy texts and they construct particular types of social relation through the relative strength of the practices they determine. The recognition of policy texts as discourses opens up greater possibilities of interpretation and action than a more prescriptive approach to policy analysis allows.

Methodology

Our theory of knowledge is a sociological approach that derives from empirical studies related to social theories and personal realities. We try to get to know the sub-culture of the classroom and school and take the view that people's personal realities and beliefs (Walford, 2007b) are embodied in speech and behaviours. The observations and analysis of the micro, we believe, is linked to macro discourses, policies and structures. We saw ethnography is a relevant and appropriate methodology to support our Foucauldian theoretical frame.

This ESRC (RES-000-23-1281) research analysed the thick (Geertz, 1973) policy and pedagogic environments through our ethnographic methodology which is predominantly qualitative. Data collection took place in six primary schools enabling us to follow annual assessment periods and the critical creative events within the school year across five Local Education Authorities. The whole database, across the six schools included fifty two days observation and collection of fieldnotes, fifty four recorded conversations with teachers and other significant adults and nineteen recorded group conversations with about seventy learners from two of the schools (See Table 1 opposite):

Table 1– Research Data

Schools/Data	City(C) Suburban Estate Two form	Istead(I) Rural One form	Hampstead(H) Rural One form	Morden(M) Suburban 3 form	Victoria(V) Urban 2 form	Westside(W) Urban 2 form
Researcher	BJ	EZP	EZP	EZP	GT	Consultant
Teacher Transcribed Conversations 54	19	3	4	1	11	16
Typed Fieldnotes – Days 46*	20	6	9	3	7	1
Transcribed children's conversations in groups 19	13	0	0	0	6	0

BJ = PI, GT = Collaborator, EZP = Researcher

Each researcher also had fieldnotes that were not transcribed and entered into the digital software.

Each school in the paper is identified in the text by the initial letter of its pseudonym; the Yr. refers to the year group taught by the teacher; each teacher's name begins with the school identification letter; DH and HT indicate deputy head or Headteacher; FN = fieldnotes; learner's names are not identified in full.

We transcribed all recorded conversations with management, teachers and pupils that we saw as being of theoretical significance. As this article focuses mainly on learner perspectives much of the raw data included comes from that collected from the two schools where we engaged with learners. However, the overall analysis was carried out on all the data.

Our analysis proceeded in the sequence: data collection – analysis – data collection – analysis. The process provided 'spiralling insights' (Lacey, 1976) as it sought to generate theory from the data using the method of 'constant comparisons' (Glaser and Strauss, 1967). Data storage, retrieval and analysis were supported by the use of the qualitative data analysis computer package Atlas Ti.

The formation of performative identities

We largely follow Snow and Anderson's (Snow and Anderson, 1987) construction, with some modifications, distinguishing among social identities, personal identities, and self-concept. Social identities are 'attributed or imputed to others in an attempt to place or situate them as social objects' (Ball, 1972: 1347). These are largely 'imputations based primarily on information gleaned on the basis of appearance, behaviour, and the location and time of the action'. In the context of our research, we find the notion of an 'assigned social identity' (Ball, 1972) useful. These are imputations based on a *desired* or *prescribed* appearance. Personal identities refer to the 'meanings attributed to the self by the actor,' and are 'self-designations and self-attributions brought into play during the course of interaction' (ibid.). They may be consistent or inconsistent with social identities. The self-concept is the 'overarching view of oneself as a physical, social, spiritual, or moral being', and is 'a kind of working compromise between idealized images and imputed social identities' (ibid.,: 1348).

Foucault rejected any notion of an essence of being, asserting that self and identities are constructed in particular contexts affected by non discursive institutions, texts and discourses.

Although our perspective of identity, outlined above comes from an interactionist perspective, which Foucault rejects in favour of a relational basis for the formation of identity, it is not inconsistent with his approach to the construction of subjectivities. The interactionist perspective accepts the idea that selves and identities are constructed in contexts, similar to the idea of the situational self (Nias, 1991, Scott, 2010) but Foucault is addressing a more fundamental question of being and becoming. Essentially, what Foucault advocates is a social constructivist account of the self. For Foucault, the subject is constituted not in language, as Lacan (1977) would have it, but through many different types of practices. While some of these individualizing practices are discursive, others are institutional. For

Foucault, the process through which subjects and their identities are armed is deeply ingrained in the culture and, as Olssen (2006) notes via Racevskis (1991), 'one that is immanent in the dominant epistemological mode of the modern period in particular' (ibid.,:23). Identity formation, like other aspects of subjectivity, is therefore inextricably enmeshed in political strategies and is involved with the power-knowledge effects applied by discourse (Olssen 2006).

While an interactionist perspective (Mead, 1934) conceives of the social self as a shifting formation of multiple identities this does not preclude the possibility of actors constructing and *believing* in a coherent sense of self through biographical identity work (Scott, 2010: 227). Pollard and Filer (1999) add to our conception of a developing learner identity by describing young children's learning career as 'a continuous spiral' (ibid.: 22) in which identity is seen as a representation of the self-belief and self-confidence which learners bring to new learning challenges and contexts.

Foucault sees social relations as inter-related dependencies (Olssen, 2006) and we use our understanding of the situated self and the creation of an assigned social identity as a micro perspective of Foucault's more macro oriented dependencies. His inter-related dependencies in the social and historical process have three aspects: first the *extra discursive* which concerns relations between the discursive and the whole play of economic, political and social practices (political values – in our case governmentality); second the *intra-discursive*, which concerns relations between objects, operations and concepts (in our case curriculum knowledge) within the discursive formation – the school; thirdly, the *inter-discursive*, which concerns relations between different discursive formations (in our case performativity and identity development – the subjective). Rather than seeking to find the articulating principle of a cultural complex, Foucault was interested in discerning how cultural formations were made to appear 'rational' and unified, how particular discourses came to be formed, and what rules lay behind the process of formation. These interests are the focus of this article.

Governmentality – the extra discursive

Pre-discursive practices such as National Curriculums and testing and assessment systems are linked, in a process referred to as 'enchainment', to discourses (Olssen, 2006). On the one hand pre-discursive practices establish and imply norms, controls and exclusions. On the other hand they render true/false discourse possible. While such practices thus act as constraints upon discourse they are unable to totally explain the discursive context of explanation and belief, which is that practices underdetermine the discursive context of their explanation of which one example is the enterprise text (Olssen, 2006).

Peters (2001) summarising Burchell (1996), says this enterprise text constitutes the distinguishing mark of the current style of governmentality and is a pre-discursive text, while 'education and training are key sectors in promoting national economic competitive advantage and future national prosperity. They are seen increasingly as the passport for welfare recipients to make the transition from dependent, passive welfare consumers to an enterprising self' (ibid.:.85), termed by Burchall as 'a technology of the self' (in Bragg, 2010). There is a clear message in this 'enterprise discourse' (du Gay, 1997) 'which generalises market conduct to other areas of life and values particular qualities such as being self-reliant, taking initiatives, risks, and personal responsibility' (Bragg 2010: 349).

The school cultures, in our research, were imbued with awards and rewards, of cracking learning barriers, and for producing performances both for each other, for parents, for the community, for funders, for celebrations, for targets, for corporate image, as well as against each other internally in the shape of sports and other competitions and against other schools. A powerful discourse of 'learning to strive' branded the journey through the pervasive homilies and target setting for learners and teachers. People, including learners played the game with apparent joy and the raising of self esteem and gained satisfaction from the process of performance outcomes. The latter is highly prized when the local community or group are important to them (Griffiths, 1993) and in the case of primary schools, parents, teachers and peer evaluation of learners had become important to their view of their self-concept – personal identity.

Identity construction meant, in this case, a clear understanding of performativity (Reay and William, 1999), the degree of understanding indicating the level of agency involved, particularly in relation to Standard Assessment Tasks (SATs):

Jo   The SATS are a test of what the teachers have been teaching us and how good our teachers are teaching us. If the teacher doesn't teach you hardly anything or if you don't understand quite as much because it hasn't been explained you'll get another level.

R.   But who tests the teacher?

Jo   The government.

R.   How do you know that?

Jo   Because my mother told me that the teachers get tested that's why we do SATS.

G.   Our teacher told us that our SATS go to the government and if we mess it up the government won't be happy with our work, that's what Miss E. said.

R.   Does that worry you?

G.   Yes, in case our work's rubbish and if I only got 4 questions right out of 20 I don't think the government would be happy with us. (City-Yr.5).

Governmentality is imposed through the strong performativity practices (Jeffrey and Troman 2009) which focus on status and the discourse confirms this, 'someone in Number 10 is probably happy when we get good results' (J-Victoria-Yr.6).

R.   Why are people making you do these SATS?

Ma. To see where you are.

R.   But you know where you are, you've been told.

Ma. Making sure for secondary school, maybe.

C.   So our school can show the secondary school and they can place you in a higher group or a lower group.

C.   It would be good for them if we got higher results, City school would have a good name for itself among other schools.

Ma. You don't want other people thinking our school is no good because people are getting low SATS results, kids won't come to this school. (City-Yr.6)

The discourse of improvement, challenge, and progression through levels of achievement pervaded their discourse:

I.   I think having a target is good so you know what you need to learn, to improve so I think it's a good idea.

Ch. I wanted to know what my target was because I thought it would improve my handwriting.

R.   Why do you want a higher grade?

C.   So you can move forward and then do harder stuff and then you don't have to do stuff that's too easy. I want harder work.

I.   I want a higher grade because then people will think you are getting better at things and people will think better of you (City-Yr.5).

This discussion could sum up the economic, political and social aims of global governmentality, that of improving oneself, working hard as an aim in life and social acceptance through levels of attainment, self subjectification (Bragg, 2010). There are three specific ways in which these values are processed.

Stratification
The practice of stratification (Riddell, 2005) is embedded within the governmentality process. (see Table 2).

Table 2 – Key Stages

	Key Stage 1	Key Stage 2
Level 1		
Level 2 a-c	Years 1+2 Aged 5-7	
Level 3 a-c		Years 3+4 Ages 7-9
Level 4 a-c		Years 5+6 Ages 9-11
Level 5 a-c		Years 7-9 Ages 11-13

Classification and objectification involve the human sciences, which developed after the start of the nineteenth century and which ensure the provision of expert authoritative knowledge, and an assortment of dividing practices which objectify; the subject, providing classifications for subject positions (mad, normal, intelligent, unintelligent, high flyer, slow developer, etc.) (Olssen, 2006). In education these operate through whole range of techniques, including examinations and other forms of assessment, streaming practices, and the like.

K.   I think it's quite easy for the higher groups but for the lower groups it's harder because they don't know much. You know that girl walking past, she's in the lower group.

R.   What do you think she feels being in the lower group.

J.   She might feel embarrassed. People might say 'we're in the high group' and 'that's easy' and stuff like that and she might feel disappointed about not being in the higher groups.

K.   And she might start to cry maybe, and she might tell her mum and then her mum might tell the teacher and then we'll be in trouble, so we mustn't say nasty stuff to other children otherwise we might be in trouble. (City-Yr.3).

The power of the norm is the new law of modern society. It adds to *parole* (language) *tradition* (text). 'The perpetual penalty that traverses all points and supervises every instant in the disciplinary institutions compares, differentiates, hierarchizes, homogenizes, excludes. In short it *normalizes*' (Rabinow, 1984: 195). Normalization imposes homogeneity but it individualises by making it possible to measure. In the primary school learners are sorted in into groups in classrooms according to ability in language and maths, even in classes as young as seven, increasing differentiation and polarisation and cleverness is directly associated with SATs performance (Reay and William, 1999):

R.   So what are these SATS all about?

Th.   It's getting ready to go in Yr. 3.

R.   But why do you have to do these SATS to do that?

Th.   To see how good we are and then we can learn more things.

J.   To see how clever we are.

R.   Are you clever? (general, 'yes')

Th.   I'm a bit second best and Jade's like the other one a bit third best, because I'm a bit better than Jade but Jade's a bit better than David.

J.   He's clever.

R.   How do you know that?

J.   Because he's on the highest table, because we have highest to lowest tables we sit at.

Th.   Jade and I are sort of the same because we are on the same table but I'm going to move up to spelling group. If you're on roses you get the hardest and if you're on Jack's table, tulips, you get middle-ish and if you're on peaches for spellings it's quite easy, they're for the other groups. (City-Yr.2)

Stratification embeds the idea of differentiated levels of competence rather than ability and acts as an effective disciplinary technique for improvement:

R.   What about people on lower grades, what do you think it's like for them?

I.   It's hard but sometimes I think if people are on lower grades it's because they don't listen to Miss R. 'cos many people on low grades are people who don't listen, they're day-dreaming.

C.   Like I said they don't listen and then they get it all wrong so then you probably don't go up a grade.

Ch.   People that have higher grades can help people who are on lower grades when they finish their work they can help them with spelling and joined up.

R.   What I asked you was what does it feel like for them.

C.   I think I would feel bad 'cos most people have higher grades and I would be low down on the grade table.

I.   I think if you have a low grade you probably feel quite embarrassed that you're not listening and you will probably feel quite bad in your self to know that you can do better but you're not doing good (City-Yr.5).

Everything is levelled (assessed) to start with and gradual but steady inclines are negotiated with extra pulling and pushing needed for learners to gain new level labels.

R.   So you're in the second group for spellings. Are you happy being seconds? (general yes)

Jack. I'm kind of first.

R.   And you Jade?

Jade. And Theresa is the first group.

R.   Does it worry you that you're a second?

Jack. Actually I'm a third in spelling and if get to Oranges I'll be second.

Th.   Sometimes I get a bit angry 'cos the teachers give me really hard spellings on Friday and you get them wrong.

R.   Who are you angry with?

Th.   No I get angry with myself 'cos I can't spell it (City-Yr.2).

Each annual report states clearly the levels each learner attains in each subject and sub category (See Table 2).

R.   So if your teacher says you're a level 2 can you get up to a level 5?

T   You'd get up to a level 3 or 4, if you wanted to get a level 5 you would have to work really hard.

R.   If you work really hard can you get from level 2 to level 5?

T   Probably.

R.   Kimberley you're working hard, you're going to get a level 5 then?

K.   People keep saying I'll get a level 5 but I don't think I will, I might in English but I don't think I will?

R.   But you're trying so hard, why are you trying so hard?

K.   'cos if you get a level 5 you will be in the top class.

R.   And does that matter to you.

M.   Yes, 'cos if you have a higher class in the secondary school you can learn more, 'cos they teach more stuff and that (City-Yr. 6).

Knowing more and being clever is equated with levels and differentiation becomes embedded in the determination of other's as well as one's own self-identity:

R.   You don't have to answer this – do you want to be a level 5 and why?

C.   Yes, so I can learn more and be like my cousin, my cousin's in a higher grade and she's really good and I want to be like her, she can do a lot of things, she can do more than me (City-Yr.6).

Best effort

A second aspect that becomes embedded is 'doing your best', an aspect of 'performative regulation', (Scott, 2010), a conceptual synergy of Foucault's disciplinary power (Foucault, 1977), Strauss's negotiated order (Strauss, 1978) and Goffman's interaction order (Goffman, 1983). Scott (2010) argues that this concept advances the poststructuralist motion of performativity, theorised by Butler (1990) in which identity is performatively constructed, by showing that 'while identities can be modified, adapted or reinvented, actors' performative repertoires may be constrained by the dramaturgical deployment of an institutional rhetoric, which defines both actor-reinventor and his/her array of possible selves' (Scott, 2010: 227). Doing your best acts as a driver for performativity – an ethical approach:

R: What would it feel like to go down a group?

C.   You'd feel a bit annoyed with yourself 'cos you want to get the best things happening to you and you'd feel disappointed in yourself and then when you go up a group you feel really pleased with yourself because you've done really well.(City-Yr.6).

Doing your best becomes problematic when learners strive to do so but are still identified as having failed and at the same time learners have to act agentically to determine whether it makes sense to strive for a top level if the work is going to get harder and possibly lead to another failure.

C.   Sometimes when you go up a group it can be quite nerve wracking 'cos you want to do well but you get harder spellings.

Ma. But you might not want it to be too easy, you might want a challenge so you might want to be in the top group, (City-Yr.6).

Being seen to have tried your best and not giving up becomes embedded in their self concept.

    R.   Why didn't you just take the time off school?

    D.   You wouldn't have got a mark.

    R.   Is that what your teacher told you?

    D.   Yes 'cos if you came in the next day, you'd only have done half and you wouldn't get all the marks you could have got.

    R.   And why would you want to get the marks?

    D.   'cos then you'd know you'd tried your best.

    R.   And is that important to you D.

    D   Yes (City-Yr.6).

Doing your best is contrasted with achieving. They are contrary discourses, e.g.: you must succeed to win but if you fail you are told never mind 'you did your best', 'I'm not really worried 'cos at least I tried my best if you get a low mark, you get a low mark' (City-Yr.6). This is a lived exhortation. They live the contradictions of a capitalist life (Mills, 1959) – striving to do their best and having to accept failure (Maguire and Pratt-Adams, 2009, Reay and William, 1999). At the same time doing one's best is never quite good enough for there is always another rung to be climbed.

Self responsibility

They are then, thirdly drawn into self assessment for improvement, where the discourse makes it their responsibility for achievement (Beach and Dovemark, 2007), the individualising of performance (Fielding, 2008, Hartley, 2007, Hartley, 2008), another major disciplinary technology.

G. We are given reports for maths, science and literacy. You get that twice a year and you get five smiley faces to colour in and the teachers get another five. You say how well you think you've done and they put in what you have done and your parents look to see what you think you are good at, against the teachers. And compare them really.

R: So do you find that useful?

T. Yes because you get to say how much you think you're improving. (Victoria-Yr.6)

They are clear about the advantages of performativity as they gradually develop performative identities, 'doing member' (Garfinkel, 1967):

R. If you were a teacher would you make your children do these tests?

C. Yes I would because it's important to know what level they're on and what they need to learn on and what they need to practice on and they need to work on to make them better (City-Yr.4).

The teleological element of education for future social and economic status involved in performativity is clear to see from the discourses used by these primary learners, 'We do SATS so when we grow up we actually know very hard maths and if we don't do SATS then we won't know very hard sums' (City-K-Yr.3).

Their responsibility for achieving at school is clear and has clear consequences, indicating the use of a discourse of governmentality for the development of future economic wealth:

K. I think the same, if they're not intelligent they might not be able to be anything when they grow bigger, if they're not intelligent.

R. How do you become intelligent?

K. When you go to university you become intelligent, if you don't learn much at school and have low grades that means you go to a children's home and you won't have to live in a nice home, so you have to learn all your grades (City-Yr.3).

They have a thoroughly sound understanding of the importance of learning for future careers and their responsibility for developing these careers now, indicating clearly the way the improvement and performativity discourse is replicated and becomes hegemonic:

C. You might end up working at Burger King if you don't get a good mark.

Ma. If you can't count, you can't work in a bank.

Ma. If you can't write you can't write a story.

R.   What about if you want to be a builder?

M.   You don't need literacy or maths but you need science to be a builder.

C.   You'd have to be quite a good drawer too to draw plans and you have to write down your plans. (City-Yr.6)

The extra discursive relations of social, political and economic practices are seen through the discourses of learners as they articulate their aspirations and the uses to which education can be applied. The main discourses used to define and describe learning were those associated with hard work, endeavour, challenge, rewards and achievements. Discourses pertaining to exploration, investigation, innovation, argument, discussion, collaboration, contributions connected to something such as creative learning (Jeffrey and Woods, 2009) were marginalised, particularly for Year 6 learners.

The construction of knowledge relations – intra-discursive
Foucault forces us to consider that it is not just educational principles but also school premises and modes of organisation that are important for understanding the constitution of identity. And rather than representing the school as an agency of reproduction, Foucault sees it as a form of disciplinary and bureaucratic governance that both reproduces and constitutes identity.

Relations between objects, operations and concepts – the intra-discursive – were of particular interest in what was a dominant form of teaching and learning – testing – but not the only one experienced – see Jeffrey, 2008 on creative teaching and learning Testing pedagogies, and the processes attached to them had their own particular construction, sometimes contradictory to other forms of teaching and learning and produced their own specific forms of experience. We identified some of those practices concerned with, space and time, performative knowledge, routinisation and rituals and strategic engagement.

Space and Time
The intra-discursive relations could be seen in the environmental use of space and the organisation of that space (Lasch and Urry, 1994). In one school the tables and chairs in the year six classes were organised in the shape of a horseshoe with

the teacher and the boards at the open end. The teacher sees each learner easily and there was were no spaces to hide acts of resistance or subversion behind the backs of others and all learner utterances were directed to the middle space totally occupied by the teacher who could easily reach a learner in a split second without losing any positional control. This form of total control also encouraged open dialogues and a feeling of being part of the whole for other subjects:

> The horseshoe shape of the desks in the classroom, set up by the arts specialist, is kept for science for the afternoon. I talked to her after school about how different it seemed to make the classroom from either the desks in rows or in groups, ie: more collective with more control for the teacher, more involving as the learners faced each other and the teacher, more opportunity to see each other's reactions and to engage directly with each other rather than through the teacher. It reminded me of those legal problems set on the TV with various constituents who debate an issue with the facilitator in the middle (FN-City-27 February 2007).

> She does a whistle stop tour of fractions. The whole school is still very teacher led and not child centred. Is the performativity disciplining? How is it? In what ways? Why do it? Why not pretend. Is the horseshoe class arrangement 'the gaze' or engagement or both? How far are they recreating the discipline? Why? This is a mixed ability group. (FN-City-23 April 2007).

Phenomenological – subjective – time was marginalised and sidelined in favour of technical-rational time (Hargreaves, 1994):

> Tables with fluffy toys .....Victorian hall (also used for lunches). Jane is giving out instructions and stresses that no extra time would be allowed. Sixteen children all wearing school uniform. Roger adjusts the standard clock so it will easily show 20 minutes i.e: set for 9.40am even though it is 9.35am, for the test to end at 10.00am. The hall is former church hall - big stained glass window at one end – wall bars at one end – multipurpose space. The Victorian payment by results inspection visits would probably have taken place here (FN-Victoria-Yr.6-9 May 2006).

Testing situations create test identities, participants who play the role of testee, inscribing governmentality:

> C. writes out the 4 times table to find out how may packs of 4 in 50 instead

of using the calculator. Josh turns another page and is halfway through in less than 20 minutes. I suspect he isn't following the instructions. He appears to read the questions but has not used the calculator at all. He is possibly playing the role of being tested without having the correct answers or using the appropriate methodology (FN-City-Yr.6-18 May 2007).

The classroom environment in those Yr. 6 classes were dedicated to knowledge absorption:

There is another board of famous figures – Shakespeare, Einstein, Keats, Marlow, Dickens, Gallileo with a list of children attached to each. These must be groups. Yet little work is theirs. All the revered work is factual knowledge, there are no arguments, different views. It's like a learning factory. There is also a do's and don'ts board (FN-City-11 May 2007).

However, for the SATs most boards are covered up so as not to assist them in their tests and the learners join in the process of performativity, 'D. asks why the "do's and dont's board" has not been taken down as it may help them. Their teacher doesn't answer but tells them that they cannot put up their hand and ask anything during a SAT' (FN-C-15 May 2007). Fast learning is a premium to manage the SATs time restrictions:

They are given a 1 minute challenge – 3/8 of 400mm. Is it the speed and momentum of the mental challenge that dominates? Why not let them have the day to do it? (FN-City-23 April 2007).

Knowledge, routinisation and rituals

Foucault's concept of practice refers to a pre-conceptual anonymous, socially sanctioned body of rules that govern one's manner of perceiving, judging, imagining and acting. As our identities and bodies are constructed through such discursive practices the partitioning of truth from falsehood is much more difficult in Foucault's view than has been previously thought and something that is never finally assured. In addition discursive practices are always complex articulations of the truth but in a particular historical juncture. Hence Foucault analyses how discursive practices constitute a perspective within a particular normative context of possible thought and action and how they become legitimised as true expressions (Olssen, 2006).

SATs achievements are institutionalised through specific programmes to improve learner's test results and the focus on correct answers to test questions is intense and more investigative discourses and relations are discarded as knowledge becomes narrowly conceived.

> An adult – supply teacher – is working with two Yr.6 pupils on science – the schools Flying High Project, those on the cusp of Level 4. He gives them questions about orbits, eg: what keeps the earth in orbit round the sun? Why does the moon's appearance change shape as it orbits the earth. One of the boys G. says 'Did you see the moon change colour last night. It was all red'. Adult says 'It was very picturesque, a lovely colour'. G. says, 'my dad said if the weather had been warmer it would have been redder. He looked it up'. The adult says 'anyway let's get on'. He doesn't follow up the child's interest at all. How long does it take for the earth to rotate around on its axis? And he says 'You've got to learn the words, that's what we want you to learn, so I can't explain it differently. (FN-City-Yr.6-21 March 2007).

The pre-SATS journeys for Yr. 6 and sometimes shorter ones for other years are about playing the game, revising constantly, regurgitating some answers but also learning to apply facts. Testing is seen as a challenge and a chance to focus on a number of short recalls and more intricate problems, opportunity to test the success of the journey and the process of it. Both teachers and learners appear to accept the challenge and the struggle of testing journeys even when they know they are handicapped. As the intensity of the testing practice develops so does the development of a routinised practice, one in which the relationship with knowledge and teaching and learning becomes deadening experience, a distancing of the self from the learning process. SATs preparation is a disciplinary technology focused on the tests not the knowledge with which they are engaging:

> They are handed back their science mock tests from yesterday and they finish those they didn't do and check them. Their teacher says 'make sure you fill in all the parts'. He reads out the questions. One boy H. tells me he can read them and then looks closely at them. The teacher says 'every hand should be up now'. You know it's not a bar or a pie graph. It's a bouncy ball graph' and they have to comprehend – read the tables. Is this scientific knowledge or mathematical technology? They all concentrate except for two boys who fiddle with a pen and play with rulers. These are no cheers of smiles of delight just coping. They have to answer some questions about temperature. They are asked what equipment they would use – a thermometer – and I ask them if they have ever used one in school and they say 'no' (FN-City-Yr.6-11 May 2007).

Routinisation is a feature of the wave of practice sessions dedicated to preparing for SATs and instilling National Curriculum knowledge:

> Claire prepares the afternoon lesson during the lunch break by logging on to the BBC schools internet education site for science aged 10 to 11 entitled 'Fighting the spread of disease'. She then makes up some unfinished sentences on a paper board, 'To prevent becoming ill from the food you could …'. 'To prevent becoming ill from insect bites you could ……' 'To prevent the spread of colds and flu you could ……' 'To prevent catching diseases you could…' All this preparation is for a teaching assistant to take the class this afternoon.

> The children carry on with their lunch in the classroom, seemingly totally uninterested in what she's doing. Learning appears to be a routine operation, a workplace. Teachers appear to balance their lessons rather than integrating them. It is a seamless experience of changing activities. Another science sheet appears on a board concerned with micro organisms. The task is to complete a table. They then have to look at some science pictures on the screen and complete sentences. These are all task orientated (FN-City-Yr. 6-17 April 2007).

The influence of the discourse extends to the extra discursive as SATs achievements out of school develops:

R: Yes. You were told to do some revising as well.

D: Homework.

K: Yes. On like websites or in the books that you can buy.

R: Where would you buy your book?

D: WH Smith.

R: OK and what websites? What would you use?

D: BBC revisewise.

R: OK. That covers SATs. And have you used that one a lot?

K: Yes and sometimes we use it in ICT.

R: Use it in school but also ... ?

D: And out (City-Yr.6).

The ritual of school performativity, like school experience generally, is taken up by children and embedded in their life outside schools. Just as young children 'play schools' in their own time so the older performative learners play performativity in their lives outside school for this is the lived reality of a learner's life.

Strategic Engagement

Both teachers and learners develop strategies for managing this process, entering a grey area between truth and falsity that is a bedrock of the process of testing competence and knowledge, secondary adjustments (Goffman, 1961).

> C. continues to tap her calculator and S. joins in. Calvin, their teacher, whispers to C. about an answer and after he leaves, she rubs out the circle although she was meant to circle 'all' the amounts. He does the same with A. on a different question and watches her as she uses the calculator and points to one of the circles where the instructions say 'write in the missing signs'. He encourages her to use a calculator (FN-City-18 May 2007).

A mutual instrumentalism (Pollard *et.al..*, 2000) developed, 'Calvin asks for volunteers to go with a supply teacher for revision for whatever they want and 2 boys answer the call' (FN-City-11/5/07). And the learners are not averse to fabricating results as they try to make sense of the imperative to perform well:

> R.   This is comprehension, two types of comprehension, one where you are allowed to look at the text to answer the questions and one where you read it and then they take it away.

> D.   I read it all, I read it twice actually and then I couldn't remember it once it got taken away so what I did, it was kind of cheating but it wasn't really cheating, I looked back to answers before and I just slightly changed them so they wouldn't be recognisable. (City-Yr.6).

Fabrications (Ball, 2000) are enacted by young people just as they are by teachers. This learner's comments on his grades were untrue apart from his 'n' for English.

R.   So what did you think of your report?

D.   Good, mostly. For maths I got 4 for English I got none, an 'n' for English for Science a 4.

R.   So what did your parents think of it?

D.   Good, they thought it was really, really good.

R.   Even though you got an 'n' for English.

D.   They knew I was going to get an 'n' because I've got a disability, reading and writing, dyslexia, they thought my level 4s were good. I feel all right (City-Yr.6).

Their strategies are understandable to adults and to learners as is the game (Olssen, 2006) and it defines people as well as constructing a contextualised learner identity:

R.   I noticed that 17 people put less than they actually got right, what do you think that says about those 17 people?

L.   They don't have faith in themselves.

A.   They're like nervous, they don't trust themselves 'cos they think like they got it wrong, but I've never in my life got 19 out of 20, so that's why I guessed low numbers 'cos I'm not that good at spellings.

R.   I noticed that some people changed their spellings and gave themselves a higher mark, why would they do that?

A.   They just want to make like they can spell better than everyone in the class.

J.   'cos they want to be good spellers.

A.   They want to be better than others, they want to think they're the best in class but they're not they just cheat (City-Yr.6).

Teachers began to act out of character as they became determined to succeed at a task, particularly where it was not a Yr. 6. SAT but an annual testing.

A.   We had to do it twice because we kept getting the spellings all wrong.

R.   What did you get wrong?

C.   There were words like 'idea' and people got the easy ones wrong.

A.   And we spelt 'any' eny.

R.   And Miss said you'd got to do it again.

C.   And one person got 20 out of 20 and one got 18 and she ripped the others up and put them in the bin.

R.   What did you think of that?

A.   She could have kept the ones she ripped up so she could have showed us where we went wrong (City-Yr.5).

Foucault's focus on practices as the main indicator of the power of texts such as policy is to show both the inconsistencies and contradictions which go to make up the identities of those in these particular contexts. Studying the relations between objects, operations and concepts, in this case learners, testing and knowledge shows how a particular text is managed and it also shows the strategies used to manipulate the imposed text.

In this case it has shown how the relation between knowledge and learning has been constructed to produce indifference and strategies to subvert the dominant text and a concept of knowledge that is framed by test questions.

Subjective Experience – inter-discursive

Different discourse formations such as performativity and identity construction is the third area of dependency identified by Foucault – inter-discursive relations. Learners experience dilemmas, tensions, and constraints as they try to manage conflicts and symbiotic relations between different influential texts as well as the intensity of life within one particular dominating text exemplified in the last section and the cultural imperatives indentified in the first section. These inter-discursive relations may mean support for one text at the same time as supporting apparently contradictory positions or practices from another influential text. For some in Year 6 the process of revision appears to be too much, especially for those who find SATs difficult:

R.   You've done lots of practice tests though haven't you?

L.   A bit too much, we do them every day all day.

D.   We've done tests for two months, no longer than that, all day, non stop apart from playtimes and lunch.

R.   Have you enjoyed any of it?

D.   No, because it doesn't stop all day? (City-Yr.6).

Later on, after it was all over, a different evaluation is made, a form of consequential identities (Dennis and Martin, 2005) noted by (Scott, 2010):

R.   Was it worth all that practicing? If you had to do it again would you, all that practicing of tests, day in day out?

D.   Yes, yes I wouldn't mind, you have to do it anyway, again, you have to do your GCSEs and that's what normal study is. My brother has to do GCSE work and he's like, 'can you help me'. (City-Yr.6).

Howe, during the process of revision and regular testing any variability of results in practice tests creates confusion and uncertainty and the cause is interpreted as student failure and responsibility:

I: Right. So do you feel confident that it will be different next week, you could have a different grade?

P.   I think so, yes.

I: So you've done a lot of work.

P.   I don't really know because my tests have been up and down.

I: Right. It's not always the same scores.

P.   Yes, because sometimes I don't read the question properly all the time (Victoria-Yr.6).

This uncertainty about competence gnaws away at the view of the self (Ball) and reflects a relevant and related self-identity perspective focused on pupil constructions of ability. Hamilton notes (2002) via Harre (1998) that learners perceptions as self-definition constitute their construction of ability. The first is the contextualised self, the second is the attributes of the individual and the third is the self seen by others (Hamilton, 2002). The examination or SATs test brings all these to the fore:

D. It makes you very nervous.

I: Why is that?

D. Because it's a lot of pressure. Because say if you got a really good mark, its quite pressurising so you need to get another good mark and if you got a bad mark its pressurising because you need to do better. So either way it's kind of scary.

P. And sometimes it can be really annoying because in your practice tests you get really high marks and in your proper ones you can get really low marks. Then you wish the test before had been the proper one. (Victoria-Yr.6).

A dissonance develops over ability constructs (Hamilton, 2002). Learners are conscious of the inbuilt feelings of failure that courses through a performative text, 'I know that feeling though, you want to get that level but you put yourself down and say you know you're not going to be able to do it' (City-P-Yr.6) so, this is done so that one can maintain an acceptable social performative identity.
Learner's performative (Jeffrey and Troman 2009) learning identities became the relay (Bernstein, 1971) though which social relations are formed:

R.   Do you know other peoples' levels?

(Together). Most peoples', but some didn't want them read out.

R.   So you had a choice. Why did you choose to have your level read out?

C.   I wanted to find out my grade.

R.   But you could have asked your teacher afterwards.

C.   Most people were having their grade read out and I thought I might as well have mine because I might have a good grade.

I.   I thought I might have a good grade and I wanted my friends to know.

R.   Why would you want your friends to know?

I.   I don't know, so they're impressed.

C.   You might want your friends to know so you can help each other get good grades. (FN-City-Yr.5-5 April 2007)

There is a governance of the soul (Rose, 1989) as Reay and William (1999) note. There are a number of identity activities going on here. Firstly an action designed to increase belonging, to establish communities of meaning (Cerulo, 1997) adapting their social identity to the particular context in which they find themselves (Snow and Anderson, 1987). Secondly, a desire to establish a particular position in the social situation, to be noted and recognised, a wish to promote the 'you' (the wishful identity) rather than the 'I' (the impulsive self) and the me (the social self), (Wiley, 1994).

However, at the same time learners play the game (Foucault, 1980) and some gain a great deal of satisfaction, or in Griffith's (1993) characteristics of identity choose to regard their success as a raising of self esteem, a consonance between self and the way others see them (Hamilton, 2002), defining themselves in terms of scores (Hanson, 1993) as Reay and William (1999) note:

A.   Do you know what, I'm so excited about I'm getting my level. In my Maths test I got 19 out of 20, I was really chuffed with myself because I can't believe I got that, because it's getting close to SATS and I'm getting better at learning because my brother, who is in Yr. 10 is teaching me stuff at Yr.7 level. I really get excited, I don't know why, I couldn't believe I got 19 in my spelling. (City-Yr.6).

Highs and lows are experienced, valued and sometimes cause traumatic reactions:

Ma. It makes you nervous. Sometimes when you're nervous you get lower marks, you panic and you can't like concentrate as much as you were going to. When you panic you can't concentrate properly and when you can't concentrate you start to panic about the questions and you can't answer them and you have to go on and answer the question really quickly. (City-Yr.6).

But they have also absorbed the 'challenge' discourse, central to taking responsibility for learning:

R. Did you like doing your SATS, (all chorus 'yes'). Why did you like doing them, what did you like about it?

Le. 'cos all the classes were silent 'cos when we usually do work like writing they're normally noisy and always talking.

L. They help you learn more 'cos when you go up to a higher class like when you are in Yr. 4, they help you learn more in Yr. 4.

M. I liked it because I like doing tricky maths stuff and English and I like doing the times tables as well and I think it was really good (City-Yr.3).

They develop a continuous conflicting performative identity that, for most of them, sways back and forth between self congratulation and self denigration:

J. It's scary, it's hard, when they say you have to get it right and you don't. You feel bad, 'cos you haven't got it right and then when the teacher tells you it's easy and everybody should know it and you've got it wrong, it's upsetting and annoying 'cos you knew that you knew it but you hadn't written it down.

R. What does it make you feel about yourself?

J. It makes you feel that you're not very good at that subject.

G. Sometimes I feel that I'm doing something completely different from everybody else, it was sort of funny and I wasn't happy.

Jo. Sometimes if you get a question on what the lesson has been about and if you don't understand it you'll be quite embarrassed in front of the class. Yes it has happened to me. (City-Yr.5).

The micro processes of talk become the macro structure of the organisation (Boden in Cerulo 1997). Performative identities are a continuous mixture of developing confidence, having it shattered, feeling successful and confident to experiencing panic and anxiety, from being assigned high status to feelings of rejection but all the time knowing that both self worth and social identities are based on striving for better and continuous improvement.

R.   So next week you're going to have your SATS, are you looking forward to it.

D.   No.

L.   I'm not worried about them. I just know I'm going to get an N, nothing.

R.   I thought they were all numbers.

L.   Yes but you can get an N for Not Levelled. N in Science N in Literacy and N in English. When we practiced in Year 6 he gave out all our levels and he called out my name and I looked at my sheet and it was N N N, No Levels and that's true.

R.   So have you told your parents that? (yes) what did they say?

L.   They said when you do it next time try harder.

D.   I said to my mum I'm going to get an N in my SATS and she goes, don't put yourself down already you don't know because it hasn't happened yet.

R.   How do you feel about being a 'No level'?

D.   I'm not really bothered, they don't really mean anything.

L.   Sorry but it means you will get a good job, so the cleverer you are you will pass your GCSEs.

R.   So how do you feel about getting a 'no level'?

L.   Not that happy because I know I can do a lot better but I know I'm going to get an N.

D.   You try 'cos of the feeling inside.

R.   What's this feeling inside Daniel?

D.   Like you want to get a level, at least a Level 4 but you don't reckon you will get a level, you're afraid you'll get a Level N. (City-Yr.6).

Foucault's relational approach portrays actors as embedded and identity as developing in concrete social practices where stability is always transitory and precarious (Olssen, 2006). What Foucault clearly conveys us that individual subjects create themselves in relation to social, political, and regulatory structures of their environment. Ethical action and agency are regarded as political, and as forms of power which is itself represented as a force that circulates. Both in his books and in interviews Foucault presents a picture of individuals who are interconnected and interdependent with each other and with the structures of social and institutional control—where freedom, itself considered political, is conceived of as self mastery within a set of societ.al. constraints.

Conclusion

The construction of performative learning identities occurs during the educational and social practices of teaching and learning practices and evidence from the discourses exemplify that construction, but at the same time these discourses confirm and embed those practices and therefore contribute to the formation of performative identities. The influence of these educational and social practices upon young people from 7-11 is both extensive and significant. They have absorbed the values of aspiration, continual effort and improvement as a way of life; they have a view of knowledge as that which can be tested; an awareness of the significance of differentiation and stratification and they have learned to fabricate their educational practice to further performative objectives. At the same time they see the value of testing and target setting as a means to achieve those objectives and regard learning as a progression from level to level and as a way of being hierarchically organised and assigned. Tests rob the National Curriculum of saying anything useful about students (Reay and William, 1999). Leaner's personal identities are being recreated constantly as their social identities are altered to cope with both the assigning of imputed identities and the social imperatives in educational settings. Their self worth – their view of themselves – is then developed in the context of their social practice.

However, the personal identity theory we have used, as indicated in our introduction, may be consistent or inconsistent with social identities, which are assigned social identities, such as the performative one, 'attributed or imputed to others in an attempt to place or situate them as social objects' (Ball, 1972: 1347). In other words individuals may challenge the imputed identity or ignore it.

These young children probably did not arrive into schools with performative identities but have constructed them as they have become enculturated, 'self-designations and self-attributions brought into play during the course of interaction' (Ball 1972: 1347). These young learners have also constructed other personal identities such as that of the creative learner as shown in our past research (Jeffrey and Woods 2009; Jeffrey 2008) and in the current research (Jeffrey and Troman 2009). Both these discourses and others are imputed identities, that of a performative learner or of a creative learner, which learners take on as they experience everyday discourse practice and engage in social acclimatisation (Snow and Anderson 1987). Researching young learners gives an insight into the power and influence of teaching and learning practices – discourses – have on the practices of the self (Olssen 2006). These young leaners cannot avoid the discourses, nor do they try to resist them very often, but seek to find ways to maintain social relations and social cohesion.

The value of a Foucauldian perspective is that is shows that the construction of performative identities is not just a corresponding reproduction of macro values but that respondents find some satisfaction from the social practices, that they differentiate between them from time to time and that they construct strategies to cope with them and manipulate them and at the same time may recognise the subjective affect they have upon themselves and their peers. Foucault doesn't see power as structured or binary between dominators/dominated or as exclusively repressive. As well as being repressive, power is also productive and far from being contained in the state or repressive apparatuses power is exercised at all levels of society. There are therefore no alternative readings of performativity in Lyotard's terms and as seen through the perspective of Foucault's discourses for the focus is how it works, not whether it is a positive or a negative policy and process. It is not a policy to reject or condemn but rather we need to consider the way in which policy discourses and market performativity is experienced as practices of the self.

Acknowledgements
This article was first published in the *European Education Research Journal* (2011) Vol. 11 (4).

10 The end of 'strategic compliance'? The impact of performativity on teachers in the English Further Education sector

Kevin Orr

Introduction

Further Education (FE) in England is a sector of education that is 'fascinating, turbulent, insecure but desperately important' (Coffield *et.al.* 2008: 4), which has over three million students. Kennedy (1997: 1) described it as what is not school and not university, though even those boundaries are porous. It remains, though, a heterogeneous sector where the majority of vocational training and adult education occurs, as well as academic study between the ages of 16 and 19. Its intake is predominantly working class (Avis, 2009). Keep (2006) described how the former New Labour government (1997-2007) treated FE like 'the biggest train set in the world' with their constant initiatives and more than any other sector of English education FE has been subject to control, compulsion and codification from the centre.

While the professional standards for Higher Education in England are set out in a four-page booklet, the professional standards for FE amount to forty pages. Since 2001 there have been two acts of parliament directly pertaining to the sector and more than ten government departments or agencies, which were often very short-lived, have had statutory involvement in the sector. Much of the content and even the means of assessment of initial teacher education (ITE) courses for FE is mandatory as is, for example, the requirement for FE teachers to record thirty hours of continuing professional development each year in order to maintain their licence to practise. implementation of these initiatives has involved a performative system of inspections and targets with which teachers must comply, well beyond even what is expected in schools or universities.

This chapter considers the impact of performativity on FE teachers' comprehension of professionalism and on their practice three longitudinal case studies and the use of and Shain's (1999) concept of 'Strategic compliance' amongst staff in FE, is discussed more fully below. The three teachers in these case studies, one in construction, one in literacy, the other in sports studies, gained their teaching qualifications in 2006 and 2007. This has meant that the period of their careers has coincided with the official discourse of education in England placing a rhetorical emphasis on learning over teaching and, most significantly, their careers have coincided with a period of constant flux in the FE sector. After decades of 'benign neglect' (Lucas, 2004) the rate of policy change affecting English FE under the previous New Labour government (1997-2010) became frenetic. The sector became identified with the government's twin projects of tackling social justice through widening participation in education and of enhancing the workforce's skills in response to the demands of globalisation. Though there has been little development of policy by the new Coalition government (elected in May 2010) the rate of change has continued as a response to the global economic crisis. In a process similar to what Klein (2007) termed Shock Doctrine, this crisis and its consequences have been used to justify and enable significant attacks on the conditions of FE teachers and to further curtail their professional autonomy. Through exploring these factors and how these three particular teachers have experienced them this chapter will argue that burgeoning performativity has left little if any space for professionals to defend traditional educational values while 'strategically complying' with organisational change.

Professionalism in FE

Stronach *et.al.* (2004:109) described professionalism as a 'construct born of methodological reduction, rhetorical inflation and universalist excess'. This description seems especially apposite in relation to professionalism in the English FE sector, which Gleeson and James (2007: 451) called 'an elusive and paradoxical concept'. Gleeson *et.al.* (2005: 446) identified how much of the discourse relating to FE teachers considers them to be 'either the recipient of external policy reform or as an empowered agent of professional change' and they cite Bathmaker (2001) who has described how FE practitioners are discussed as both 'devils' whose poor practice needs to be closely controlled and as 'dupes' who have carelessly jettisoned their professional values by submitted to new managerialist regimes. Robson (1998) was amongst those to argue that professionalism in FE has its own form, what has been termed the 'dual professionalism' of FE teachers. Most teachers have entered FE having been established professionals in previous careers, as was the case of two of the participants in this study, and many maintain and prioritise that original professional allegiance. This is because, as Robson *et.al.* (2004: 187) argue, their previous experience gives them the credibility required for their new teaching role and that credibility has more currency in FE than pedagogy. Furthermore, Gleeson *et.al.* (2005: 449) recognise that becoming an FE teacher 'is, for many, less a career choice or pathway than an opportunity at a particular moment in time'. Many FE teachers have started teaching a few hours a week part-time while still employed as a hairdresser, mechanic or plumber before becoming full-time. Their continuing identity with their former profession may prevent some from considering themselves as professional *teachers*.

The notion of dual professionalism may, moreover, tacitly reveal a central aspect of the tradition of FE. English FE colleges, like the one in this study, very often find their origins in the mechanics institutes and technical colleges of the nineteenth and early twentieth centuries where skilled craftsmen or artisans would pass on their knowledge (Simmons, 2008: 367; Orr and Simmons, 2009: 5). There was no requirement for specific teaching qualifications nor, indeed, an expectation. Emphasis on subject knowledge over pedagogy was carried over into the post-Second World War FE sector (Bailey, 2007); its priorities are suggested by FE teachers not requiring any teaching qualification in order to practise until 2001, in very sharp contrast to English school-teachers. As a result of this heritage, a distinctive culture of professionalism relating to teaching in FE never emerged. Summing up the position of FE teachers Colley *et.al.* (2007: 186) accurately noted how their professionalism

> faces a triple jeopardy: teaching *per se* is of low status in the hierarchy of professions; FE is of low status in the hierarchy of education sectors; and many FE teachers are also positioned marginally by their 'accidental' entry into the profession, and continued identification with their former occupations.

This lack of a distinct culture of professionalism along with the relatively weak position of the sector in relation to schools and universities may have left FE teachers particularly to a regime of performativity. In 2001, Clow (417) concluded that 'as it stands at the moment FE teachers are unlikely to agree a definition of their professionalism without external support.' The new overarching professional standards for teachers, tutors and trainers in the lifelong learning sector published in 2006 by Lifelong Learning UK (LLUK), the government-funded agency with responsibility for the FE sector, may be considered as an example of 'external support'. Their form, however, exemplifies the performative nature of reforms in FE. The LLUK standards, which cover FE teachers and which became statutory in 2007, equate professionalism not with autonomy or judgment based on specialist knowledge, but rather with adhering to a centrally controlled list of practices. They contain 190 statements of the 'skills, knowledge and attributes' (LLUK, 2006: ii) required by teachers in the sector, which amount to a required taxonomy of professional behaviour including a commitment to: '[s]tructure and present information clearly and effectively' (LLUK 2006: 5). The content and tone of this and other documents that relate to FE suggest what Avis (2003, p. 315) termed 'a truncated model of trust' in FE teachers, who therefore had to be tightly controlled through performative measures. Far from this enhancing the professionalism of FE teachers, Nasta (2010: 453) concluded that 'all recent policy initiatives to regulate FE teachers have taken place within a fragmented and impoverished professional culture'.

The instrumental case studies of three FE teachers during the period 2006 to 2011, described more fully in the next section, attempt to identify and evaluate the developing impact of performativity on individual practitioners in FE. The lived experience of these teachers tells a story characterised by disconcerting rapidity and constancy of change in the FE workplace, through cuts in provision; staff turn-over; promotion; or altered terms and conditions. So rapid and constant has this change been, associated with the burgeoning of performativity, that these three teachers have rarely had time to establish patterns of work, let alone to act strategically to defend professional values.

The place of case studies

The value of case studies to research the FE sector has been disputed. Avis (2006) criticised them, particularly in relation to the prodigious Transforming Learning Cultures (TLC) in FE research project (see James and Biesta, 2007) because, Avis would contend, such studies risk separating individuals from broader political circumstances that may determine much of their lives. In response to Avis, Colley (2006: 109) argued that a case study approach does not necessarily preclude critical theoretical analysis of society and, as is the intention in this study, the 'unique "close-up" experiences…offer a fractal expression of the whole set of social relations', which analysis on a larger scale might ignore or distort. That is, study of the microcosm may reveal the workings of the whole organism. This resonates with Thomson *et.al.* (2010: 639) who argue in relation to schooling that 'policy sociologists might gain from … research at the micro/vernacular levels' to illuminate how policy becomes 'embedded' in the particular. This research has attempted to examine the 'micro/vernacular' of how three FE teachers have experienced performativity in the sector over a period of five years of political flux and transition as an exemplar (Flyvberb, 2006: 219) or an 'examination of an instance in action' (MacDonald and Walker, 1977: 181 in Merriam, 1988: 11).

Closely related to the rise of performativity in FE is managerialism, which Avis (2002: 75) referred to as 'a central plank in the PCET [Post-Compulsory Education and Training] settlement in which there is an attempt to construct a social block around managerial interests'. The ascendancy of managerialism in FE stems primarily from 1993 when the then Conservative government controversially brought FE out of the control of local authorities and colleges became individually incorporated institutions. It was argued at the time that this would give college managers greater autonomy in developing their institutions but led to what Hillier (2006: 28) described as a 'frenzy of activity' and 'cut-throat competition' between colleges as each attempted to maximise its revenue by recruiting as many students as it could at the expense of other institutions. Hillier (2006: 30) recalled accurately that this 'strategy [was] known throughout the sector as "getting bums on seats"'. Over the five years following incorporation the number of students rose by 33%, while at the same time around 20,000 full-time staff left the sector (Betts, 1999 cited in Lucas, 2004: 80). Those staff that remained were normally transferred to poorer contracts. Gleeson *et.al.* (2005: 447) argue that incorporation 'radically altered democratic accountability in favour of government, business and corporate interests'. This was a break from the past. Randle and Brady (1997: 232) wrote:

> Traditionally, staff and managers aspired to a common set of educational values, encompassing the notion of professional expertise and some discretion in design, delivery and assessment of provision ...[which is] being replaced by a new type of manager primarily concerned with resource management, particularly financial resources.

This may be overstated, but Ainley and Bailey (1997) have vividly described how managers in FE became valorised over teachers, senior management teams over academic boards. After the incorporation of colleges the numbers of managers grew, principals became self-styled chief executives, and the salaries of teachers and managers diverged. Managerialism in FE was then and is still associated with, for example, statistics for student recruitment, retention and achievement eclipsing all other measures of educational value, including the professional judgement of teachers. Managers had the solutions, while teachers were often considered the problem. As Ball (2008: 49) contends, 'Performativity is a culture or a system of "terror". It is a regime of accountability that employs judgements, comparisons and displays as means of control, attrition and change.' At the time of these changes, Elliott (1996: 16) noted that teachers in FE

> felt that, for the college managers, business methods had become an end in themselves, sustaining a 'control' ethos and a managerialist culture. A common complaint was that senior college managers seemed to have lost sight of the core business of student learning and achievement – they no longer saw students as students, but as units of funding.

Over fifteen years later, the participants in these case studies were making similar complaints about the priorities of the college that directed their practice.

Mike, one of the participants in this research, asked with exasperation in 2011: 'How can you have a business plan for a college that doesn't take into account qualifications? ... that is the way it is turning.'

Alongside the long-term legacy of incorporation, the immediate background of the global economic recession, which started in 2009, is especially pertinent to these case studies. The recession has been used by the Coalition government as justification for major cuts to funding throughout the English public sector (see Jones, 2010: 793) including cuts to the funding of FE. As the data below shows, this has led to further insecurity and disconcertedness that may have allowed changes to be made to the sector that were hitherto unacceptable to staff. Looking at how neoliberal politicians and economists operate to manipulate circumstances at times of crisis, Klein (2007: 21) states:

> It is in these malleable moments, when we are psychologically unmoored and physically uprooted, that these artists of the real plunge in their hands and begin their work of remaking the world.

The account of an official of the UCU, the main trade union for FE teachers, suggests a comparable if less dramatic process in the sector. 'We believe colleges are using the current environment, where they think people are fearful, to cut deeper than they need' (Mourant, 2011: 4). Newcastle College produced a surplus of £6m in the year 2010-2011 and awarded the chief executive of the group that runs the college a pay rise, including bonus and retention payment, of £73,000. At the same time the college was seeking 200 full-time equivalent job losses (ibid.). The three participant teachers felt subject to similar threats of unemployment. Their lives have been directly affected by reductions in funding and changes to work patterns, what Jones (2010: 793) calls a 'solution of massive shock therapy', endorsed with little quarrel by the Labour opposition as being necessary to reduce the national deficit. This 'therapy' has included the further incursion of performativity into the FE sector.

The teachers who participated in this research, one in sports, one in plumbing and one in adult literacy, were initially selected from a larger cohort as being broadly representative of FE's diversity and because all three were consciously committed to enhancing their teaching practice. Between 2006 and 2007 all three achieved a teaching qualification awarded by the same university, though the routes they followed to that qualification were different. Unlike the vast majority of schoolteachers in England, 90% of FE teachers are employed without a teaching qualification, which they then must achieve through part-time study whilst already employed as teachers (UCET, 2009). This is normally referred to as an 'in-service' course. Mark, the plumbing teacher, and Andrea, the adult literacy teacher, both followed this route over two years at the college where they were employed to become qualified with the Certificate in Education. Danny, the sports teacher, completed a one-year, full-time 'pre-service' course based at the university but with lengthy placements at an FE college. All three teachers , therefore, new to teaching in 2006 and the time of the most recent interviews (in late 2010 and early 2011) all three were working in the same college, referred to here as City College, though Danny had previously been placed and then worked in different institutions.

City College, situated in a major northern post-industrial conurbation, has recently merged to form, according to its website, a huge 'super college' with 80,000 mainly part-time students at its many campuses around the city. The college offers a huge variety of courses ranging from basic numeracy to degrees in digital design. Policy reforms have shaped the architecture of City College through a well-funded construction programme closely tied to the priorities of the former New Labour government. The college has had a Skills Zone devoted to basic numeracy and literacy; an impressive new Higher Education centre situated on a separate campus; and the college broadly divides adult from 14-19 provision also on separate campuses, all following national initiatives. As noted above, the official discourse related to FE has emphasised learning and the learner over the teacher and teaching; even the officially sanctioned professional body is called the Institute for Learning. Biesta (2009: 3) has described this distortion as 'learnification', or 'the translation of everything there is to say about education in terms of learning and learners'. This discourse, again associated with the former New Labour government, made concrete in City College's new buildings with their huge communal areas for students, warehouse-sized computer-based learning 'workshops' and, in rather stark contrast, cramped staffrooms for teachers. This discourse of learning may also act subliminally to further justify the poor conditions and status of FE teachers by marginalising their role in teaching.

Initial data for this ethnographic study came from observations of the participants' teaching and interactions in the workplace followed by extended semi-structured interviews. Their progress has been followed through two subsequent interviews and observations of their changing work-settings at interval of around eighteen months. The interviews were transcribed and all data were analysed using both a priori and grounded codes broadly relating to control, agency, practice, flux in the workplace and workplace relationships. The trajectory of each of the participants is set out briefly below before considering how performativity has affected these teachers' practice and agency. The impact of performativity will be considered through Gleeson and Shain's (1999: 482) concept of strategic compliance, which they identified amongst staff in FE and which they described as 'a form of artful pragmatism which reconciles professional and managerial interests'. Strategic compliers remain committed to traditional professional values such as dedication to their students and to their subject but at least partially conform to the performative demands of managerialism in order to create space to defend what they value in their educational practice. The concept recognises both that practitioners have agency and ethics, but that they are also subject to the circumstances within which they operate: within these circumstances strategic compliers do 'not comply for the "sake of their own skins"' (460) but make decisions to conform or not based upon the needs of their learners. As Avis (2005: 211) puts it, strategic compliance works on a notion of pragmatism to 'wrest progressive possibilities from the conditions in which FE is placed.' All three of these teachers, the reconciliation of professional and managerial interests, which is at the heart of the concept of strategic compliance, has been highly problematic as their careers in FE have developed. These case studies suggest that while commitment to their learners and to traditional values of social justice through education remain, the encroachment of performativity on teachers' agency and practice has meant any space for strategic compliance is small and threatened.

Mark

Despite ostensibly performing and being qualified as a teacher at the time of his first interview, Mark would not describe himself as teacher. He was a plumber, reflecting the idea of 'dual professionalism'. At first he explained this by referring to his contract, which described him as a trainer not as a teacher (with consequently smaller salary), and to his prior work as a plumber. He also mentioned 'issues of self-esteem'. Even in the latest of the interviews he still would not call himself a teacher, but neither any more would he call himself a plumber, though he continued to update his industry qualifications. Roth and Lee (2007: 215) explained, 'Whichever identities are salient for an individual during a particular context exist in a complex dance with one's sense of agency and position within the social world.'

Mark's position in the social world was contradictory. He took on the role of trainer in the plumbing department in his early thirties having been a plumber since leaving a local grammar school at sixteen. His apprenticeship had involved day-release at an FE college. In the first two interviews Mark was explicit about gaining the social status of working in education despite a pay-cut that meant he had to continue to work in the evenings and at weekends as a plumber. As explained above, he undertook ITE part-time at City College whilst employed there and had gained his teaching certificate within two years of starting at the college. He immediately went on to gain an honours degree through part-time study and latterly was frustrated that this had not increased his opportunities at the college. After three years at City College Mark was made 'zone leader' but at the time of the second interview in 2008 he was unsure of what this meant as regards responsibility or how it would affect his pay and conditions:

> That's to be negotiated, but we don't know what is going to happen and my hours are about to be reduced so I can take on some of the responsibility and we've had a lad who has handed his notice in yesterday so that might be on the back burner a bit and I might have to carry on… I'll still have to do the zone leader responsibility but I'll probably not get my teaching hours reduced just yet.

Mark appeared largely passive within these putative changes, which may be explained by his prior experience of relatively short-term contracts whilst working in construction '*on the tools*'. He was used to jobs changing or ending and to moving on to other employment. Even as zone leader, however, Mark's role was mainly as a teacher and he taught long hours while also being expected to fulfil many management and administrative duties over which he had little influence. He described his typical day in 2008:

> I'd come in at twenty to nine or something like that and if it was a theory session I would have done some preparation the night before… If it was a practical session it would be a case of getting out there ten minutes before the lesson starts just to get my stuff out and looking at the tracking document that we use so that I know who is doing what.

Practice controlled by documentation, what Mark refers to here as tracking documents, which came from elsewhere and so were beyond the control of the individual teacher were consistent across all three participants. After teaching until late afternoon Mark would be: 'doing paperwork or sorting out a few schemes of work or lesson plans for certain individuals that are being observed in the next few days. That's about it.'

During the first encounters Mark was happily isolated within the college; he described feeling 'uncomfortable' if he had to visit other parts of the college. This situation had transformed by 2011 as he had been promoted to a slightly more senior middle management role, which curtailed his freedom by reducing his anonymity:

> Now the principalship know my name … which I am not quite happy about… As a consequence, obviously there are people who e-mail me or

phone me up who I've never heard of, or I have heard the names but never had any contact with or ever needed to. Now all of a sudden I do.

Changes in roles and burgeoning early-career responsibility within relatively low-level positions were also experienced by Danny (see below), accompanied by increasingly performative tasks. Mark said in 2011:

> I am sat at a desk all day doing paperwork, I am sat in pointless meeting after pointless meeting, meetings about meetings about meetings and it's just not what I signed up for.

Cuts in funding were also having consequences:

> ...everyone is under more stress than they were. We are getting told obviously, we need more students in, we need more success rates but you're not getting as much resources, you're not getting as much manpower to do all this with and obviously that is causing a lot of stress.

Mark had still been able to set his own timetable and maintained significant control over aspects of his work. He was, nevertheless, frustrated by the reduction in his teaching, which had 'kept [him] sane', and he believed strongly that the quality of his teaching had suffered:

> ...so I'm quite an unhappy bunny in the role that I am in. I have told my management exactly that; I've had meetings [but] there doesn't seem to be any way out of it other than me to go.

Yet fear of redundancy and unemployment kept him from going:

> That is why I am staying put for now because ... you have to think yourself lucky to still have a job as it stands. So I'll cling onto it for now with a view to do something else, but for now I need to pay the bills.

Mark's plan at that time, however, was to move to another organisation, and possibly into teacher education, when he could. Mike's fears of unemployment proved well founded. Four months subsequent to the last interview Mike had lost his job through another restructuring at City College. He had found some part-time teaching employed through an agency at a college almost forty miles away.

Danny

Danny exudes a broad-shouldered self-confidence and easy charm. He had been
educated at a prestigious grammar school in Northern Ireland before going
to university in England and called his background socially and economically
'privileged'. In 2006 at the age of 21 he went straight on to the full-time pre-
service FE ITE course at a different northern university. Prior to this course
Danny had had no experience of FE, nor had he any vocational experience to
underpin dual professionalism. He trained to work as a sports and leisure teacher
and his college placement during his ITE course had been very challenging. He
was quickly given great responsibility for several difficult groups and although
Danny thrived, others might have felt abandoned. At the end he said, 'I've had
a fantastic placement in quite a few ways even though at times I felt I'd been
eaten alive.' He explained how he had learned to restrict what he referred to as
'creativity' in teaching during his placement. He graphically demonstrated his
transition from a horse ('trustworthy and friendly, perhaps too friendly'), to a
hippo ('cute but dangerous'), then to a pig ('selfish') and finally to a cross between
a Tyrannosaurus Rex and a security guard ('ferocious').

Though he retained a commitment to developing his teaching, he recognised
what was apparent in observations also, that his practice had narrowed when
he was faced with the pressures of difficult and disaffected learners and the
bureaucratic demands of the college. Danny explained that he had returned to
the didactic and less interactive methods of his own traditional education.

By the time of the second interview in early 2008 Danny had, for five months,
been working as an agency-employed teacher in a different suburban college.
Though ostensibly employed part-time, at twenty-seven or twenty-eight hours a
week he had more contact time with students than college-employed full-time
teachers, and he was a personal tutor which, he felt, 'far outweighs any other
responsibility'. Though he enjoyed his role and he felt well supported, Danny was
aware of his vulnerability as a part-timer:

> Ideally I would love to stay here because I've established myself and I put
> eight hundred percent into everything I do anyway, even though there is
> no guarantee that I'm going to be here [next year].

Like Mike, Danny's fears were well founded. In the summer of 2009 after two years
at the college he was given notice that he would not be re-employed in September
and told, '*Yeah bye, we can't afford you anymore.*' Gleeson *et.al.*(2005: 451) described
what they called 'the long interview' in the FE sector, during which teachers would
be employed for years on short-term or temporary contracts with the hope of

being made full-time and permanent. After Danny's 'long interview', he did not get the job. Consequently, he considered himself lucky to find a position as a trainer earning less money at City College having looked nationwide for work in colleges. He was soon to take on a junior management role:

> To now being in a management position after three and a half years of teaching, it's caught me a little bit by surprise because I've never been out of education.

The change in role had caused him some disenchantment and his concerns are redolent of performativity and managerialism:

> The transition … has opened my eyes … quite a bit. Not only just as going from a teaching role to a management role, seeing the intricacies of how the education system currently prioritises and works, which can be disillusioning. … The bottom line for a lot of things is money especially in this college… A lot of decisions in this college are made by the higher-ups as I call them.

The example of a decision made by a 'higher up' which ignored consequences 'on the ground' was open enrolment: 'to get a student to pass a course… after having missed the first twelve weeks of class is nigh on impossible, but yet the doors are still wide open.' As the performative demands of his role have increased, moreover, his teaching had further narrowed, though he remained very confident that he could still teach innovatively if he were being observed. Danny said:

> My actual teaching has lost its momentum and its vision. My lessons are less creative; they are less focused around the 'grade one, outstanding, think outside the box lessons' that they used to be and they are more focused around knowing that the majority of students just need to know the pass criteria.

Yet, like Mark, Danny had retained conscious control over significant aspects of his work as demonstrated by how he would defend his staff:

> Any time I get any hint that a member of staff in my staff room is running a course that might not be viable, I do anything I can to try to make sure that it becomes viable or that they become 'un-missable' for the college.

Despite the cuts, Danny felt secure in his own job because his section attracts many students and was therefore generally viable, but he was highly pressurised and was frustrated and bitter at the limitations on his influence; his 'future planning ability for the department is minimal'. For Danny, City College is a 'stepping stone' and within five years he plans to be elsewhere, 'still in a management role, still in sports, hopefully a few more grade one level observations and hopefully get my creativity back.'

Andrea

Andrea's circumstances at City College had changed enormously over the five years of the study and were, in 2011, paradoxical; although she apparently had the least secure role at the college, she was the most positive about her position and her practice. Andrea was from an aspirational working-class family. She had left school at eighteen and her training and professional background were in youth work but concurrently she had worked part-time at the college for several years in various ancillary to teaching roles such as teaching assistant and placement organiser. In her early forties she was appointed as a Skills For Life teacher to young students with special needs, often linked to their challenging behaviour. Out of twelve boys in one of her 2006 to 2007 groups, three had Anti-Social Behaviour Orders served on them; 'it's always on the verge of kicking off', Andrea said. In class, though, she never appeared fazed. Like Mark she followed the in-service route to gaining a Certificate in Education and she found the course engaging and inspirational. Again like Mark in his first role, Andrea's role kept her isolated from the wider college. In 2007 she said:

> I know we're a massive institution but it boils right down to the people you are with and I just care about the students and the colleagues I work with. The rest is that it's almost like we are working within a little bubble within a massive bubble.

Even within her section there was little interaction beyond a small and diminishing core of long-term staff. Andrea's then manager, with a list of things to do 'as long as her arm', had changed from being a friend to being the subject of Andrea's suspicion. She nevertheless enjoyed her job and had none of Mark's reticence in calling herself a teacher: 'I can feel the reward and the satisfaction that I'm getting and they outweigh anything that I've ever done before, to be honest.' Andrea could shape her own teaching, too. Though she had to follow a set National Curriculum with her special needs students, Andrea modified it based upon her judgement of their personal record files before entering the course, 'otherwise it's a bit dry, looking at telephone directories and things like that.' Her sessions displayed, above all, Andrea's warmth towards the learners.

Keen to develop her knowledge and her career, in 2008 Andrea gained a specialist qualification in literacy teaching but in the same year she lost her job in the first sweep of redundancies at the college. These redundancies preceded both the election of the Coalition government and more widespread public-sector cuts by at least two years. This sweep was connected to a reorganisation after the merger of the two colleges mentioned above, which also brought in new contracts that divided those who taught sixteen to nineteen year-olds, who kept their holidays and were paid slightly better, from those who taught adults, with fewer holidays and poorer pay. Mark and Danny had found themselves on either side of this divide, Mark with adults and Danny with sixteen to nineteen, and though they were resigned and even content with this, they both mentioned how it had left many unhappy. Andrea was, however, only without work for a few weeks when she was telephoned while on holiday abroad to be offered a job in the 'Train to Gain' team as a peripatetic adult literacy teacher working with employees in their workplaces. She consequently found herself on one of the ostensibly poorer 'adult' contracts:

> I was one of those people who would have been a little bit better off in many ways because I was already on a shit contract. It couldn't get any worse for me, shit contract, shit hours, no child care, I had to sort out my own child arrangements.

Even though the college had a well-known history of sacking those prominent in the trade union over the previous decade, Andrea resisted this change to contract as a union activist and she expressed clearly how the recession was being deployed as justification:

> It is incredibly divisive and I think it is wrong to have to tolerate that. I think ultimately [the college] are exploiting the economic crisis and they almost make you feel that you should be grateful that you are in a job and … some of the messages that you read from the principalship, that was the inference and that is how we interpreted it as a union.

Although the changes were eventually pushed through, Andrea still spoke out when management explained the changes to staff:

> They were not meetings, just a monologue of them telling us how it was and how lucky we were. I was seething inside … I just said I know what

you said and that this is the way it is and I know we should be grateful but you can't account for how unhappy everybody is. You can't account for how divided you have made us feel and how the morale has never been so low ..., [the vice principal] was really affronted.

Andrea also drew attention to the well-publicised 10% pay rise that those in the principalship had awarded themselves:

How that was a complete poke in the eye and how affronted [staff] felt about that and did [senior management] not realise what idiots they were for ... doing that at such an insensitive time?

Her name was taken at the end of the meeting and although she remains in her job, Andrea believed it unlikely that she could ever be promoted. Performativity demands compliance, not criticality or agency. The union, once again, has been broken through sackings and with it the resistance to the changes:

People are more despondent and distrusting now and unfortunately are just recoiling now and are just burying their heads and trying to forget about it. It is almost like we almost had an opportunity to make a difference or make an impact and it didn't work out.

Nonetheless, Andrea '[loved] coming to work' and was enjoying being part of a well-motivated and supportive team who have the interests of their learners to the fore. In her new role she has been able to develop her teaching practice as never before:

It is almost like this is the way it needs to be and how it should be...I feel like I can be a kind of text book teacher in a way and some of the things that we were taught and learnt about [on the ITE course], you can almost put into play, you have that autonomy to do that.

That autonomy may at least partly be attributed to her entirely teaching off site and alone ('we kind of lay low on Train to Gain') but also partly to having 'a very open-minded manager'. Unlike Mark and Danny, Andrea had never taken on management duties. Train to Gain was, however, an initiative created and promoted by the previous New Labour government with whom it is closely associated. Andrea considered it to be beneficial for learners but described it as 'like a money pit. It is just not an economically viable programme at all', so it is vulnerable to political change. Andrea remained, though, sanguine believing that within the area of basic skills for adults she will always have work, possibly in new apprenticeships. Andrea was keen to get a better paid job and like the other participants in their most recent responses, she saw her near future beyond City College and would like to gain ESOL qualifications to work in that area.

Performativity and practice

Many of the themes that arise from these case studies mirror those that Avis (2005, p. 210) identified from the literature on FE in the early 1990s:

- Loss of control
- Intensification of labour
- Increased administration
- Perceived marginalization of teaching
- Stress on measurable performance indicators

Similarly, Randle and Brady (1997: 237) drew on Derber's (1983) notions and described the proletarianization of FE teachers and identified their 'powerlessness to define the final product of one's work'. This chimes with Orr (2012) who has used the Marxist understanding of alienation to analyse the circumstances of FE teachers and the regular complaints in these case studies of too much paperwork and too little autonomy are indicative of that. Connected with this, too, is the encroaching language of business. The acute job insecurity is, though, a relatively new factor: each of the three had faced redundancy in the two years to June 2011, but circumstances of constant change have come to characterise FE. The impact on these individuals has been stark, especially as regards their teaching. Mark regretted the loss of his teaching and described his practice as having regressed as a result of spending so little time in front of students.

In early interviews Danny spoke of his own inspirational if unorthodox schoolteachers in Northern Ireland. That Danny in 2011 repeatedly equated a good session with what OfSTED consider to be a grade 1 suggests that these arbitrary performative measures had now even determined what he considered a good teacher to be. So the grade from OfSTED eclipses professional knowledge or judgement. Here, performativity has not 'got in the way' of being a good teacher; it has redefined the nature of a good teacher. Yet apparent in their most recent accounts was both a commitment to teaching as being valuable and a strongly articulated desire to foreground this. Their identities as educators and therefore valued, was important to them. Danny's description of the contradictions is vivid:

It is kind of like a cattle herding system, fantastic right, milk you, do this, do that, fantastic, fine and at the end of it you're thinking what have you really achieved how many lives have you actually changed. I've managed to convince or rather push people towards university that never considered the thought. So, those are my little 'get- ups' and I need these kind of things to know I am making a slight difference. But because of all the things, the infrastructure currently in place, my level and ability have stayed the same… I have all these other things in the back of my head like the elephant in the corner saying, 'well, you could spend the three hours doing that or you could spend the three hours doing paperwork that you haven't been able to do yet.' Usually the paperwork wins.

Mark and Danny's professionalism as teachers has diminished as a direct consequence of the performative pressures of their role reducing their capacity to teach. What Colley *et.al.* (2007: 174) wrote may illuminate this:

While a great deal has been written about *becoming* or *being* a professional, competing versions of professionalism almost invariably entail – as do 'common sense' understandings – an implicit assumption that professional status is permanent once it has been attained.

Despite this 'common sense', Colley *et.al.* describe the trajectory out of the profession of their participants through 'agentic exits' (185); that is, a decision to leave FE teaching based upon unwillingness to comply with changes to educational priorities. Mark and Danny had not left the profession and did not intend to, but they had partly left teaching, even though they both identified some control over the organisation of their work. Colley *et.al.*'s concept of 'unbecoming professionals' is helpful as it recognises flux in the situation of teachers whose professionalism may not necessarily develop from where it started. It may regress. Andrea's story is, though, different. Due in part to working outside the college campus and due to her supportive manager and colleagues, Andrea fulfilled what the college require and she still defended her own professional values. She completed the extensive administrative aspect of her work while also creatively finding extra time to teach her students. Her practice was thriving in the space to make autonomous professional judgements, literally away from performative pressures. Andrea's freedom from surveillance was, however, contingent on being part of a specific and highly vulnerable initiative and whether she can be said to be acting strategically, that is for the long-term, is at best moot. She had escaped the performative demands experienced by Mark and Danny, but she is on a part-time, temporary contract and she has antagonised senior managers. Her freedom to flourish as a professional may be short-lived. Andrea was unlikely to keep that role nor the independence it allows, but her circumstances as well as those of the other participants belie any notion of strategy, which raises the question of strategic compliance.

Gleeson and Knight (2006) have questioned the dualism that sees professionals in the public services either as victims of reform or strategic operators planning routes around the performative obstacles set in their path whilst simultaneously maintaining their values. Neither element of this dualism describes the situation or the practice of Danny, Mark or Andrea; it is surely difficult to perceive in their practice 'an artful pragmatism which reconciles professional and managerial interests' (Gleeson and Shain, 1999: 482). Such reconciliation within City College seems impossible given the overwhelming hegemony of managerialism and its concomitant performative demands. The three teachers are coping, and even thriving in Andrea's case, within their constraints by taking advantage of short-term opportunities as they arise whether that is when Andrea finds extra time for her students or when Danny defends his staff from redundancy. This cannot, however, be considered as strategic as it has no overall or long-term goal. These teachers are, at best, able to act tactically but their actions are barely disturbing managerial interests. Moreover, given the situation of City College where staff are subject to banal performative requirements with the very real threat of redundancy, strategic compliance can hardly be considered as a progressive option for teachers. As Avis (2005: 217) has argued, the concept of strategic compliance concedes the right to manage to managerialist managers and so 'professionalism becomes impoverished and is reduced to a mechanism of continuous improvement.'

In City College, performativity has apparently met less resistance as teachers have feared for their jobs and so tolerated what they had found before to be unacceptable. The three teachers highlighted here remain, though, committed to their students and to developing their teaching. Nevertheless, if these case studies 'offer a fractal expression of the whole set of social relations' (Colley, 2006: 109) within FE, they suggest that the impact of policies which have promoted control over teachers' practice through performativity have fundamentally distorted educational priorities.

11

'It's not a factory!' Performativity in education and support provision for marginalised and excluded youth in a UK former coal-mining community.

N. Geoffrey Bright

Introduction

The last ten years or so has seen extensive and illuminating exploration of the impact of performativity in a variety of education settings nationally and internationally (for examples focussing on different sectors and from different perspectives see: Troman, 1996, 1997; Ball, 1998, 2000, 2001, 2003; Gewirtz and Ball, 2000; Mahony and Hextall, 2000; Woods and Jeffrey, 2002; Brehony, 2005; Webb and Vuillamy 2006; Troman *et.al.*, 2007; Strain, 2009; Wilkins, 2011). In general, the emphasis of work following Ball's broadly Foucauldian inquiry has not been on the merely practical character of performance cultures but more widely on the way that performativity can be seen as a key discursive component of what Ball has called a *'generic global policy ensemble'* (Ball, 2008, 39). That ensemble 'rests on a set of basic and common *policy technologies...*that work to bring about *new values, new relationships and new subjectivities* in arenas of practice' (ibid.: 40, all original emphases). Performativity is implemented through one such policy technology which itself has three strands: a pervasive culture of targets and auditing; a regime of regulatory mechanisms such as inspection; and a general marketisation of the environment. As such, it insinuates the key aspects of the neo-liberal economic project into everyday life right across the public sector and in so doing reconstitutes institutional and individual worlds.

Within education research, the majority of work on performativity has tended to interrogate the shaping of subjectivities among 'professional' practitioners – teachers, lecturers – and has generally been situated as a response to issues arising out of an established literature on professionalism. Consequently, there has been less of a focus on the impact of performativity on para-professionals, support staff and the variety of 'multi-agency' practitioners working outside the school system, or indeed among children and youth themselves – even though all of these groups might be seen as 'policy actors' in Ball's terms. Indeed, while the picture of performativity as thoroughly embedded within mainstream settings such as schools is now well developed – with Wilkins (2011) recently assembling preliminary evidence of the emergence, even, of a 'post-performative teacher' – the grip of performativity in the marginal, 'poor relation' settings of alternative out-of school provision, youth support and 'foundation learning'[1] is less well researched.

In light of that, the discussion presented in this chapter seeks to develop our understanding of how performativity reaches into the lives of those situated in that sector; not only the 'tutors' and support staff, but also the young people who find themselves on the margins of the system simply because, in the words of one of my participants, they 'either *couldn't* or *wouldn't*, perform' in school. It does that, also, in a very specific context of marginalisation: that of the now post-industrial UK coalfields.

A Coalfield Ethnography

The data drawn on here originates from a doctoral intergenerational ethnography of education and youth transitions among 'marginalised'[2] young people, mainly in four former pit villages – Beldover, Coalbrook, Cragwell and Longthorne[3] – in a coalfield area of Derbyshire, England. The study was conducted between 2006 and 2011 and attempts an ethnographic project aiming at a set of objectives that are, hopefully productively, in some tension with each other. First, in 'analysing the disputed and contested policy and practice space around young people "put at a disadvantage"' (Smyth, 2010: 4), it proposes what Smyth identifies as a 'critical policy ethnography'. As such, it concerns itself with 'a broad social and educational policy arena as it is being enacted, rolled out, experienced and re-worked through the lives of a particular category of young people' (ibid.). Such critical policy ethnography obviously draws on Ball's 'policy sociology'. There, attention is given to 'policy rhetorics and discourses', looking at the way they 'work to privilege certain ideas and topics and speakers, and exclude others' (Ball, 2008: 5) and how they are 'contested, interpreted... inflected, mediated, resisted and misunderstood...' (Ball, 2008: 7) when implemented locally. Tracing such discursive contestations is, thus, central to the ethnographic project as I've envisaged it.

Secondly, in a post-industrial context *par excellence*, the study seeks to interrogate the 'dialectics of discourse and the everyday' in Dorothy Smith's phrase (Smith, 1987). It does so by way of an interpretive approach exploring the relationship between 'discourse-in-practice' operating at meta (institutional, cultural or policy) level and as locally enacted, situated, 'discursive practice' operating at a micro (interactional) level. It looks, therefore, at the 'myriad *hows*

---

1. Foundation Learning is learning provision for those currently below UK 'Level 2'. Level 2 is, for example, the minimum level for entrance to apprenticeship training.
2. My study focuses on those either excluded from school, 'at risk' of exclusion or – being over the school leaving age – finding themselves 'NEET' (not in employment, education or training) or in the 'foundation learning' sector.
3. All names of places (at a level lower than county) have been changed as have the names of all persons.

and *whats'* of everyday life, oscillating between 'bracketing' the one level – say, the meta – and then the other – the micro (Hollstein and Gubrium, 2007, 496).

Thirdly, the ethnography attends to processes of local, classed, cultural production, seeing the *locally enacted* as occurring within an affective frame something like a 'structure of feeling' (Williams, 1975, 1977) or similar, perhaps, to Thrift's 'spatiality of feeling' (Thrift, 2008); that is, as having a very significant *affective* aspect. In light of that, the study seeks, overall, to work the troublesome edge between policy discourse, material cultural practice and the 'bloom-spaces' (Gregg and Seigworth, 2010: 9), 'transmissions' (Brennan, 2004) and 'atmospheres' (Anderson, 2009) of affect that are so obvious in the embodied choreography of '*dis*-affection' as it presents in the locality. Thus, it aims to come at locally textured fieldwork 'data' in a manner approaching that canvassed recently by Lawrence Grossberg whereby the local remains situated within a broader historical conjuncture but the affective, as 'feeling', is admitted 'as part of [the] study' (Grossberg, 2010: 335).

What follows from this for the purposes of *this* discussion, is that it will look at the impact of performativity on a group of practitioners and young people whose lives are *affectively* related either directly and knowingly, or atmospherically and unknowingly, to socially remembered or unconsciously embodied resistant histories, notably of the miners' strike of 1984-85 and the subsequent campaign against pit closures. Even though the local economy in the area studied has changed enormously, these histories still echo into the present. Indeed, they are more resonant now as the current conjuncture (an apparently intractable crisis of globalised capitalism) impacts in the locality through a tougher culture of performativity within the ever diminishing public sector and as rising unemployment and immiseration outside it. In the light of this, the argument will be made that the responses to performativity outlined here can't be fully encompassed by the kind of discussion focussing on the relationship between performativity and 'professionalism' that occupies much of the literature. Even a professionalism conceived as constructed, contested and fluidly shifting can't quite accommodate the particular complexities of historicised meaning-making considered in this chapter.

A common touchstone of defiance: the setting

I have described the characteristic nature of the coalfield area in which my study is set in detail elsewhere (Bright, 2010, 2011a, 2011b, 2012). Nevertheless, that description bears some repetition again here because, as I hope to show, it affects the way that performativity – arising as a phenomenon of globalised capitalism – is internalised and resisted. I've noted before, for example, that while the former coal mining villages have been energetically 'rebranded' as increasingly desirable 'historic market towns' since the pits closed in the 1990s, the now non-existent industry still casts a shadow and the coalfields remain blighted by severe socio-economic problems relating to unemployment, long-term sickness and poverty. Beldover, Coalbrook and Cragwell all saw their pits close in within a couple of years of each other in the early 1990s. Twenty years later the wards around the sites of the former collieries still exhibit levels of deprivation that remain among the 1% most deprived nationally and, generally, more than a third of the working age population are still 'inactive' due to illness, disability or caring responsibilities. Unemployment is increasing, particularly among young people, and more than 50% of the population possess no qualifications. Basically, deprivation in these localities – described by one participant as 'villages Santa Claus forgot' – reaches the very worst urban levels, a decline described by another participant as a fall from 'model village to brown [heroin] city' (for accounts of coalfield decline see Beatty *et.al.*. 2005; Bennett *et.al.*. 2000; Gore *et.al.*. 2007; Murray *et.al.*. 2005).

I have also pointed out before how coalfield communities have been viewed as exceptional in different disciplinary literatures and have argued that such exceptionality operates on the formation of contemporary social identities in a number of ways: first, directly, in the material impoverishment to which I've just referred; secondly, indirectly, by means of 'sedimented' local and family histories (Reay, 2009: 27), and, thirdly, in an atmospeheric transmission of what Hardt has called 'affects of trauma' (Hardt, 2007: xii) relating to the end of the industry. Coal mining communities such as Beldover, Coalbrook, Cragwell and Longthorne have been modelled as paradigmatic of working class 'community' in modernity (Dennis *et.al.* 1956; Bulmer, 1975; 1982), as 'archetypally proletarian' (see Lockwood 1966) and as characterised by 'a very clear sense of the past as struggle [which] constitutes a memory that goes back at least a century' and that has the strikes of 1926, 1972, 1974 and 1984-5 as a 'common touchstone' and 'the imagery of the strike as defiance of the state [as]…a constant one' (Fentress and Wickham, 1992: 115-6). (See also the trade union histories – Page Arnot, 1961; Griffin, 1962; Williams, 1962 – studies of the 1984-85 strike – Samuel *et.al.* 1986; Waddington *et.al.* 1991; Richards, 1996 – well as work on women's roles in the characteristic coalfield 'geography of gender relations' – Massey, 1994; Seddon, 1986).

All of this adds up to what Strangleman has usefully called a 'context of singularity' (2001: 255) that not only relates to a unique history of industrial development and rapid, politically orchestrated decline, but also to a tradition of workplace and community resistance that I've argued continues to shape the disengagement – even 'counter aspiration' (Bright, 2011a; 2012) – of a group of contemporary coalfield youth even though it is more than twenty years since the pits closed. I would also contend that the same singularities influence how the group of locally originating staff who work with those young people both see themselves 'professionally' and respond to performativity in education, as we'll see here. As to what we might expect given the surge of individualism and disembedding from class (Giddens, 1991; Beck 1992) that has arguably taken place in the period separating the two generations considered here, there are, nevertheless, some strong continuities. Before we move to consider these matters in detail, however, a note about the doctoral fieldwork will be helpful.

Fieldwork

Given that ethnography is, distinctly, a repertoire of methods characteristically involving *direct* and *sustained* social contact with participants, the research project from which I'm drawing material here has been grounded in concentrated fieldwork taking place over a four year period in a variety of settings, some of which have changed and evolved during that period. Sites have included formal – but out-of-school – youth education projects, informal education and youth work venues, youth clubs, a community youth house, private homes, a miners' welfare club and the street. Research in two key sites, however, has generated the bulk of the data relevant to this chapter. Firstly, by means of a sustained link (2007-2009) with staff and learners at a community based 'pre Entry to Employment' programme – *Go 4 it!* – recruiting 14-16 and 16-18 year-olds from the local communities who are either still at school but at 'risk of becoming NEET' (not in education, employment or training) or who have finished school and are NEET. This programme, with some staff changes, has now evolved into a 'foundation learning' project funded through a different route and referred to below as *Move4ward.* Secondly, through a similarly sustained (2009-2010) participant observation of staff and young people involved with local authority 'detached' and club-based youth work provision such as the *Cavs Lasses Group* – a girls only, after-school group on the Cavendish estate, Beldover – and *Bus Stop* – a mobile youth support service, are two examples.

The former generated a series of semi-structured and unstructured interviews with young people and staff, as well as a series of short participant observation opportunities in classrooms and on 'visits'. The latter generated frequent observations over a sustained period, spontaneous conversations, and semi-structured and unstructured interviews with groups and individuals. For the preparation of this chapter, follow-up discussions were also carried out with 'Christine', the education manager who first facilitated my research at *Go4it!* in 2007, and new conversations were had with two staff members 'Maggie' and 'Pat' now working for the *Move4ward* foundation learning project. Moreover, and in general, it should also be noted that the ethnographic project referred to here itself grew out of my own lifelong connection to the localities as a member of a pit family, as a worker, as a political and trade union activist and for the last twenty five years as an education 'professional'.

Participants

In moving towards the crux of the discussion, there are some general points that need to be made about the group of participants and how they are situated in relation to one of the most surprising paradoxes evident in the data I've accumulated: namely, a peculiarly enigmatic *simultaneous presence and absence of history* in the coalfield localities studied. Now, these localities, as we've already noted, have always been *characterised* by a particularly high awareness of history transmitted through a century-long collective social memory of 'struggle' culminating in the locally bitterly divided 1984-85 strike. So, the fact that this history, an unspeakable but ever present 'elephant in the room', is both readily available and, at the same time, foreclosed – accessible to the older generation but not the youth – is significant. Indeed, the intergenerational aspect of my work brings out this difference, showing how the collective memory of resistance and upheaval remains a conscious reference point for the *staff* with whom I've spoken, while at the same time only being available through affective transmission to the young people. It should not be assumed to be having a lesser impact on them because of that, however, as, oddly, they still play out its conflicts. Signally for our purpose here, this 'hidden in plain sight' legacy of the conflicted demise of the coal industry influences the way in which both staff and young people respond to the encroaching embrace of performativity.

Now, education and support for marginal youth is itself a marginal sector in many ways. It is uncertainly related to the professional structures of mainstream schooling, special education and further education; has been shunted between different funding regimes and managed in different ways through frequently changing, temporary contractual relationships – as 'community education', as 'work-based learning', and now as part of the adult education sector but branded as 'foundation learning'. This sectoral uncertainty – registered as a feeling that 'you do expect shit to happen in your job, every day' (Maggie) – has been an issue for the staff participants that I've worked with, all of whom have been required to modify their professional identities at least once during the period of the research. Equally, though, it's worth noting that the margin – in the locality of my research at least – is also a productively liminal space where relationships and networks are often semi-formal and fluid and where a group of locally originating, and largely female, staff have adeptly negotiated their way by surprising routes from voluntary and sessional employment as youth or community workers into roles as tutors and managers.

The staff

The staff involved originally around the *Go 4 it!* project and now with the *Move4ward* foundation learning group – Christine, the manager; Maggie and Pat, the 'tutors'; Karen, a classroom support assistant; Stacey, a youth worker; Chris, a police community support officer (PCSO); Frank, a community tutor and Ray, a senior manager in the district – all originate in the local working class communities and have all had non-traditional, mature student, routes into the roles they now occupy. Prior to gaining a mixed and occasionally disparate portfolio of qualifications in youth and community work, adult teaching qualifications, access diplomas and part-time degrees, they worked variously in hairdressing, catering, factory work and clerical work. Two of the men were coal miners and another worked in coal by-product manufacturing and construction. All had a family background in coal mining and all but Pat and Maggie had been actively involved – Karen and Stacey even as young girls – in the miners' strike of 1984-85, the campaign against pit closures or trade union and labour politics. Most of the sessional youth workers supporting the mobile *Bus Stop* project and the *Cavs Lasses Group* around the Cavendish estate in Beldover, all sites of participant observation, also share a similar background.

In being linked organically to the same communities as the young people with whom they work, they are quite distinct from the professional layers of staff that one would find in a school. They also have a particular attitude towards their role, seeing the young people on their programmes as the casualties of a malignant legacy of conflict and pit closures that continues into the present, and their own work as ameliorative in very direct ways:

> I could just see it [recently] totally snowballing and being roughly in that culture that there was in the strike, you know, they were coming up and they were saying, Stace, have you got anything to eat, I'm starving? And I was going and buying bread and cheap loaves or beans, because the only meal they had had that day was at school because they had free school meals. (Stacey, youth worker).

What we might note here, really, is that in this sector of the education system and in this particular locality, the 'policy actors' negotiating the reach of performativity are a distinctive, even idiosyncratic, group in some interesting ways. The staff directly supporting *Go4it!*, *Move4ward* and the various local youth work projects, see themselves as working out with the official project of schooling. What's more, they view their role as an almost impossible one of cleaning up after the official project's failure to meet the needs of those left on the margin twenty years after the end of the mining industry. Seeing things in this way, they retain a specific and actively *affective* connection to that 'common touchstone of defiance' noted above which they carry as a reference narrative – Frank and Ray explicitly as 'socialists' – alongside, but affectively prior to, any professional discourse in which they find themselves. Even as the provision in which they are involved – often generated initially from a local campaigning, do-it-yourself culture going back, one way or another, to the 1984-85 strike – has become increasingly incorporated into Local Authority structures they see the changing cohorts of young people as 'the same group of kids'. Consequently, their socially reparative practice – based in a characteristic, local collectivist ethic that still sees knowledge and knowledge relations as essentially *social* in character – goes on. Indeed, they talk of their own work as a kind of last bastion against what they know is 'really' happening: that is, a still unfolding 'grand plan', aimed at finally dealing with the remnants of the coal mining 'enemy within':

It's part o' the grand plan in't it, eh? [bitterly and knowingly] I do wonder if, like, in ten years time we're gonna be almost back in Victorian days... an' all benefit's getting chopped. You know is it part o' this grand plan o' this Tory government and now they're in they're gonna make it that. You know, there's that sector o' community that's got fuck all basically, there's them in middle that's got a bit, but there's these up 'ere that's got everything and to me I see it all around, there's people that's got nothing, really got nothing. I mean, I nip down Coalbrook market, say Wednesday, to get a sandwich or something and you see some o' faces, Geoff, o' people, and you think, oh, my God, what a life you lot have had! Poverty and anxiety...people just look so ground down, and ill, and tired...in last two or three years, you know, in Beldover. (Christine, *Move4ward* manager).

One might reasonably expect, then, that the self-positioning deployed by these staff – broadly espousing the 'organization, cooperation and older forms of collective relations' (Ball, 2003: 219) to which performativity runs counter – will be particularly problematic in relation to the 'intensive work on the self' (Dean, 1995, p. 581) required by performativity's 'system of 'terror'' (Ball, 2008: 51). And it is, but not straightforwardly.

Young people

But what of the young people – Karl, Dave, P-J, ASBO-Jonnyo, Cocker, Lianne, Beth, Heartbreaker, the 'Cavs lasses'; the 'Model crew' and the many others – that I've sat with, talked with and listened to over a five year period? How are they positioned in the discursive frame of performativity? What's more, how do they position themselves? These are young people who describe themselves as from 'round here', from places that are 'not exactly *tough* tough, but [have]got a name' where '[e]veryone just knows everyone', '[where] it's a bit rough and that..', '[where we] just all stick together really' (Dave). They see themselves as 'a bit rough, but not idiots' in Cocker's terms. They can be 'little fuckers' (Karl) or a 'bit of a bastard' (Dave) or, like Beth – who refuses the 'plastic' identity of girls who 'are in with the teachers' – 'a cunt, me'. They are the young people who thirty years since according to Liz, a sessional youth in Beldover would have quickly been absorbed into the local economy, 'Lads'd 'a been at pit. Lasses'd 'a been in knicker factory'.

According to the categorisations of the multi-agency services that work with them, these young people 'are, or are at risk of' becoming teen parents, becoming NEET (not in employment, education or training), being involved in catastrophic drinking and drug use, and 'offending'. As far as the facts are concerned, they have commonly been permanently or temporarily excluded from school, subject to 'managed moves' or 'invited not to attend'. After exclusion, a number have been subjected to anti-social behaviour orders (ASBOs) and acceptable behaviour contracts (ABCs) after trouble with the police. More seriously, some have had custodial sentences in Young Offender institutions and have, subsequently been electronically tagged and placed under curfew on release.

Remarkably, every single young person involved with the doctoral project – around a hundred or so that I've spent some time with – is familiar, *as a matter of course*, with some combination of the following: family breakdown; long term unemployment; chronic disease; disability; alcoholism; sexual abuse (including rape); overdose related death; arrest and strip search; parental imprisonment; suicide or accidental death; eviction; domestic violence. Referred to sneeringly in some professional canteen discourse as part of a 'hillbilly', 'RAF' ('rough as fuck'), culture of the 'in-bred', these young people are supposedly without aspirations and are commonly positioned as prone to the embrace of the racist right.

What can be said with accuracy is that they almost exclusively come from families that were involved with the coal mining industry who, subject to what Beverley Skeggs has described as 'spatial apartheid' (Skeggs 2004: 180), still live in the 'pit rows', 'white city' estates and 'colliery model villages' of former pit housing in the denigrated space that I have previously described as 'the Model' (Bright, 2011a). They are working class youngsters, basically, whose lives are similar in many ways to the early lives of the staff who now work with them – a phenomenon that is as common in this sector as it would be unusual in schools and which somehow draws staff and learners together in a symbiotic, sometimes collusive resistance to performativity.

The reach of performativity: 'I'm thinkin', God, we must be bloody mad!'
The foregoing description of the participants and their characteristic relationship to their roles notwithstanding, it's important to acknowledge, nevertheless, that most of the elements ordinarily noted in research on performativity in schools are discernible to some extent in this sector, too. Among staff, the 'regress of mistrust' recognised by Power (1994) is clearly visible, extending here even to the self in this fascinating conversation with *Move4ward* tutors Maggie and Pat, which is worth quoting at length:

> Maggie. We were youth workers. [...] *that* was the job that I went into [...] All of a sudden to then just put the pressure on staff [to change] ... It's now 'functional skills' and we were told: you'll be delivering functional skills – 'cos you don't have to be *qualified* to deliver functional skills. But we've still got to get them to the same Maths and English certificate that, before, previously, *qualified* literacy and numeracy tutors were come in, bought in, like, externally to deliver that for us, 'cos *we weren't* qualified! When it changed to functional skills, all of a sudden, overnight we *became qualified* to deliver! It didn't make any sense to us, 'cos we still had to get 'em to the same point.

> GB. "So how did you feel about that?

> M. We were a bit pissed off to start wi', weren't we?

> Pat. Then we just sort o' accepted it [lengthy pause] ...you know, talking about it now I'm laughing ...cos...

> M. It's funny when you look back in't it?

> P. You think to yourself, blinking 'eck! What? How did this happen? I came in ...You know, as Maggie says, we came in as youth workers!

> M. [laughing, to Pat] See you've forgotten, an't you?

P. I just put things behind me...I'm laughing now, thinking oh my God, would anybody else put up wi' that? You know, would anybody else?

M. Teacher training! We had to do that!

P. Teacher training! Do that, or lose your job!

NGB. Was there clear pressure to do that? Not 'you can do it if you want'?

M. No, we had to do it. That became part of the job description overnight.

P. You know...but the thing is, the young people that we're working with are still them difficult young people that need that personal development side of it. You know, why are they cramming to get done in three month what school hasn't done and family hasn't done in the last 16 years? And they want us to get it all in, to get 'em up up to a level 2 [...] But I'm thinking ...and talking like you've just gone through all that... I'm thinkin' 'God, we must be bloody mad!'

M. You know, they can't read and write and they want us to be able to get 'em to read and write wi'in space o' three month. I'm saying: *what*?

There is much in this about the doubtful character of professional identities in the sector; about the haphazard, illogical shifts of status between being qualified and being unqualified; about having one's identity shaped by the technical-bureaucratic apparatus of the job description 'overnight'. There is also something of the 'institutional schizophrenia' noted by Blackmore and Sachs (1997) as well as what Ball sees as the 'potential 'splitting' between the teachers own judgements about 'good practice' and student 'needs' and the rigours of performance (Ball, 2003: 221).

Troman and Woods' (2001) research in the primary education sector, as well as remarking a similar progressive erosion of trust, also notes the 'security-seeking' tactics that are attendant upon it, here evident in the same conversation with Maggie and Pat:

Maggie. I *make* her change, 'cos I'm adaptable. I say come on, a change is good and then she's alright, 'cos Pat's one for getting a bit unsure and saying 'I don't think I can do this' and I go 'course you can, you're doin' it already...

'[E]xistential anxiety and dread', again identified by Troman and Woods (ibid.), is particularly sharp in this extract from Frank's long, bitter and troubled condemnation of the symbolic violence of performative culture:

> But what's actually changed me [...] what I've actually found out in the last 10 years, 15 years, is that this area of work is the...we *should* be the *most* open, honest. This is what we portray, as tutors, teachers, learners, facilitators...is that were honest, open and as transparent to colleagues as we can be. Well, *it's the biggest back-stabbing, two-faced, under-handed, I'll-get-one-over-on-you organisation I have ever worked in my life*! I do regard it as that. It is so two-faced. We say one thing, we mean another. There's always someone now trying to put their foot on your head, and not to try to drive it into the soil, [but] to actually try to bloody drown you with it. You know, to keep it on, to further their own games, their own needs. That's the culture now in this [...] It's all about: am I satisfying my boss? Is my boss satisfied with what I'm doing? I'll shit my britches if [not]! (Frank, Community Tutor).

Among the key, 'mechanics of performativity' (Ball, 2003: 220) is that of a general intensification of pressure, something again pretty obvious in the data here as the hard arithmetic of outputs is linked to 'draw down' of funds in a way that increases the possibility of sudden punitive sanction for failure to perform:

> Yeah, at the end of the day if you don't meet those outputs, and you don't get your funding, bottom line is: no funding, no job, and we've seen that 'cos other teams have gone. That's a real reality for people, that. If this year you're the team that's underperforming you might be the next for the chop. Every so often that can raise its head, like we're coming to the end of the year, we're under performing as a whole team... (Christine-Education Manager).

For Christine, the 'data base', supported by somebody 'coming out to see me every week and look over my shoulder' works as the Foucauldian panoptican:

> X [the manager] has wanted it uploaded every week. Every week: every unit every kid's done. So at the end of the teaching week, which is Wednesday, on Thursday Maggie and Pat look at sorting folders out. Tick it all on a sheet and that goes to K and she has to load it all electronically...*then* ...*then*...when they've got three units that ticks *another* box. That then, it's a tracking system, ticks another box, you know, that you've earned £50. So that, at any one point, the manager [at county HQ] can look how many

units we've delivered and how many kids we've got [and] how much *money* we've earned. (Christine).

We are looking here, of course, at the pressures to fabricate performative selves, a project that is evident in 'day-to-day social relations and practices' (Ball, 2003: 226) within these various youth support projects but remains, though these pressures are far from negligible, stubbornly incomplete among staff in my study. 'Ethical practices' noted by Ball as a 'casualty' of performativity, in fact, generally remain robust – certainly in the fundamental area of relationships with learners – precisely because they are not articulated to any jeopardised professional ethics but rather to class and local culture. Among the staff, responses to performativity are broadly resistant, varying from working the spaces purposefully left in their lesson plans, to jumping through the hoops if need be, as Maggie canvasses here:

I call it 'the hoop', you've got to jump through the hoop and then you can get your dollars at end o' day can't you? But that's something I don't agree with. But what do we do, Geoff, when we want to get paid? (Maggie, Tutor).

In this, there is clearly some ethical discomfort, but it is more about what one has to do in a classed world to make 'a dollar' than it is about compromising the partisan ethic of collective care which remains the core of the practice that I've observed. Indeed, if there is any ethical elasticity among practitioners on projects such as *Go4it* and *Bus Stop* it is rooted in that very partisanship and exercised in favour of the young people. There are, of course, momentary instances where what appear to be the beginnings of fabricated performative identities are discernible, where some pleasure is felt in the controlling power of the data base; in the status of a new, incorporating, job title such as 'senior co-ordinator'; in the mastery of making a difficult adaptation:

Christine. But the tracking X set up is fantastic in that respect! And, I mean, we go on it. Me and K go on it and look at where we all are and we've had spread sheets at team meetings.

NGB. So you can see your performance at a glance?

C. Yeah, at a glance every week, in the early days this academic year K 'd say it went from like 'Oh, look we're up to three thousand, Ooh, look five thousand' And she even said yesterday, she inputted some units and she said 'our team's so far earned fifty five thousand' 'cos it's that accurate. (Conversation with Christine)

I do like change [...] I know wi' other project, when ever anything goes off they all panic, they all just panic, but I just sit back and think 'Oh, new challenge. I like that![...] I get a little bit 'boredom threshold'! (Maggie – Tutor)

While these processes can here, again, be seen to be 'folded into complex institutional, team, group and communal relations and [to] penetrate mundane day-to-day interactions' (Ball, 2003: 223) the fabrication of new subjectivities still stops short. In a field note, I have Maggie contemplating the benefits that might have accrued to her in embracing the requirements of performativity, particularly in taking on a teacher training qualification:

I do look at it like you've got qualified in another area [as a tutor]. I feel quite confident to apply for a job in a school.

The telling surprise here, though, is that the school role she imagines herself now potentially applying for is not that of a teacher but of a classroom assistant, not because her qualification leaves her ineligible (though the move wouldn't be straightforward) but because she cannot imagine herself crossing the social class divide between teaching assistant and teacher (for which 'professional status' is a proxy) and which would therefore compromise her relationships with 'the kids' and threaten her own working ethic and jeopardise her local identity.

The young people

Moving back again to the perspective of the young people, it's equally the case that phenomena noted in school-based research looking at learner responses to performativity, are clearly visible – though, with these young people responses are presented as if in negative image. After all, what distinguishes Dave, Beth, Rianne, Heartbreaker and the others is, quite simply, their *persistent failure to meet the performance standards*, whether of 'strong' or, in Jeffrey and Troman's terms, 'weak' performativity. Jeffrey and Troman's work (2009), again in the Primary sector, has drawn attention to the fact that by age 11'[l]earner's understanding of performativity is acute' (Jeffrey and Troman, 2009: 8) as:

[t]he construction of performative learning identities [which occur] during the educational and social practices of performative teaching

and learning and the discourses used exemplify that construction but at the same time ... confirm and embed those performative practices in daily practice and therefore contribute to the formation of performative identities. (Jeffrey and Troman, 2009: 24).

Jeffrey and Troman provide, indeed, a powerful picture of a performative project almost complete in its success: one whereby prevalent discourses of improvement (ibid.: 9), of 'effort' (ibid.: 11) – embedded as 'doing your best' – and of 'responsibility' (ibid.: 12) supported by regimes of 'performative stratification' draw learners into 'playing the game' in a way that propels the conclusion that:

> [t]he influence of these educational and social practices upon young people from 7-11 is both extensive and significant. They have absorbed the values of aspiration, continual effort and improvement as a way of life; they have a view of knowledge as that which can be tested; an awareness of the significance of differentiation and stratification and they have learned to fabricate their educational practice to further performative objectives. (Jeffrey and Troman, 2009: 24)

Now, the very existence of groups of young people like the excluded youth of Beldover, Cragwell and Coalbrook is profoundly problematic for the performative project. They stand out, after all, as the blatant, embodied evidence of the project's less than complete success.

'If you do anything wrong you go in there': Dividing practices in 'isolation'

Looking at the school careers of these young people we can see that performative stratification facilitated through ever harsher 'dividing practices' (Rabinov, 1984) within school becomes indispensible as 'best effort' and 'self-responsibilty' fail to gain any purchase. So-called 'learning support units' play a very significant role here. Staff such as the *Go4it!* staff know this, as do the young people. Indeed, Christine was well aware that the school 'unit' had been *the* significant recruitment link in terms of the *Go4it!* programme, allowing local secondary schools – pressed by increasingly performative cultures and, in two cases, eager to recover reputations after special measures – to offload, or 'dump' in her terms, non-performing learners:

> So they sent them [a group of young men]...but *en bloc* [...] I got this [impression] that all they wanted, was them out of school and as long as they were doing something, and whenever we took them out on trips, I

think we could've taken them to the moon, but they wouldn't have cared. There was no interest [...] We invited them several times: if you ever want to come down and have a look. But nothing. I think they were just glad to get rid of them. (Christine, *Move4ward* Manager).

This phenomenon was immediately apparent to Christine and her staff, as they recognised how exclusion within schools was being achieved through learning support structures which were supposed, obviously, to be *supportive,* but were, in fact, anything but:

Well, we went up to Beldover, to visit the new intake of pre-16s. Well, yeah, I was a bit surprised. We walked in the first morning and the students [in the Learning Support Unit] were sat reading comics, and when I asked the staff [member] who'd been working in schools for a number of years, she said that's what happens in most learning support units. They just give them a comic to read, or a book that they might be interested in. They don't really get any structured learning, some of them all day, not just a few hours. They just put them there to keep them away from the rest of the class. That's generally what happens. (Christine, *Move4ward* Manager).

The young people themselves see such 'support' as a sham and view being 'sent to the 'unit' as punitive. More importantly, they are aware that it is about removal from the classroom as a step, if need be, towards removal from school:

...cos we'd got like this room where you go in. If you got done they put [you] in.[...]. (Rianne, young person, *Go4it!*)

[You] just sit and copy stuff [...] [They] Gi' y' a piece o' paper like this one 'ere, tell you to write that down an when you've finished tell you to write it again. An' I used to get to third line and stop 'cos I never used to like it...Well, if you do anything wrong you go in there and then if you, say, do anything wrong in there you get excluded. If you do summat too bad before you go in there you get excluded anyway. (P-J, young man, *Go4it).*

Being placed in learning support serves neatly both to exclude young people from the classroom *de facto* and at the same time construct them as 'at risk' of exclusion ('attendance in learning support' would, for example, be seen as contributing to a formal assessment of 'risk' which would then help justify their potentially permanent removal from school 'in their own interest').

A double dynamic

Basically, then there is a kind of double dynamic operating here, bringing these particular staff together with these particular young people in the developing frame of performativity. As a way of bringing this out, I'd like to focus on the cases of Christine, the *Go4it* and more recently *Move4ward* manager, and Karl, one of the NEET youngsters previously permanently excluded from school.

As for Christine, her own biography is notable. The daughter of a coal miner and married to mining engineer who himself had progressed from face work to colliery under manager, she had been active in the campaign against pit closures and was linked to community-based projects in Coalbrook and around the other communities in the north of the coalfield. Over a period, she undertook part-time qualifications enabling her to teach in post-compulsory education, finally completing a part-time degree in education in which she gained first class honours. She had been employed in a number of project manager roles on fragile contracts since the early 2000s.

Now, at risk of simplifying the material that discussion with Christine has generated – a rich fabric of complex, extensive, interwoven ruminations on gender, class and community as they impacted on a woman from a pit family – it's noteworthy that a key, recurrent and evidently troubling theme is that of 'staying and leaving' (Bauman's, 2001, 'paradox of community'). Christine has reflected in depth – her speech and comportment ebbing and flowing between the accents and mannerisms of the 'local' and the 'professional'– on the challenge of simultaneously performing roles that both stay within (as mother, wife) and move beyond (as worker, manager, 'professional') the gender conventions of the community. In this, she is acutely sensitive to the dilemmas provoked by the embrace of performativity and passionate about the damage it causes in education:

> But you know this thing – performativity? – it's happening in all public sector in't it? I think it's just getting to a lot o' people now that it's year in, year out. You've got outputs to reach, you've got less money but you're still gettin' same people [...] But how can you have an output system wi' people that you're caring for? It just does not make sense [...] It's not a factory! We're talking about people here, aren't we? Just everybody's upset, fed up of targets, outputs, and I think that just generally gets people down. People are being squeezed, really being squeezed. You're not working wi' iron and metal and coal, you're working with human beings that have got skin and feelings and brains'. (Christine, education manager).

The conflict is not merely between a set of *professional* ethics (based on notions of education as a public good) and the requirements of performativity, indeed it perhaps owes least to that. It is, rather, about a conflict between a class ethic rooted – problematically, certainly, as it is shaped in the patriarchal, coalfield 'geography of gender relations' (Massey, 1994) – in transmitted classed and gendered notions of collective care, 'the tenderness' as PCSO 'Chris', formerly a Coalbrook miner, put it. Indeed, it is interesting how Christine's spontaneous rhetoric places the 'factory' of performativity in the brute, masculine, and now redundant, domain of 'iron and metal and coal', demarcating it firmly from the affective work with 'human beings that have got skin and feelings and brains' which is now the necessary post-industrial emotional labour of residual solidarity carried out in this locality largely by women such as herself.

Karl, on the other hand offering a young person's perspective, was aged 17 when first spoken to in 2007. Bright and alert, he was easily 'spun out' by anyone who displayed an air of authority. He had been permanently excluded from Coalbrook school in year 9 after periods in 'learning support' and short term exclusions for a series of infractions of school disciplinary codes that he called 'taking no shit'. After that he had been supported by the 'behaviour support service' for excluded pupils but left 'unofficially' before completing the programme. At the time of our conversations, Karl was 'sorting his sen out' after a protracted period of heavy drinking and amphetamine use funded through petty crime. Like a number of the young people, he wasn't living at home, but between his 'mates'' and his 'Nan's' homes. He had been among a large group of boys excluded together from Coalbrook school as the school took measures to improve its image after a poor inspection 'performance'. Karl said he struggled to understand why he couldn't 'do owt right' at school, particularly as other support staff that he came across later saw him in quite a different way from the way in which he felt he was viewed at school:

So when I went to [behaviour support] they said to me...both o' women... they says 'I can't see why your sat 'ere in this room wi' us, cos y' must be one o' nicest lads I've ever sat an' spoke to...Says 'I can't believe any o' this stuff I've read about in your school report. An' I says, 'Well, all depends 'ow y' get tret. That's it. If y' gonna get tret like shit, then your gonna treat them like shit aren't you? (Karl, Coalbrook).

Indeed, he sensed performativity in school as an unidentifiable, malevolent force:

I don't know, it were, like, I 'ad to get away from summat[4] but there were

4. See glossary of local terms (after References)

234

nowt theer. It were like I were tryin' to hide from summat but there were nowt theer to hide from. You know wha' I mean? (Karl, young person, *Go4it!* project, Coalbrook).

This puzzling, constant pressure of hiding from 'summat theer' when there 'were nowt theer to hide from', testifies to the normalising aspect of performativity in Karl's school which, at the time, had the highest level of exclusions in Derbyshire. Karl is plaintively aware of his inability to perform appropriately for the mainstream but internalises it as being difficult to 'handle':

Yeah, I think it would 'ave been better if I could 'ave gone somewhere else, not into a mainstream school. Where I could 'a just sat there, could 'ave done summat wi'like people who knew 'ow to 'andle. It were more because people never used to listen or even if you'd not done nowt [nothing] wrong they used to gi' y' all this an' all that. An' that's what ya used to do more. Used to think, why are ya not listenin' to me? Why bother? (Karl, Coalbrook).

Permanent exclusion was a 'terrible big thing', precipitating him into a downward spiral:

An' that's what got me down as well 'cos I'm thinkin', well, sempt everything were all on top on me... thought on'y way to ger out o' it were jus' take drugs... (Karl).

In his view, all he'd done, in line with the local culture ('it were way I were brought up') was, like many of the other young men and women, to 'fight back at' (Sophie) an urban middle class culture imposed by people 'higher than you' (P-J) who 'like, all come from these, like, posh estates where nowt bad goes off' (Dave) but who have no legitimacy, originate from an elsewhere of 'Chesterfield or Sheffield, or somewhere' (P-J), don't understand the 'old nature' (Cocker) of pit village culture and don't know what it was like to 'live in a shit hole' (Dave).

I think it's because they've come from, say, like a different background to what most people 'ave in Coalbrook as well. To grow up in Coalbrook it is, well, it is a bit rough when you grow up young. When you don't 'ave a lot o' shit y' appreciate shit more, you know worra mean? An' I think it's because they've come from a different area. An' in a different area it's a totally different ball game, innit? (Karl, Coalbrook).

The tortuous reverse symmetry between Christine and Karl and between the staff and the young people generally lies, I would suggest, in this: just as the essentially *classed* thrust of performativity in school excludes working class boys and girls like Karl, Beth, P-J, Lianne, Dave, Sophie, Cocker from its domain – pushing them out under the more directly disciplinary gaze of the 'new architecture of regulation' (Ball, 2008: 41) of CCTV-swept streets and curfewed neighbourhoods – so it generates the very need for projects such as *Go4it!*, *Bus Stop* and the *Cavs Lasses Group*. Yet, as those projects develop and succeed in providing a locally meaningful space in which the young people can get 'back on track', the overflow of performative pressure from the mainstream steadily squeezes the space of ethically driven, community based, semi-formal support provision, requiring 'harder' outcomes – work readiness, measurable 'functional' skills of numeracy and literacy – than it is possible to achieve within the severely time limited programmes. Thus, it jeopardises the *classed* reparative project of the staff, leaving them unable to develop what is effectively a *nascent* critical pedagogic project into anything that might be linked to the resistant histories of the locality.

In my observation of the *Go4it!*, *Move4wards*, *Bus Stop* and the *Cavs Lasses Group* projects, young people invariably thrive in atmospheres of 'relationality' (Smyth, 2010) where the core ethics of those histories are transmitted. Inevitably, though, in small scale, uncertainly professional settings with no structures of collegiality or collective organisation, the sheer pressures of performativity prevent the emergence of any meaningful activist practice (Sachs, 2003 and Avis, 2005). Thus any pedagogic critique of the double dynamic of performativity as it works to both exclude the youngsters and terrorise the staff, remains undeveloped.

Conclusion
We have seen, then, how an ethnographic study of the educational margin in a marginal area reveals a picture of a performative culture steadily but unevenly encroaching from the mainstream sector. Though what has become the 'foundation learning' sector has never been thoroughly professionalised – or, alternatively, comprehensively *de*professionalised as has, say, the further education sector – aspects of performativity are, nevertheless, clearly visible among the informal vigour of such projects as *Go4it!*, *Move4ward*, *Cavs Lasses Group Bus Stop*. The effects of an audit culture of 'outcomes' and 'targets' is plain to see, meets with much resistance, some compliance and generates a mixed group of victims and survivors in its wake. Also evident is a cruelly instrumental funding regime of 'no outcomes, no funding; no funding, no job'. Regulation through formal inspection, meanwhile, is less common than in mainstream settings. However, observation –

'going through the data base' – is a function regularly carried out by more senior managers from county hall and is both welcomed and resented.

Indeed, most of the effects noted by Ball (2008: 52) and others are part of the changed everyday culture of the different types of provision brought together as foundation learning and youth support. Increased pressure, intensification of work, more paperwork, intensified surveillance – all of these are without doubt having an impact on the staff and young people. Changes in social relationships, however, are probably less complete. While there is a vague air of competitiveness creeping into the everyday culture of projects such as those observed here, it is still novel enough to be seen as funny. As to the gap between senior staff and teaching staff noted by Ball (ibid.) the situation in a typical foundation learning project is not really comparable with a school given the a much smaller scale of operations. There is mistrust to be sure, but what is more common – and no doubt healthier in the long run – is an unwillingness to be impressed by 'managers' that is part of the working class culture in which staff grew up. Similarly, local history bequeaths a stubborn refusal to be terrorised by instrumental reminders of 'no funding, no job'. This is, after all, a setting where the collective memory is of uncertain, episodic employment; strikes; lock outs and the wage vicissitudes of the 'butty system'[5]. This brings me to the key point I want to bring out of this discussion.

We'll remember that 'policy rhetorics and discourses', while they are incorporated and fabricated into new subjectivities are '...contested, interpreted and enacted in a variety of arenas of practice and ... inflected, mediated, resisted and misunderstood...' (Ball, 2008: 5,7). That contestation occurs, of course, within specific spatialities/structures of feeling. While cultures in the foundation learning and youth support sector are increasingly performative in character, projects like the ones referred to here, do seem able to avoid the full discursive weight of performativity for a number of contextual reasons. Such projects are, to be sure, short term, small scale, and float around the sectors of the education system because 'nobody wants [them]' (Pat). More importantly, though, in the area of this study at least, they are staffed by a group of locally originating staff who – while they are 'encouraged to think about themselves as individuals ...calculate about themselves, "add value" to themselves, improve their productivity, strive for excellence and live an existence of calculation' (Ball, 2003: 217) – are in the main bound to an unspoken ethical commission with their learners that is both genuine and a defence against the professionalism from which they are still themselves excluded. Indeed, that commission is not part of a professional code

---

5. The traditional payment system in coal mining in this area where by colliers would be paid not directly by the coal company but by the 'butty', a kind of charge hand.

but is more to do with an affective affiliation to 'community' that only makes complete sense in relation to the touchstone of shared collective memory which stands counter to any 'ethical re-tooling' required by performativity.

This ethical dimension, still obdurately drawing on unfashionable practices of solidarity and modernist grand narratives such as social justice, refuses the 'thorough exteriorization of knowledge' noted by Lyotard as a requisite of the post-modern condition (Lyotard 1984: 4). Because of this, working lives in projects like these don't seem so troubled by the 'ontological insecur[ity]' (Ball, 2003: 220) that has been observed elsewhere. The various education and support projects that I've observed over the past five years all seem to retain a place for what Smyth *et.al.* (2000: 140) call the 'primacy of caring relations in work with pupils and colleagues', an affective atmosphere in which many serially excluded young people seem to thrive.

Even if those working in this enclave are prevented by the very drive of performativity from developing fully critical forms of practice, they do manage to stay loyal to pedagogies of social progress through collective care while at the same time 'performing performativity' with, as they say round here, their 'fingers crossed behind their backs'. They respond to performativity neither as 'incorporated', nor 'empowered', nor as 'activist' professionals. And they are certainly not 'post-performative' in Wilkins' (2011) sense. They perform performativity at arm's length without espousing the project of 'resourcing the entitled middle class self'"(Skeggs 2004: 135) that is an inherent part of the professionalism about which they remain ambivalent and which is hard to take seriously when you have uncertain professional status, 'live 'ere' and are rooted in marginal communities with resistant histories. For the time being, they manage to 'do' performativity somehow *alongside their lives*, which are significantly bound to those of the youngsters with whom they work and with whom they have much in common. Their commitment is, therefore, as Christine says, to a 'long haul' reparative project. Quite *how long* they'll be able to work in this way, though – particularly if their practice remains unarticulated to a wider critical pedagogical project – remains to be seen. As youth support becomes incorporated into larger, ever more outcome-driven structures and as these staff find themselves working alongside others from much more thoroughly performative settings in centrally managed multi-agency teams, their room to manoeuvre around the spaces of the margin will inevitably be reduced. Consequently, retaining the powerfully affective commitment to 'benefit[ting] these kids and really improv[ing]' their lives – a principle deeply sedimented in the local culture but increasingly jeopardised by deindustrialisation and deepening economic crisis – will not be easy.

Acknowledgements

The author wishes to acknowledge the help of Derbyshire County Council youth and adult education staff in gaining access to the ethnographic sites referred to in this chapter. He also wishes to record his indebtedness to colleagues at the 2011 Oxford Ethnography Conference for providing feedback on an early draft of this text.

Glossary of local terms

The Model – Specifically the 'colliery model village' housing in Beldover, Coalbrook and Cragwell built by the Beldover or Coalbrook Coal Company in the last decade of the nineteenth century. Sometimes the term is used more broadly to designate a space/place of 'roughness' or potential 'trouble'.

The Cavs – The Cavendish Estate in Beldover. A 'white city' estate of the type built by the National Coal Board in many Derbyshire pit villages after the Second World War. So called because of the white painted prefabricated material from which the houses were built.

Aye – Yes

Gi' – Give

Nowt – Nothing

O' – Of
'ole – Hole, as in 'shit hole'

Owt – Anything

Summat – Something

Theer – There

Wi' – With

Bibliography

Ainley, P. & Bailey, B., (1997) *The Business of Learning.* London: Cassell.

Alexander, B. K., Anderson, G. L., & Gallegos, B. P., (2005) *Performance theories in education; power, pedagogy and the politics of identity*, New Jersey: Lawrence Erlbaum Associates.

Allan, A. and Cullen, F., (2008) Picturing innocence? Innocent pictures? Representation and the use of self directed photography in studies of children's and young people's cultural worlds *ESRC Research Development Initiative Seminar, Advancing the use of visual methods in research on children's cultural worlds*, University of Cardiff 16 April 2008.

Allan, J., Ozga, J. and Smyth, G., (eds.) (2009) *Social Capital, professionalism and Diversity*, Rotterdam: Sense.

Allen, V.L. & van de Vliert, E., (eds.) (1984) *Role Transitions: Explorations and Explanations*, New York: Plenum.

Anderson, B., (2009) Affective atmospheres. *Emotion, Space and Society.* 2: 77-81.

Apple, M. W., (2000) Can Critical Pedagogies interrupt rightist policies?, *Educational Theory, 50* (2): 229-254.

Apple, M. W., (2001) *Educating the "Right" Way: Markets, Standards, God, and Inequality*, York: RoutledgeFalmer.

Apple, M.W., (2001) Comparing neo-liberal projects and inequality in education, *Comparative Education*, 37(4): 409-423.

Archer, M., (1995) *Realist social theory: The morphogenetic approach*, Cambridge: Cambridge University Press.

Archer, M., (2000) *Being human: The problem of agency*, Cambridge: Cambridge University Press.

Arnot, M., and Reay, D., (2007) A sociology of pedagogic voice: Power, inequality and pupil consultation. *Discourse: Studies in the Cultural Politics of Education,* 28(3): 311–25.

Atkinson, P., Coffey, A., Delamont, S., Lofland, J. and Lofland, L., (2001) Editorial Introduction, in P. Atkinson, A. Coffey, S. Delamont, J. Lofland and L. Lofland. (eds.) *Handbook of ethnography,* London: Sage.

Austin, J.L., (1962) *How to do things with words*, Oxford: Oxford University Press.

Avis, J., (2002) Imaginary Friends: managerialism, globalization and post-compulsory education and training in England. *Discourse: studies in the cultural politics of education,* 23 (1): 75-90.

Avis, J., (2003) Rethinking trust in a performative culture: the case of education, *Journal of Education Policy,* (3): 332.

Avis, J., (2005) Beyond performativity: reflections on activist professionalism and the labour process in further education, *Journal of Education Policy*, 20(2): 209-222.

Avis, J., (2006) From reproduction to learning cultures: post-compulsory education in England, *British Journal of Sociology of Education* 27 (3): 341-354.

Avis, J., (2009) *Education, Policy and Social Justice*, London: Continuum.

Bagley, C., (2006) School choice and competition: A public market revisited. *Oxford Review of Education*, 32(3): 347-362.

Bailey, B., (2007) The establishment of centres for the training of teachers in technical and further education in England, 1933-1950. *Journal of Vocational Education and Training*, 59 (3): 279-294.

Ball, D., (1972) Self and identity in the context of deviance: The case of criminal abortion, in R. A. Scott, & J. D. Douglas, (eds.) *Theoretical perspectives on deviance.* New York, Basic Books).

Ball, S., (1990) Introducing Monsieur Foucault, in Ball, S., (ed.) *Foucault and education: disciplines and knowledge,* London: Routledge.

Ball, S., (1997) Good school/bad school: paradox and fabrication. *British Journal of the Sociology of Education,* (3): 317-336.

Ball, S., (1998) Big policies/small world: An introduction to international perspectives in education policy. *Comparative Education,* 34(2)**,** 119-130.

Ball, S. J., (1993) Education markets, choice and social class: The market as a class strategy in the UK and the USA. *British Journal of Sociology of Education,* 14(1): 3-19.

Ball, S.J., (1994) *Education reform: a critical and post-structural approach,* Milton Keynes: OUP.

Ball, S.J., (1999) 'Global trends in educational reform and the struggle for the soul of the teacher!' paper presented at the British Educational Research Association Annual Conference, University of Sussex at Brighton, September 2-5.

Ball, S. J., (1998) Performativity and fragmentation in 'postmodern' schooling in *Postmodernity and the fragmentation of welfare,* J. Carter (ed.) 187-203. London: Routledge.

Ball, S., (2001) Performativities and fabrications in the education economy: towards the performative society, in Gleeson, D. and Husbands, C., (eds.), *The performing school: managing teaching and learning in a performance culture,* London: RoutledgeFalmer.

Ball, S. J., (2000) Performativities and fabrications in the education economy: Towards the performative society? *Australian Educational Researcher.* 27(2): 1-23.

Ball, S. J., (2001) Grandes politicas, un mundo pequeno. Introduccion a una perspectiva internacional en las politicas educativas. in *Neuvas tendencias en politicas educativas: Alternativas para le escuela publica,* . M. Andrada, M. Narodowski and M. Nores, 103-128. Buenos Aires: Granica.

Ball, S. J., (2001) Performativities and fabrications in the education economy: Towards the performance society, in Gleeson, D. and Husbands, C., (eds.) *The Performing School: Managing Teaching and Learning in a Performance Context*, London: RoutledgeFalmer.

Ball, S. J., (2003) 'The teacher's soul and the terrors of performativity', *Journal of Education Policy*, 18 (2), 215-228.

Ball, S.J., (1994) *Education reform: a critical and post-structural approach*, Milton Keynes: OUP.

Ball, S. J., (2008) *The Education Debate*. Bristol: Policy Press.

Ball, S. J., (2009) The governance turn: (Editorial). *Journal of Education Policy*, 24(5): 537-538.

Ball, S.J., (1999) 'Global trends in educational reform and the struggle for the soul of the teacher!', paper presented at the British Educational Research Association Annual Conference, University of Sussex at Brighton, September 2-5.

Bassey, M., (1999) *Case Study Research in Educational Settings*, Buckingham PA: Open University Press.

Bathmaker, A. M., (2001) Neither Dupes Nor Devils: Teachers' Constructions of their Changing Role in Further Education. *Paper presented at Conference of the Learning and Skills Research Network*, Robinson College, Cambridge: 5-7 December.

Bauman, Z., (2001) *Community: seeking safety in an insecure world*, Cambridge: Polity Press.

Beach, D. & Dovemark, M., (2007) *Education and the commodity problem*, London: Tufnell.

Beatty, C., Fothergill, S. and Powell, R., (2005) *Twenty years on: Has the economy of the coalfields recovered?* Sheffield: Sheffield Hallam University.

Becher, T. and Trowler, P., (2001) *Academic tribes and territories: Intellectual enquiry and the culture of disciplines*, Buckingham: SRHE and OUP.

Beck, Ulrich., (1992) Risk society: Towards a new modernity. London: Sage

Bennett, K., Beynon, H. and Hudson, R., (2000) *Coalfields regeneration: dealing with the consequences of industrial decline*. Policy Press: Coalfields Community Foundation.

Bentham, J., (1787) *Panopticon: or, The Inspection-house*, Dublin Thomas Byrne.

Bernauer, J. and Rasmussen, D., (1988) *The final Foucault*, Cambridge: MIT Press.

Bernstein, B., (1971) On the classification and framing of educational knowledge, in M. F. D. Young (ed.) *Knowledge and control: New directions for the sociology of education.* London: Collier Macmillan), 47-69.

Bernstein, B., (1996) *Pedagogy, symbolic control and identity; theory, research, critique*, (London: Taylor and Francis).

Bhabha, H. (1994) *The location of culture.* London: Routledge.

Biesta, G.J.J., (2004) Education, accountability and the ethical demand: Can the democratic potential of accountability be regained? *Educational Theory,* 54(3): 233-250.

Biesta, G.J.J., (2006) *Beyond learning: democratic education for a human future,* London: Paradigm Publishers.

Biesta, G., (2009) Good education: what it is and why we need it, *Inaugural lecture 4 March 2009,* Institute of Education.

Biesta, G.J.J., (2010) *Good education in an age of measurement: Ethics, politics, democracy,* London: Paradigm Publishers.

Biesta, G.J.J & Tedder, M., (2006) *How is agency possible? Towards an ecological understanding of agency-as-achievement. Working paper 5,* Exeter: The Learning Lives project.

Biesta, G.J.J. & Tedder, M., (2007) Agency and learning in the lifecourse: Towards an ecological perspective, *Studies in the Education of Adults,* 39: 132-149.

Blackmore, J. and Sachs, J., (1997) Worried, weary and just plain worn out: gender, restructuring and the psychic economy of higher education. Paper presented at the AARE Annual Conference, Brisbane.

Blatchford, P., Russell, A., Bassett, P., Brown, P. and Martin, C., (2007) 'The role and effects of teaching assistants in English primary schools (Years 4-6) 2000-2003. Results from the Class size and pupil-adult ratios (CSPAR) KS2 project' in *British Educational Research Journal* 33 (1): 5-26.

Blumer, H., (1969) *Symbolic Interactionism: Perspective and Method,* Berkley: University of California Press.

Bottery, M. and Wright, N., (2000) *Teachers and the state: towards a directed profession,* London: Routledge.

Bottery, M., (2003) The leadership of learning communities in a culture of unhappiness. Paper given to the ESRC Seminar Series *Challenging the orthodoxy of school leadership: Towards a new theoretical perspective,* National College for School Leadership, UK.

Bourdieu, P. and C, J.C., (1977) *Reproduction in education: Society and culture,* London: Sage.

Bourdieu, P., (1977) *Outline of a theory of practice,* Cambridge: Cambridge University Press.

Bourdieu, P., (1986) Forms of capital, in Richardson, J.G., (ed.) *Handbook of Theory and Research for the Sociology of Education,* New York: Greenwood Press.

Bourdieu, P., (1990) *The logic of practice,* Cambridge: Polity Press.

Bourdieu, P., (1998) *Acts of Resistance: Against the new myths of our time,* tr. Richard Nice, Cambridge: Polity Press.

Bourdieu, P., (2001) *Practical reason,* Cambridge: Polity Press.

Bowe, R., Ball, S.J. with Gold, A. (1992) *Reforming Education and Changing Schools: Case Studies in Policy Sociology,* London: Routledge.

Boyd, B. & Norris, F., (2006) From development to improvement – a step too far? The evolving contribution of Quality Improvement Officers to the school improvement agenda in Scottish local authorities, *Scottish Educational Review,* 38(2): 213-224.

Bragg, S., (2010) 'student voice' and governmentality: The production of enterprising subjects. *Discourse: Studies in the Cultural Politics of Education,* 28(3): 343-358.

Brain, I. & Comerford-Boyes, L., (2006) Teachers as mediators between educational policy and practice. *Educational Studies,* 32(4), 411-423.

Brehony, K., (2005) Primary schooling under New Labour; the irresolvable contradiction between excellence and enjoyment. *Oxford Review of Education.* 31(1): 29-46.

Brennan, T., (2004) *The transmission of affect.* Ithaca and London: Cornell University Press.

Bright, N. G., (2010) 'Just doing stuff'? Place, memory and school disaffection in a former UK coal-mining area. *International Journal on School Disaffection.* 7(1): 44-52.

Bright, N.G., (2011a) 'Off The Model': Resistant spaces, school disaffection and 'aspiration' in a former coal-mining community. *Children's Geographies.* 9(1): 63-71.

Bright, N.G., (2011b) 'Non- Servile Virtuosi' in insubordinate spaces: School disaffection, refusal and resistance in a former English coalfield. *European Education Research Journal.* (4).

Bright, N.G.,(2012) 'Sticking together!'- Policy activism from within a UK former coal-mining community. *Journal of Educational Administration and History.* (Forthcoming)

Bubb, S. and Earley, P., (2010) *Helping Staff Develop in Schools.* London: Sage Publications.

Buckingham, D. & Jones, K., (2001) New labour's cultural turn: Some tensions in comtemporary educational and cultural policy. *Journal of Education Policy,* 16(1): 1-14.

Bulmer, M., (1975). Sociological models of the mining community. *Sociological Review.* 23.

Burchell, G., (1996) Liberal government and techniques of the self, in A. Barry, T. Osborne & N. Rose (eds.) *Foucault and political reason; liberalism, neoliberalism and rationalities of government.* London: UCL Press, 19-36.

Burnard, P. and White, J., (2008) 'Creativity and performativity: counterpoints in British and Australian education', *British Educational Research Journal,* 34 (5): 667-682.

Burns, J., (2000) *'Improvement through inspection'? An investigation of teachers' perceptions of OfSTED as a vehicle of improvement*, Oakhill, Staffs: University of Central England.

Busher, H., (2006) *Understanding educational leadership: People, power and culture*, Buckingham: Open University Press.

Busher, H., (2007) Contestation and hope: the control of teachers' practices as a site of colonial struggle, *'Developing theory in organisational research and practice in educational settings'*, Bath: University of Bath, 13th-14[th]June 2007.

Busher, H. and Cremin, H., (2009) Using participants' photo-narratives to elicit their perspectives on social interactions in schools. Paper given at *1st International Visual methods Conference*, Leeds, UK: Leeds, September 2009.

Busher, H., Lawson, T.,Wilkins, C., Acun, I., (2011) Pedagogy, empowerment and discipline: comparative perspectives of novice teachers in England and Turkey reflecting on 'the other' *Compare* (3), DOI: 10.1080/03057925.2011.552905.

Butler, J., (1990) *Gender trouble: Feminism and the subversion of identity*, New York, Routledge.

Butler, J., (1993) *Bodies That matter: on the discursive limits of 'sex'*, London: Routledge.

Butler, J., (1997) *The psychic life of power*, Stanford, California: Stanford University Press.

Byrom, T., Thomson, P., and Gates, P., (2007) 'My school has been quite pushy about the Oxbridge thing': voice and choice of higher education *Improving Schools* 10 (1) 29–40.

Carr, D., (2005) Personal and interpersonal relationships in education and teaching: a virtue ethical perspective, *British Journal of Educational Studies, 53*(3): 255-271.

Carr, W. and Hartnett, A., (1996) *Education and the struggle for democracy: the politics of educational ideas*, Keynes: Open University Press.

Casey, C., (1995) *Work, Self and Society after Industrialism*. London: Routledge.

Clandinin, J. and Connelly, M., (eds.) (1995) *Teachers' Professional Knowledge Landscapes*, New York: Teacher.

Castanheira, M. L., Crawford, T., Dixon, C. N., & Green, J. L., (2001) Interactional Ethnography: An Approach to Studying the Social Construction of Literate Practices. *Linguistics and Education,* 11(4): 353-400.

Cerulo, K. A., (1997) Identity construction: New issues, new directions. *Annual Review of Sociology,* 23: 385-409.

Chapman, C., (2002) OfSTED and school improvement: teachers' perceptions of the inspection process in schools facing challenging circumstances, *School Leadership and Management,* 22(3): 257-272.

Charmaz, K., (1996) Foreword. in Prus., R. (ed.), *Symbolic Interaction and*

Ethnographic Research: Intersubjectivity and the Study of Human Lived Experience, Albany: State of New York University Press.

Charon, J., (1995) *Symbolic Interactionism: An Introduction, An Interpretation, An Integration,* London: Prentice Hall.

Citizenship Foundation (1997) *Citizenship and civic education,* London: Citizenship Foundation.

Cleaver, E., Ireland, E., Kerr, D., & Lopes, J., (2005) citizenship education *Longitudinal Study: Second Cross-Sectional Survey 2004. Listening to Young People: citizenship education in England* (No. DfES Research Report 626). London: DfES.

Clow, R., (2001*)* Education Teachers' Constructions of Professionalism, *Journal of Vocational Education and Training,* 53 (3): 407-419.

Coffey, A., (2001) *Education and social change,* Buckingham: Open University Press.

Coffield, F., Edward, S., Finlay, I., Hodgson, A., Spours, K. and Steer, R., (2008) *Improving Learning, Skills and Inclusion: The impact of policy on post-compulsory education,* London: Routledge.

Cohen, L., Manion, L., & Morrison, K., (2000) *Research Methods in Education,* London and New York: RoutledgeFalmer.

Colley, H., (2006) From childcare practitioner to FE tutor: biography, identity and lifelong learning, in C. Leathwood and B. Francis (eds.) *Gender and Lifelong Learning: Critical Feminist Engagements,* London: RoutledgeFalmer.

Colley, H., James, D. and Diment, K. (2007) Unbecoming teachers: towards a more dynamic notion of professional participation, *Journal of Education Policy* Vol. 22, (2): 173–193.

Cooper, B., (2002) *Teachers as Moral Models? The Role of Empathy in Relationships Between Pupils and Their Teachers,* Thesis (PhD), Leeds Metropolitan University.

Cowie, M., Taylor, D. & Croxford, L., (2007) 'Tough, Intelligent Accountability' in Scottish Secondary Schools and the role of Standard Tables and Charts (STACS): A Critical Appraisal, *Scottish Educational Review,* 39(1): 29-50.

Croghan, R., Griffin, C., Hunter, J. & Phoenix, A., (2008) Young people's construction of self: Notes of the use and analysis of the photo-elicitation methods, *International Journal of Social Research Methodology,* 11 (4): 345-356.

Dale, R., (2009) Introduction, in Dale, R. & Robertson, S., (eds.) *Globalisation and Europeanisation in Education.* Oxford: Symposium Books.

Davies, I., (1999) What has happened in the teaching of Politics in schools in England in the last three decades, and why? *Oxford Review of Education,* 25(1&2): 125-140.

Day, C., Stobart, G., Sammons, P., Kington, A., Gu, Q., Smees, R., and Mutjaba, T., (2006a) *Variations in Teachers' work, lives and effectiveness (VITAE) Research Brief No: RB743,* London: DfES.

Day, C., Kington, A., Gu, Q. and Sammons, P., (2005) The Role of Identity in Variations in Teachers' Work, Lives and Effectiveness. Paper presented as part of a TLRP Seminar Series.

Day, C., Kington, A., Stobart, G. and Sammons, P. (2006b) The Personal and Professional Selves of the Teachers: Stable and Unstable Identities. *British Educational Research Journal* 32(4): 601-616.

DCSF (2008) *Working Together: Listening to the voices of children and young people,* London: DCSF (http://publications.education.gov.uk/ eOrderingDownload/DCSF-00410-2008.pdf) [accessed 30 Aug2010]

DCSF, (2007) *School workforce in England,* HMSO: London. http://www.dfes. gov.uk/rsgateway/DB/SFR/s000743/SFR29_2007v3.pdf. Visited 28.4.08.

De Wolf, I.F. and Janssens, F.D.J., (2007) Effects and side effects of inspections and accountability in education: an overview of empirical studies. *Oxford Review of Education,* 33(3): 379-396).

Deakin C. R., Coates, M., Taylor, M., and Ritchie, S., (2004) A systematic review of the impact of citizenship education on the provision of schooling, in *Research Evidence in Education,* London: EPPI-Centre, Social Science Research Unit, Institute of Education.

Dean, M., (1999) *Governmentality: Power and Rule in Modern Society,* London: Sage.

Demetriou, H. and Wilson, E., (2010) Children should be seen and heard: The power of student voice in sustaining new teachers *Improving Schools* 13 (1).

Dennis, A. & Martin, J. V., (2005) Symbolic interactionism and the concept of power. *British Journal of Sociology,* 56(2): 191-213.

Dennis, N., Henriques, F. and Slaughter, C., (1956) *Coal is our life.* London; Eyre and Spottiswood (2nd edn 1969), London: Tavistock.

Denzin, N., (1989) *Interpretative interactionism,* London: Sage.

Department for Education (DfE) (1992) The New Requirements for Initial Teacher Training (Circular 9/92), London: DfE.

DfE, Department for Education (1993) The Initial Training of Primary School Teachers. London: DfE.

DfE, Department for Education, (2010) *The Importance of Teaching. The Schools White Paper 2010,* London: The Stationery Office.

DfE, (2011) *Teachers' standards, effective from 1 September 2012,* https://www.education.gov.uk/publications/eOrderingDownload/teachers%20 standards.pdf. Visited 22.08.11.

DfEE (2005) *Higher standards, better schools for all.* Report for HMSO Norwich.

Derber, C., (1983) Managing professionals: Ideological proletarianization and post industrial labour, *Theory and Society,* 12 (2): 309-341.

Devine, J., (1996). *Maximum Security: The Culture of Violence in Inner-City Schools,* Chicago, The University of Chicago Press.

DfES, Department of Education and Science, (1984) *Initial Teacher Training: Approval of Courses (Circular 3/84),* London: DES.

DfES, Department of Education and Science, (1989) *Initial Teacher Training: Approval of Courses (Circular 24/89),* London: DfES.

DfES, (2003) *Time for standards – raising standards and tackling workload: a national agreement,* London: DfES.

Donaldson, G., (2011) *Teaching Scotland's Future (Review of Teacher Education in Scotland),* Edinburgh: The Scottish Government.

Dreyfus, H. L. & Rabinow, P., (1982) *Michel Foucault: Beyond structuralism and hermeneutics,* Chicago, University of Chicago Press.

Du Gay, P., (ed.) (1997) *Production of culture/cultures of production,* London: Sage.

Duffy, B., (1999) Analysis of documentary evidence, in Bell J., (ed.) *Doing Your research project: a guide for first time researchers in education and social science,* Buckingham: OUP.

Duffy, M., (2005) Friday forum: inspection, *Times Educational Supplement,* (22 April).

Dwyer, P.J., (1995) "Foucault, docile bodies and post-compulsory education in Australia", *British Journal of the Sociology of Education,* 16(4): 467-477.

Earley, P., (1998) *School improvement after inspection? School and LEA responses,* London: Paul Chapman.

Edmond, N., (2003) 'School-based Learning: constraints and limitations in learning from school experience for teaching assistants', *Journal of Education for Teaching,* 29 (4): 113-123.

Educational Management Administration & Leadership. 37: 67-85.

Edwards, R. Nicoll, K. and Tait, A., (Migrating metaphors: the globalisation of flexibility in policy Journal of Education Policy 17: 353-65.

Elliott, G., (1996) Educational management and the crisis of reform in further Education, *Journal of Vocational Education and Training,* 48 (1): 5-23.

Elliott, J., (2001) Characteristics of performative cultures: their central paradoxes and limitations as resources for educational reform, in Gleeson, D. and Husbands, C., (eds.), *The performing school: managing teaching and learning in a performance culture,* London: RoutledgeFalmer.

Ellis, V., McNicholl, J. and Pendry, A., (2011a) *Institutional conceptualisations of the work of teacher education in England. Final Report,* Department of Education: University of Oxford.

Ellis, V., Blake, A., McNicholl, J. and McNally, J., (2011b) *The Work of Teacher Education. Final Research Report,* Bristol: The Higher Education Academy, Subject Centre for Education ESCalate.

Emirbayer, M. & Mische, A., (1998) What is agency? *The American Journal of Sociology,* 103: 962-1023.

Evans, J. and Penney, D., (1994) 'Whatever Happened to Good Advice? Service and Inspection after the Education Reform Act', *British Educational Research Journal*, 20 (5): 519-533.

Evetts, J., (2005) The management of professionalism: A contemporary paradox, paper presented at the *ESRC C-TRIP Seminar Series*, City, 19 October.

Fazzaro, C. J., & Walter, J. E., (2002) Schools for democracy: Lyotard, dissensus and educational policy, *International Journal of Leadership in Education*, 5(1): 15-32.

Fentress, J. and Wickham, C., (1992) *Social memory*. Oxford: Blackwell.

Fielding, M. (2008) Personalisation, education and the totalitarianism of the market. *Soundings*.

Fielding, M., (2004) Transformative approaches to student voice: Theoretical underpinnings, recalcitrant realities, *British Educational Research Journal*, 30(2) 295 - 310.

Flick, U., (2009) *An introduction to Qualitative research 4th Edn*, London: Sage

Flutter, J. and Rudduck, J., (2004) *How to improve your school: Giving pupils a voice*, London: Continuum Books.

Flyvbjerg, B., (2006) Five Misunderstandings About Case-Study Research, *Qualitative Inquiry*, 12 (2): 219-245.

Foucault, M., (1963) *The birth of the clinic: an archaeology of medical perception*, London: Routledge.

Foucault, M., (1972), *The archaeology of knowledge*, London: Routledge.

Foucault, M., (1976) Truth and Power, in Gordon, C., (ed) (1980) *Power / Knowledge: Selected interviews and other writings by Michel Foucault, 1972-1977*, New York: Pantheon Books.

Foucault, M., (1977) *Discipline and Punish: The Birth of the Prison, trans. A. Sheridan*, London: Allen Lane.

Foucault, M., (1977) *Discipline and punish: The birth of the prison*, London: Penguin.

Foucault, M., (1979a) Governmentality. *Ideology and Consciousness* (Autumn): 5-21.

Foucault, M., (1979b) *Discipline and punish*, trans. Allen Lane, Penguin.

Foucault, M., (ed.) (1980) *Power/knowledge: Selected interviews and other writings*, New York, Pantheon.

Foucault, M., (1986) Disciplinary power and subjection, in Lukes, S., (ed) (1986) *Power*, Oxford: Blackwell.

Foucault, M., (2000) Technologies of the self, in Rabinow, P., (ed.) *Michel Foucault*. London: Penguin, 223-51.

Frazer, E., (1999) Introduction: The idea of political education, *Oxford Review of Education*, 25(1&2): 5-22.

Freire, P., (2005) *Pedagogy of the Oppressed*, New York; London: Continuum.

Fuchs, S. (2001) Beyond agency, *Sociological Theory*, 19: 24-40.

Fullan, M., (2003) *Change Forces with a Vengeance*, London: RoutledgeFalmer.

Furlong J., (2001) 'Reforming teacher education, re-forming teachers: accountability, professionalism and competence' in Phillips, R. and Furlong, J., (eds) *Education, reform and the state: twenty-five years of politics, policy and practice*, London: Routledge/Falmer.

Furlong, J. and Smith R., (eds.) (1996) *The Role of Higher Education in Initial Teacher Training*, London: Kogan Page.

Furlong, J., Whitty, G., Whiting, C., Miles, S., Barton, L. and Barrett, E., (1996) Re-defining partnership: Revolution or reform in initial teacher education? *Journal of Education for Teaching*, 22(1): 39–55.

Gardner, J., (2011) Educational research: What (a) to do about impact! *British Educational Research Journal*, (4): 543-561.

Garfinkel, H., (1967) *Studies in ethnomethodology*, Englewood Cliffs NY, Prentice-Hall.

Garland, I., (2008) Workforce reform: exploring the boundaries between teacher and assistant roles, Thesis (PhD) University of Sheffield.

Garland, I. & Garland, P., (2009) Performativity and the roles of teachers and teaching assistants, paper presented at the *British Education Research Association Conference*, City, September.

Geertz, C., (1973) *The interpretation of cultures: Selected essays by Clifford Geertz*, New York, Basic Books.

Gewirtz, S., (1997) Post-welfarism and the reconstruction of teachers' work in the UK, *Journal of Education Policy*, 12(4): 217-231.

Gewirtz, S., (2002) The *Managerial School*: post-welfarism and social justice in education, London: Routledge.

Gewitz, S. and Ball, S., (2000) From 'welfarism' to 'new managerialism': shifting discourses of school leadership in the education market place. *Discourse*, 21(3): 253-267.

Giddens, A., (1984) *The constitution of society,* Cambridge: Polity Press.

Giddens, A., (1991) *Modernity and self-identity. Self and society in the late modern age.* Cambridge: Polity Press.

Gillborn, D., and Youdell, D., (2000) *Rationing education: policy, practice, reform, and equity*, Buckingham, Open University Press.

Gillies, D., (2008) Developing governmentality: Conduct3 and education policy. *Journal of Education Policy*, 23(4): 415-427.

Gilroy, P. and McNamara, O. (2009) A critical history of research assessment in the United Kingdom and its post-1992 impact on education, *Journal of Education for Teaching*, 35(4): 321-335.

Glaser, B. G. & Strauss, A., (1967) *The discovery of grounded theory*, Chicago, Aldine.

Gleeson, D. & Gunter, H., (2001) The performing school and the modernisation of teachers, in Gleeson D. & Husbands C. (eds.), *The performing school: Managing, teaching and learning in a performance culture* (139-158), London: RoutledgeFalmer.

Gleeson, D. & Shain, F., (1999) Managing ambiguity: Between markets and managerialism – a case study of 'middle' managers in further education, *The Sociological Review*, 47(3): 461-490.

Gleeson, D., Davies, J. and Wheeler, E., (2005) On the making and taking of professionalism in the further education workplace, *British Journal of Sociology of Education*, (4) 445-460.

Gleeson, D., and Husbands, C., (eds.) (2001). *The Performing School: Managing, Teaching and Learning in a Performance Culture*, London: RoutledgeFalmer.

Gleeson, D. and James, D., (2007) The paradox of professionalism in English Further Education: a TLC project perspective, *Educational Review*, 59(4): 451-467.

Gleeson, D. and Knight, D., (2006) *Challenging Dualism: Public Professionalism in 'Troubled' times*, Sociology, 40 (2):277-295.

Gleeson, D. and Shain, F., (1999) Managing ambiguity: between markets and managerialism—a case study of middle managers in further education, *The Sociological Review*, 47(3): 461-90.

Goffman, E., (1959) *The presentation of self in everyday life*, London: Penguin.

Goffman, E., (1991) *Asylums: Essays on the Social Situation of Mental Patients and Other Inmates*, Harmondsworth: Penguin.

Goffman, I., (1983) The interaction order. *American Sociological Review*, 48(1): 1-17.

Gold, A. & Evans, J., (1998) *Reflecting on school management*, London: Falmer.

Goodlad, J. (1994) *Educational Renewal. Better Teachers, Better Schools*, San Francisco: Jossey-Bass.

Goodson, I. F., (2003) *Professional Knowledge, Professional Lives: Studies in education and change*, Maidenhead: Open University Press.

Goodson, I. F. & Ulf Numan, U., (2002) Teacher's Life Worlds, Agency and Policy Contexts, *Teachers and Teaching*, 8(3): 269-277.

Gore, T., Fothergill, S., Hollywood, E., Lindsay, C., Morgan, K., Powell, R. and Upton, S., (2007) *Coalfields and neighbouring cities: Economic regeneration, labour markets and governance*. York: JRF.

Greenbank, P., (2003) The role of values in Educational research: The case for reflexivity *British Educational Research Journal* 29(6) 791-801.

Gregg, M. and Seigworth, G.J., (eds) *The affect theory reader*. Durham and London: Duke University Press.

Griffin, A.R., (1962) *The miners of Nottinghamshire 1914-1944*. London: George Allen and Unwin.

Griffiths, M., (1993) Self-identity and self esteem: Achieving equality in education. *Oxford Review of Education,* 19(3): 301-317.

Grossberg, L., (2010). Affect's future: Rediscovering the virtual in the actual. in *The affect theory reader,* eds. G. J. Seigworth & M. Gregg, 309-338. Durham and London: Duke University Press.

Hall, H. and Noyes, A., (2009) New regimes of truth: The impact of performative school self evaluation systems on teachers' professional identities *Teaching and Teacher Education,* 25(6) 850-856.

Hamilton, L., (2002) Constructing pupil identity: Personhood and ability. *British Educational Research Journal,* 28(4): 591-602.

Hammersley, M., (1990) *Classroom Ethnography,* Buckingham: Open University Press.

Hammersley, M., (2006) 'Ethnography: problems and prospects', *Ethnography and Education* 1(1): 3-14.

Hanson, F. A., (1993) *Testing testing: Social consquences of he examined life,* Berkeley, CA, University of California Press.

Hardt, M., (2007) Foreword: What affects are good for, in *The affective turn: Theorising the social,* P. Clough, (ed.) and London: Duke University Press.

Hargreaves, A., (1994) *Changing teachers, changing times- teacher's work and culture in the postmodern age,* London: Cassell.

Hargreaves, A., (2000) The four ages of professionalism and professional learning. *Teachers and Teaching* 6(2): 152-182.

Hargreaves, D. H., (1972) *Interpersonal Relations and Education,* London: Routledge and Kegan Paul.

Harland, J., (1996) Evaluation as realpolitik, in Scott, D. and Usher , R., (eds.) *Understanding educational research,* London: Routledge.

Harre, A., (1998) *The singular self: An introduction to the psychology of personhood,* London: Sage.

Harris, A. & Ranson, S., (2005) The contradictions of educational policy: Disadvantage and achievement. *British Educational Research Journal,* 31(5): 571-587.

Harrison, J. and McKeon, F., (2008) The formal and situated learning of beginning teacher educators in England: Identifying characteristics for successful induction in the transition from workplace in schools to workplace in higher education, *European Education of Teacher Education,* (2):151-168.

Hartley, D., (2007) Personalisation: The emerging 'revised' code of education? *Oxford Review of Education,* 33(5): 629-642.

Hartley, D., (2008) Personalisation: The nostalgic revival of child-centered education? *Journal of Education Policy.*

Helsby G., (1999) *Changing teachers work*, Buckingham: Open University Press.

Herzberg, F., (1971) Motivation-hygiene theory, in D. Pugh (ed.) *Organization theory*. Harmondsworth, Penguin.

Higher Education Funding Council for England, (HEFCE) (2008) *Sub-panel 45 Education Subject Overview Report*.

Higher Education Funding Council for England, (HEFCE) (2011) *Assessment framework and guidance on submissions*, http://www.hefce.ac.uk/research/ref/pubs/2011/02_11/ [Accessed 1 November 2011].

Hillier, Y., (2006) *Everything You Need to Know about FE Policy*, London: Continuum.

HMIe, (2002). *How good is our school? Self-evaluation using quality indicators*. Edinburgh: HMIe.

HMIe, (2006) *The journey to excellence, parts 1 & 2*, Edinburgh: HMIe.

HMIe, (2007) *How good is our school? The journey to excellence, part 3*, Edinburgh: HMIe.

Holden, C., (2004) 'Heaven help the teachers!' Parents' perspectives on the introduction of education for citizenship, *Educational Review, 56*(3): 247-258.

Holliday, A., (1999) Small cultures. *Applied Linguistics, 20*(2): 237-264.

Hollis, M., (1994) *The Philosophy of Social Science: An Introduction*, Cambridge: Cambridge University Press.

Hollstein, J.A. and Gubrium, F., (2005) Interpretive practice and social action. in. *The Sage handbook of qualitative research; Third edition,* . N.K. (eds) and Lincoln, Y.S 483-505. London and Thousand Oaks: Sage.

Hollstein, J. A and Gubrium, J.F., Interpretive practice and social action, in Denzin, N. K. and Lincoln, Y. S., (eds) (2005) *The Sage handbook of qualitative research*, London: Sage.

Howells, R., (2003) *Visual cultures*, Cambridge: Polity Press.

Hoyle, E., (1981) Management and the school, Block 3, *E323 Management Processes in Schools*, Milton Keynes: Open University Press.

Hulme, M. and Menter, I., (2008) Research Briefing No 49: *Learning to teach in post-devolution UK: ESRC Teaching and Learning Research Programme*, Swindon: ESRC.

Hulme, M. and Sangster, P., (In Press) Challenges of research(er) development in University Schools of Education: A Scottish case, *Journal of Further and Higher Education*.

Hunter, I., (1994) *Rethinking the school: subjectivity, bureaucracy, criticism,* St Leonards, Allen Unwin.

Ireland, E., Kerr, D., Lopes, J., Nelson, J., & Cleaver, E., (2006) *Active Citizenship and Young People: Opportunities, Experiences and Challenges In and Beyond School. citizenship education Longitudinal Study: Fourth Annual Report* (No.

DfES Research Report 732), London: DfES.

James, N. and Busher, H., (2006) Credibility, authenticity and voice: dilemmas in online interviewing *Qualitative Research* 6(3): 403-420.

James, N. and Busher, H., (2009) *Online Interviewing*, London: Sage

Jeffrey, B., (1999) Distancing research objects through the involvement of the self, in A.W. Massey, G. Walford (ed.) *Studies in educational ethnography: Explorations in ethnography.* (vol. 2) Stamford Connecticut, Jai Press: 163-182.

Jeffrey, B., (2002) 'Performativity and changing teacher relations', *Journal of Education Policy,* 17(5): 531-546.

Jeffrey, B. (2007) 'Creative Learning in Europe: Making use of global discourses', Cremin, T., and Burnard, P., (Eds.) (2007) *Creative Learning 3-11 and how we document it.* Stoke-on-Trent, Trentham: 35-42.

Jeffrey, B., (2008) Creative learner identities. *Education 3-13, 36*(3): 253-264.

Jeffrey, B. & Troman, G., (2004) Time for ethnography. *British Journal of Educational Research,* 30(4): 535-548.

Jeffrey, B. & Troman, G., (2009) Creativity and performativity practices in primary schools: A Foucauldian perspective. Paper presented at the British Educational Research Conference, City University, September 2009.

Jeffrey, B., Troman, G., The Embracing Performative Institution, *Journal of Organisational Ethnography* Vol.1 (2).

Jeffrey, B. & Woods, P., (1998) *Testing teachers: the effect of school inspection on primary teachers,* London: Falmer Press.

Jeffrey, B. & Woods, P., (2009) *Creative learning in the primary school,* London: Routledge.

Jessop, B., (1998) The narrative of enterprise and he enterprise of narrative: Place marketing and the entrepreneurial city, in T. Hall and P. Hubbard (eds.) *The entrepreneurial city: Geographies of politics, regime and representation.* Chichester, John Wiley.

Jones, K., (2001) Travelling policy/local spaces: Culture, creativity and interference. *Education and Social Justice,* 3(3): 2-9.

Jones, K. (2005) Remaking education in Western Europe. *European Education Research Journal,* 4(3): 228-242.

Jones, K., (2010) 'Crisis, what crisis?', *Journal of Education Policy,* 25 (6): 793 -798.

Kakos, M., (2008) *The interaction between students and teachers,* Thesis (PhD), University of York.

Kamanka, E., (1982) (ed). *Community as a social ideal.* London: Arnold.

Kearney, C., (2003) *The Monkey's mask: Identity, memory, narrative and voice,* Stoke-on-Trent, Trentham Books.

Keating, A., Kerr, D., Lopes, J., Featherstone, G., & Benton, T., (2009) *Embedding citizenship education in Secondary Schools in England (2002-08): citizenship education Longitudinal Study Seventh Annual Report* (No. DCSF

Research Report 172). London: DCSF.

Keddie, A., Mills, M. & Pendergast, D., (2011) Fabricating and identity in neo-liberal times: Performing schooling as 'number one', *Oxford Review of Education*, 37(1): 75-92.

Keep, E., (2006) State control of the English education and training system—playing with the biggest train set in the world, *Journal of Vocational Education and Training*, 58 (1): 47-64.

Kennedy, H., (1997) *Learning Works: Widening Participation in Further Education*, Coventry: Further Education Funding Council.

Kerr, D., Ireland, E., Lopes, J., Craig, R., & Cleaver, E., (2004) *Making citizenship education real. Citizenship education longitudinal study: second annual report. First longitudinal survey* (No. DfES Research Report RR531), London: DfES.

Klein, N., (2007) *The Shock Doctrine: The Rise of Disaster Capitalism*, London: Penguin Books.

Laar, B., (2006) *Inspection and accountability*, London: David Fulton.

Labaree, D. F., (2004) *The Trouble with Ed Schools*, New Haven: Yale University Press.

Lacan, J., (1977) *Écrits*. London: Tavistock.

Lacey, C., (1976) Problems of sociological fieldwork: A review of methodology of 'hightown grammar', in Hammersley M. and Woods P., (eds.) *The process of schooling*. London: Routledge, 55-66.

Lacey, C., (1976) Problems of sociological fieldwork: A review of methodology of 'hightown grammar', in M. Hammersley & P. Woods (eds.) *The process of schooling*. London: Routledge, 55-66.

Ladwig, J., (2010) Beyond academic outcomes, *Review of Research in Education*, 34: 113-141.

Lagemann, E.C., (2000) *An elusive science: The troubling history of education Research*, Chicago: University of Chicago Press.

Landy, R. J., (1986) *Drama Therapy*. Springfield: Thomas.

Lasch, S. & Urry, J., (1994) *Economies of signs and space*, London: Sage.

Lawn, M., (1996) *Modern times? Work, Professionalism and Citizenship in Teaching*, London: Falmer.

Leander, K.M. & Osborne, M.D., (2008) Complex positioning: Teachers as agents of curricular and pedagogical reform, *Journal of Curriculum Studies*, 40: 23-46.

Lenski, G., (1986) Power and privilege in Lukes, S., (ed) (1986) *Power*, Oxford: Blackwell, 243-252.

Levin, B., (1998) An epidemic of education policy: (what) can we learn from each other. *Comparative Education*, 34(2): 131-141.

Lifelong Learning UK (LLUK) (2006) *New overarching professional standards for teachers, tutors and trainers in the lifelong learning sector*, London: LLUK.

Lockwood, D., (1966) Sources of variation in working-class images of society. *Sociological Review.* 14(3): 249-267.

Lortie, D. C., (1975) *Schoolteacher,* Chicago, University of Chicago Press.

Lucas, N., (2004) *Teaching in Further Education: New Perspectives for a Changing Context,* London: Institute of Education.

Lucas, L., (2006) *The Research Game in Academic Life,* Maidenhead: Open University Press.

Lucas, N. and Nasta, T., (2010) State regulation and the professionalisation of further education teachers: a comparison with schools and HE. *Journal of Vocational Education and Training,* (4): 441-454.

Lupton, R., (2005) Social justice and school improvement: improving the quality of schooling in the poorest neighbourhoods, *British Educational Research Journal,* 31(5): 589–604.

Lyle, J., (2003) Stimulated Recall: A report on its use in naturalistic research *British Educational Research Journal* 29(6) 861-878.

Lyotard, J. F. (1984). *The Postmodern Condition: A Report on Knowledge* (G. Bennington & B. Massumi, Trans.), Manchester: Manchester University Press.

MacBeath, J., (2004) Inside Job, *The Guardian,* April 20.

MacKinnon, N., (2011) The urgent need for new approaches in school evaluation to enable Scotland's Curriculum for Excellence, *Educational Assessment, Evaluation and Accountability,* 23: 89-106.

Maguire, M. & Pratt-Adams, S., (2009) Improving the English urban primary school: Questions of policy. *Improving Schools,* 12(1): 59.

Mahony, P. & Hextall, I., (2000) *Reconstructing teaching: standards, performance and accountability,* London: RoutledgeFalmer.

Management Charter Initiative (MCI), (1997) *The Integrated Model of Management Standards,* London: MCI.

Manke, M. P., (1997) *Classroom Power Relations,* Mahwah, London: Lawrence Erlbaum Associates.

Marshall, J.D., (1999) Performativity: Lyotard and Foucault through Searle and Austin, *Studies in Philosophy and Education,* 18(5): 309-317.

Massey, D., (1994) *Space, place and gender.* Cambridge: Polity Press.

McIntyre, D., Pedder, D., and Rudduck, J., (2005) Pupil voice: comfortable and uncomfortable learnings for teachers, *Research Papers in Education,* 20, 149-168.

May, T., (1994) Transformative power: a study in a human service organization, Sociological Review, 42 (4): 618-637.

McLaren, P., (1986) *Schooling as a Ritual Performance,* London: Routledge and Kegan Paul.

McLean, M., (2006) *Pedagogy and the University,* London: Continuum.

McNally, J., (2006) From Informal Learning to Identity Formation: A conceptual journey in early teacher development, *Scottish Educational Review,* 37:79-89.

McNamara, O. and Brown, T., (2005) *New Teacher Identity and Regulative Government: The Discursive Formation of Primary Mathematics Teacher Education*, New York: Springer-Verlag Press.

McNamara, O., Brundrett, M. and Webb, R., (2008) *Primary teachers: initial teacher education, continuing professional development and school leadership development* (Primary Review Research Survey 6/3), Cambridge: University of Cambridge Faculty of Education.

Mead, G. H., (1934) Mind, self and society c. Morris, ed.

Menter, I., (2011) Four 'academic sub-tribes', but one territory? Teacher educators and teacher education in Scotland, *Journal of Education for Teaching,* (3): 293-308.

Menter, I., Brisard, E. and Smith, A., (2006) *Convergence or Divergence? Initial Teacher Education in Scotland and England*, Edinburgh: Dunedin.

Menter, I., Hulme, M., Murray, J., Campbell, A., Hextall, I., Jones, M., et al. (2010) Teacher education research in the UK: The state of the art, *Revue Suisse des Sciences de l'Education*, (1):121-142.

Merriam, S., (1988) *Case Study Research in Education*. Francisco: Jossey-Bass.

Mills, C. W., (1959) *The sociological imagination*, New York, Oxford University Press.

Moore, A., (1996) 'Masking the Fissure': Some Thoughts on Competences, Reflection and 'Closure' in Initial Teacher Education, *British Journal of Educational Studies*, 44(2), 200-211.

Moore, A., (2004) *The Good Teacher: Dominant Discourses in Teaching and Teacher Education*, London: RoutledgeFalmer.

Morley, L. & Rassool, N., (1999) *School effectiveness: fracturing the discourse,* London: Falmer Press.

Morley, L., (2003). *Quality and power in higher education*, Maidenhead: Open University Press.

Morton, S., (2003) *Gayatri Chakravorty Spivak*, London: Routledge

Mourant, A., (2011) Are colleges cutting more jobs than they need to? *Guardian* 27 June.

Mujis, D., A. Harris, C. Chapman, L. Stoll, and J. Russ., (2005) Improving schools in socio-economically disadvantaged areas: a review of research evidence, in Clarke, P., (ed.) *Improving schools in difficulty*, London: Continuum, 94-113.

Murray R., Baldwin, J., Ridgeway, K., Winder, B., (2005) Socio-economic decline and adaptation: South Yorkshire's former coalfields. *Local Economy.* (20): 344-359.

Murray, J. and Male, T., (2005) Becoming a teacher educator: Evidence from the field, *Teaching and Teacher Education*, 21(2), 125-142.

Murray, J., (1998) Integration or dichotomy of teaching and research? A case study of primary initial teacher educators, *Teachers and Teaching: Theory and Practice,* (1):143-160.

National Remodelling Team (2005) Case Studies. http://www.remodelling.org/resources/case_study_detail.php?latest. Visited 15.10.05.

Nelson, C. and Watt, C., (eds), (2004) *Office Hours: Activism and Change in the Academy,* London: Routledge.

New Criteria for Courses (Circular 14/93) (London: DfE).

Nias, J., (1989) *Primary teachers talking,* London: Routledge.

Nias, J., (1991) Primary teachers talking: A reflexive account if longtitudinal research, in Walford G. (ed.) *Doing educational research.* London: Routledge.

Nicholls, G., (2005) *The Challenge to Scholarship,* Abingdon:Routledge.

Nieveen, N., (2011) *Teachers' professional development in curriculum design in the Netherlands,* Paper presented at the European Conference for Educational Research, Berlin, 14 September, 2011.

O'Brien, M., (2011) Professional responsibility and an ethic of care, in C. Sugrue, & T. Sobrekk (eds.), *Professional Responsibility – new horizons of praxis,* London: Routledge.

Oancea, A., (2010) *The BERA/UCET Review of the Impacts of RAE 2008 on Education Research in UK Higher Education Institutions,* London: BERA/UCET.

OECD, (2007) *Quality and Equity of Schooling in Scotland.* Paris: OECD.

OfSTED. (2005). *A new relationship with schools.* London: HMSO.

OfSTED Office for Standards in Education (2006) *Towards Consensus? Citizenship in Secondary School,* London: OFSTED.

OfSTED Office for Standards in Education (2010) *Citizenship established?* London: OFSTED.

Olssen, M., (2006) *Michel Foucault: Materialism and education,* London: Paradigm Publishers.

Olssen, M., Codd, J. and O'Neill, A. M., (2004) *Education Policy – Globalization, Citizenship and Democracy,* London: Sage.

Orr, K. and Simmons, R., (2010) Dual identities: the in-service teacher trainee experience in the English further education sector, *Journal of Vocational Education and Training,* 62 (1): 75-88.

Orr, K., (2012) Coping, Confidence and Alienation: the early experience of trainee teachers in English FE, *Journal of Education for Teaching,* 38 (1):51-65

Osborn, M., Croll, P., Broadfoot, P., Pollard, A., McNess, E. & Triggs, P., (1997) Policy into practice and practice into policy: Creative mediation in the primary classroom, in G. Helsby & G. McCulloch (eds.), *Teachers and the national curriculum* (pp. 52-65), London: Cassell.

Paechter, C., (2007) *Being boys, being girls: Learning masculinities and femininities,* Abingdon: McGraw Hill.

Page-Arnot, R., (1961) *The miners in crisis and war*. London: George Allen and Unwin.

Patience, S., (2007) *Participatory Video for pupil voice: An experiment in emancipatory research*, M.A. Dissertation, University of East Anglia.

Perryman, J., (2006) Panoptic performativity and school inspection regimes: disciplinary mechanisms and life under special measures, *Journal of Education Policy*, 21(2): 147-161.

Perryman, J., (2007) Inspection and emotion, *Cambridge Journal of Education*, 37(2): 173-190.

Perryman, J., (2009) Inspection and the fabrication of professional and performative processes. *Journal of Education Policy* (5): 609-629.

Perryman, J. (2011) The Return of the Native: The Blurred Boundaries of Insider / Outsider Research in a British Secondary School. *International Journal of Qualitative Studies in Education* 24(7): 857-874

Peters, M., (2001) *Postmodernism, Marxism and neoliberalism: Between theory and politics*, Lanham, Md., Roman and Littlefield.

Peters, T. J. & Waterman, J. R. H., (1982) *In search of excellence*, New York, Warner Books.

Pignatelli, F., (1993) What can I do? Foucault on freedom and the question of teacher agency, *Educational Theory*, 43: 411-432.

Pink, S., (2001) *Doing visual ethnography*. London: Sage.

Pink, S., (2009) *Doing sensory ethnography*. London: Sage.

Plowright, D., (2007). Self-evaluation and OfSTED inspection: developing an Integrative model of school improvement, *Educational Management Administration Leadership*, 35(3): 373-391.

Pollard, A. & Filer, A., (1999) *The social world of pupil career*, London: Cassell.

Pollard, A., Broadfoot, P., Croll, P., Osborn, M. & Abbott, D., (1994) *Changing English primary schools: The impact of the education reform act at key stage one*, London: Cassell.

Pollard, A., Triggs, P., with, Broadfoot, P., Mcness, E. & Osborn, M., (2000) *What pupils say: Changing policy and practice in primary education*, London: Continuum.

Power, M., (1994) *The Audit Explosion*, London: Demos.

PricewaterhouseCoopers (2001) *Teacher workload study*, at http://www. teachers.gov.uk/docbank/index.cfm?id=3165. Visited 23.4.08.

Priestley, M., Edwards, R., Miller, K. & Priestley, A., (2012) Teacher agency in curriculum making: Agents of change and spaces for manoeuvre, *Curriculum Inquiry*. 43(2): 191-214.

Priestley, M. & Humes, W., (2010) The Development of Scotland's Curriculum for Excellence: Amnesia and déjà vu, *Oxford Review of Education*, 36(3): 345-361.

Priestley, M., (2011a) Whatever happened to curriculum theory? Critical realism and curriculum change, *Pedagogy, Culture and Society*, 19(2): 221-238.

Priestley, M., (2011b) Schools, teachers and curriculum change: A balancing act? *Journal of Educational Change*, 12(1): 1-23.

Pring, R., (1999) Political education: relevance of the humanities, *Oxford Review of Education*, 25(1&2): 71-87.

Prosser, J., (2006) *Image-based research: a sourcebook for qualitative researchers* London, Routledge.

Prosser, J., (2009) Visual methods: A road map, *Introduction to Visual Methods workshop, ESRC Research Development Initiative, Building Capacity in Visual Methods*, University of Leicester 13-14 January 2009.

Prus, R., (1996) *Symbolic Interaction and Ethnographic Research: Intersubjectivity and the Study of Human Lived Experience*, Albany: State University of New York Press.

Pyhältö, K., Pietarinen, J. & Soini, T., (In Press) Do comprehensive school teachers perceive themselves as active professional agents in school reforms?, *Journal of Educational Change*.

QCA Qualifications and Curriculum Authority (1998) *Education for Citizenship and the Teaching of Democracy in Schools*, London: Qualifications and Curriculum Authority (The Crick report).

QCA Qualifications and Curriculum Authority (n.d.) A framework of personal, learning and thinking skills, URL: http://curriculum.qcda.gov.uk/uploads/PLTS_framework_v2_tcm8-936.pdf

Quality Assurance Agency for Higher Education, (2000) *The standard for initial teacher education in Scotland, benchmark information*, Gloucester: QAA. http://domus.srce.hr/iuoun/images/dokumenti/standardi/teachereducationscotland.pdf [Accessed 1 November 2011].

Rabinow, P., (1984) (ed.) *The Foucault reader*, New York, Pantheon.

Racevskis, K., (1991) *The final Foucault*, Cambridge Mass., The MIT Press.

Randle, K. and Brady, N., (1997) Further Education and the New Managerialism, *Journal of Further and Higher Education*, (2): 229-239.

Reay, D., (1998). Micro-politics in the 1990s: Staff relationships in secondary schooling. *Journal of Education Policy*, 13(2): 179-196.

Reay, D., (2009) Making sense of white working class underachievement. In *Who cares about the white working class?* Ed. K. Páll Sveinson, London: Runnymede Trust.

Reay, D. & William, D., (1999) 'I'll be a nothing': Structure and agency and the construction of identity through assessment. *British Educational Research Journal*, 25(3): 343-354.

Reeves, J., (2008) Between a rock and a hard place? Curriculum for Excellence and the Quality Initiative in Scottish schools, *Scottish Educational Review*, 40(2): 6-16.

Reynolds, M., (1999) Standards and professional practice: The TTA and initial teacher training, *British Journal of Educational Studies*, 47(3):247–260.

Richards, A., (1996) *Miners on strike*. Oxford, Berg.

Riddell, J., (2005) Government policy, stratification and urban schools: A commentary on the *five year strategy for children and learners. Journal of Education Policy*, 20(2): 237-241.

Riley, K.A., Docking, J, & Rowles, D., (2000). Caught between local education authorities: Making a difference through their leadership, in Riley, K.A., & Louis, K. S., (Eds.) *Leadership for change and school reform*107-128. London: RoutledgeFalmer.

Riley, K. and Rustique-Forrester, E., (2002) *Working with Disaffected Students: Why students lose interest in school and what we can do about it,* London: Paul Chapman Publishing.

Roberts, L., Basit, T. N., McNamara, O., Carrington, B., Maguire, M. and Woodrow, D., (2006) Did they jump or were they pushed? Reasons why minority ethnic trainees withdraw from initial teacher training courses, *British Educational Research Journal*, 32(3): 387-410.

Robertson, S., (1996) Teachers' work, restructuring and post-Fordism: Constructing the new professionalism, in Goodson, I. F. and Hargreaves, A., (eds.) *Teachers' professional lives,* London: Falmer.

Robinson, S., (2011) Diluting education? An ethnographic study of change in an Australian Ministry of Education Discourse, *Studies in the Cultural Politics of Education* 32(5): 797-807.

Robinson, W., (2004) *Power to Teach: Learning through Practice*, London: Routledge.

Robson, C., (1993) *Real world research,* London: Blackwell.

Robson, J., (1998) A profession in crisis: status, culture and identity in the further education college, *Journal of Vocational Education and Training*, 50 (4): 585-607.

Robson, J., Bailey, B. and Larkin, S., (2004) Adding Value: investigating the discourse of professionalism adopted by vocational teachers in further education colleges, *Journal of Education and Work*, 17 (2): 183-195.

Rose, N., (1989) *Governing the soul: The shaping of the private self,* London: Routledge.

Rose, N., (2000) *Powers of freedom: Reframing political thought,* Cambridge, Cambridge University Press.

Rosenholtz, S., (1989) *Teachers' workplace,* New York, Longman.

Roth, M. and Lee, Y-J., (2007) 'Vygotsky's Neglected Legacy': Cultural-Historical Activity Theory, *Review of Educational Research*, (2): 186-232. RoutledgeFalmer.

Rudduck, J. and McIntyre, D., (2007) *Improving learning through consulting pupils.* Pearson Publishing.

Rudduck, J., (2004). *Pupil Voice is Here to Stay* [online] http://www.qca.org.uk/11478.html

Sachs, J., (2003) *The Activist Teaching Profession*, Buckingham, Open University Press.

Sikes, P., (2006) Working in a 'new' university: In the shadow of the research assessment exercise, *Studies in Higher Education*, 31 (5): 555–68.

Sahlberg, P., (2010) Rethinking accountability in a knowledge society, *Journal of Educational Change*, 11: 45-61.

Sammons, P., Hillman, J. & Mortimore, P., (1995), *Key characteristics of effective schools; a review of school effectiveness research,* London: Institute Of Education and OfSTED.

Samuel, R., (1986) Introduction to *The enemy within pit villages and the miners' strike of 1984-5,* (eds.) R.Samuel, B. Bloomfield and G.Boanas. London and New York: Routledge.

Sarup, M., (1993) *An Introductory Guide to Post-structuralism and Postmodernism,* New York; London: Harvester Wheatsheaf.

Schechner, R., (2002) *Performance studies, an introduction,* London: Routledge.

Scott, C. 2007. Stakeholder perceptions of test impact. *Assessment in Education* 14, no. 1: 27-49.

Scott, S., (2010) Revisiting the total institution: Performative regulation in the reinventive institution. *Sociology,* 44(2): 213-231.

Scottish Executive, (2004) *A Curriculum for Excellence*, Edinburgh: Scottish Executive.

Scottish Executive, (2006) *A Curriculum for Excellence: Progress and proposals,* Edinburgh, Scottish Executive.

Scottish Funding Council (SFC), (2010) *Intake targets for the controlled subjects in higher education institutions for the academic year 2010-11.*

Sebba, J. and Robinson, C., (2011) Evaluation of UNICEF UK'S Rights Respecting Schools Award paper presented to *British Educational Research Association Annual Conference*, Institute of Education, University of London: London UK, 7-9 Sept 2011.

Seddon, V., (1986) *The Cutting Edge: women and the pit strike.* London: Lawrence and Wishart.

Senge, P. and Scharmer, C.O., (2006) Community action research: Learning as a community of practitioners, consultants and researchers, in P. Reason & H. Bradbury (eds.) *Handbook of action research* (pp. 195-206), London: Sage Publications.

Shepherd, J., (2011) Michael Gove unveils plan to convert weakest primary schools into academies, *The Guardian Newspaper*.

Shore, C., and Wright, S., (1990) Audit culture and anthropology:

neo liberalism in British Higher Education, *The Journal of the Royal Anthropolological Institute*, 5: 557-75.

Simmons, R., (2008) Golden Years? Further education colleges under local authority control, *Journal of Further and Higher Education*, (4): 359-371.

Skeggs, B., (2004) *Class, self, culture*, London: Routledge.

Slater, J., (2004) Two day warnings of laser inspections *Times Educational Supplement*, February 13.

Slee, R., (ed.) (1988) *Discipline and schools: a curriculum perspective*, South Melbourne, Macmillan.

Smart, B., (1986) The politics of truth and the problem of hegemony, in D. Couzens & Hoy, (ed.) *Foucault: A critical reader*. Oxford, Basil Blackwell, 157-173.

Smith, D.E., (1987) *The everyday world as problematic.* MA: Northeastern University Press.

Smyth, J. & Shacklock, G., (1998) *Re-making teaching: Ideology, policy and practice*, London: Routledge.

Smyth, J., Dow, A., Hattam, R., Reid, A. and Shacklock, G., (2000) *Teachers' work in a globalising economy*. London: Falmer Press.

Smyth, J., Down, B. and McInerney, P., (2010) *Hanging in with kids in tough times: Engagements in contexts of educational disadvantage in the relational school.* New York: Lang.

Smythe, A. & Holian, R., (2008) Credibility issues in research from within organisations, in Sikes, P. and Potts, A., (eds.) *Researching education from the inside: investigations from within,* London: Routledge.

Snow, D. & Anderson, L., (1987) Identity work among the homeless: The verbal construction and avowal of personal identities. *American Journal of Sociology,* 92(6): 1336-1371.

Sparks, A., (1987) Strategic rhetoric. *British Journal of the Sociology of Education,* (1): 37-54.

SQA, (2009) Personal correspondence in response to request for information. St Leonards, Allen Unwin.

Starratt, R., (2007) Leading a community of learners, *Educational Management Administration and Leadership,* 35(2): 165–83.

Statistical First Release (2011) *School workforce in England November 2010 (provisional)* 6/2011, Department for Education. http://www.education.gov.uk/rsgateway/DB/SFR/s000997/index.shtml. Visited 22.8.11.

Stoll, L., & Fink, D., (1996) *Changing our schools; linking school effectiveness and school improvement*, Milton Keynes: OUP.

Strain, M., (2009) Some ethical and cultural implications of the leadership 'turn' in education: On the distinction between performance and performativity.

Strangleman, T., (2001). Networks, place and identities in post-industrial mining communities. *International Journal of Urban and Regional Research* 2: 253-267.

Strauss, A. L., (1978) *Negotiations: Varieties, contexts, processes and social order*, San Francisco CA, Jossey-Bass.

Stronach, I., Cope, P., Inglis, B. and McNally, J., (1994) The SOED 'Competence' Guidelines for initial teacher training: Issues of control, performance and relevance, *Scottish Educational Review*, 26(2):118-133.

Stronach, I., Corbin, B., McNamara, O., Stark, S. and Warne, T., (2004) Towards an uncertain politics of professionalism: teacher and nurse identities in flux, *Journal of Education Policy*, 17(1): 109-138.

Swaffield, S. and MacBeath, J., (2005) School self-evaluation and the role of the critical friend, *Cambridge Journal of Education*, 35(2): 239-252.

TDA (2007a) *Professional standards for HLTA status.* http://www.tda.gov.uk/upload/resources/pdf/t/tda0426_the%20standards.pdf. Visited 30.4.08.

TDA (2007b) *Professional standards for teachers: Qualified Teacher Status* http://www.tda.gov.uk/upload/resources/pdf/s/standards_qts.pdf Visited 1.5.08.

TDA (2007c) *The revised standards for HLTA Status.* http://www.tda.gov.uk/support/hlta/resources_2007.aspx. Visited 1.5.08.

TTA Teacher Training Agency (2004) *Qualifying to Teach: Professional Standards for Qualified Teacher Status and Requirements for Initial Teacher Training*, London: TTA.

Thomas, D., (1995) Teachers' stories studies. In Thomas, D., (ed.), *Teachers' stories*, Buckingham: Open University Press.

Thomson, P. and Gunter, H., (2005) Researching students: voices and processes in a school evaluation Paper presented to the Symposium: 'Speaking up and speaking out: international perspectives on the democratic possibilities of student voice'. AERA, Montreal April 2005.

Thomson, P. (2002) *Schooling the Rustbelt Kids: Making the Difference in Changing Times*, Stoke on Trent, Trentham.

Thomson, P., Hall, C. and Jones, K., (2010) Maggies's day: a small scale analysis of English education policy, *Journal of Education Policy*, (5): 639-656.

Thrift, N., (2000) Performing cultures in the new economy. *Annals of the Association of American Geographers*, 90(4): 674-692.

Thrift, N., (2008) 'Spatialities of feeling', in Thrift, N., *Non-representational theory: Space/politics/affect*, London and New York: Routledge.

Travers, C. J., and Cooper, C. L., (1996) Teachers under pressure: stress in the teaching profession, London: Routledge.

Troman, G., (1996) The rise of the new professionals? The restructuring of primary teachers' work and professionalism. *British Journal of Sociology of Education.* 17(4): 473-487.

Troman, G., (1997) Self-management and school inspection: complementary forms of surveillance and control in the primary school, *Oxford Review of Education,* (3): 345-363.

Troman, G., (2000) Teacher stress in the low-trust society, *British Journal of Sociology of Education,* 21(3): 331-353.

Troman, G., (2008) 'Primary teacher identity, commitment and career in performative school cultures', *British Education Research Journal,* 34(5): 619-633.

Troman, G., Jeffrey, B. and Raggl, A., (2007) Creativity and performativity policies in primary school cultures in *Journal of Education Policy* 22(5): 549-72.

Turner-Bisset, R., (2007) 'Performativity by stealth: a critique of recent initiatives on creativity', *Education 3-13,* (2): 193-203.

Troman, G. & Woods, P., (2001) *Primary teachers' stress.* London: Routledge.

Ulvik, M. and Smith, K., (2011) What characterises a good practicum in teacher education? *Education Inquiry,* 2(3):517-536.

Universities' Council for the Education of Teachers, (UCET) (2009) *Submission to the skills commission inquiry into teacher training in vocational education,* London: UCET.

van Zanten, A., (2005) New modes of reproducing social inequality in education: The changing roles of parents, teachers, schools and educational policies, *European Educational Research Journal,* 4(3): 155-169.

Vanderstraeten, R., (2001) The school class as an interaction order, *British Journal of Sociology of Education,* 22(2),: 267-277.

Vanegas, P. (1996) 'An Exploration of the Educational Policy Process: Teachers in Columbia', paper presented at the *British Educational Research Association Conference,* University of Lancaster, September.

Vongalis-Macrow, A., (2007) I, Teacher: Re territorialisation of teachers' multi-faceted agency in globalised education, *British Journal of Sociology of Education,* 28: 425–439.

Waddington, D., Wykes, M. and Critcher, C., (1991) *Split at the seams? Community, continuity and change after the 1984-5 coal dispute.*Milton Keynes: Open University Press.

Walford, G., (2007a) 'Classification and framing of interviews in ethnographic method', *Ethnography and Education* 2(2): 145-157.

Walford, G., (2007b) The nature of educational ethnography, in Walford G., (ed.) *How to do educational ethnography.* London: Tufnell Press, 1-15.

Walkerdine, V., (1988) *The mastery of reason,* Cambridge: Routledge and Kegan Paul.

Wall, K. & Higgins, S., (2009) Pupils' views of Templates: A visual method for investigating children's thinking, *ESRC Seminar, Leicester University, Jan 2009*.

Walsh, P., (2006) Narrowed horizons and the impoverishment of educational discourse: teaching, learning and performing under the new educational bureaucracies in *Journal of Education Policy* 21(1): 95-117.

Webb, K., (1979) Classroom interaction and political education, *Teaching Politics*, 8, 221-232.

Webb, R. and Vulliamy, G., (2006) The impact of New Labour's education policy on teachers and teaching at Key Stage 2. *FORUM: For Promoting 3–19 Comprehensive Education* 48(2): 145-158.

Wenger, E., (1998) *Communities of Practice: Learning, Meaning, and Identity*, York: Cambridge University Press.

White, P., (1999) Political Education in the Early Years: the place of civic virtues, *Oxford Review of Education*, 25(1&2): 59-70.

Whitty, G., (2000) 'Teacher professionalism in new times', *Journal of In-Service Education*, 26 (2): 281-294.

Wilcox, B. & Gray, J., (1996) *Inspecting schools; holding schools to account and helping schools to improve*, Buckingham: OUP.

Wiley, N., (1994) *The semiotic self*, Cambridge, Polity Press.

Wilkins, C., (2011) Professionalism and the post-performative teacher: New teachers reflect on autonomy and accountability in the English school system, *Professional Development in Education*, 37(3): 389-409.

Wilkins, Chris., (2011) Professionalism and the post-teacher: new teachers reflect on autonomy and accountability in the English school system. In *Professional Development in Education* 37(3): 389-409.

Williams, J.E., (1962) *The Derbyshire miners*. London: George Allen and Unwin.

Williams, R. (1977) *Marxism and Literature*. London: Oxford University Press.

Williams, R., (1975) *The country and the city*. St. Albans: Paladin.

Willmott, H. (1993) Strength is ignorance; slavery is freedom: Managing culture in modern organisations. *Journal of Management Studies* Vol 30 215-52.

Woods, P. A., (1998) *School choice and competition: Markets in the public interest*, London: Routledge.

Woods, P. A., (2007) Academy schools and entrepreneurialism in education. *Journal of Education Policy* 22(2): 237-259.

Woods, P., (2004) Creative teaching and learning: Historical, political and institutional perspectives. *Creativity in Education Seminars - ESRC*. Exeter.

Woods, P. & Jeffrey, B., (1996) *Teachable moments: The art of creative teaching in primary schools*, Buckingham, Open University Press.

Woods, P. and Jeffrey, B., (2002) 'The reconstruction of primary teachers' identities', *British Journal of Sociology of Education*, 23(1): 89-106.

Woods, P., Jeffrey, B., Troman, G. & Boyle, M., (1997) *Restructuring schools, reconstructing teachers,* Buckingham, Open University Press.

Wragg, E.C., Haynes, G.S., Wragg, C.M. and Chamberlin, R.P., (2000) *Failing Teachers?* London: Routledge.

Youdell, D., (2006) Subjectivation and performative politics - Butler thinking Althusser and Foucault: Intelligbility, agency and the raced-nationed-religioned subjects of education. *British Journal of Sociology of Education* 27(4): 511-28.

Young, M., (1998) *The Curriculum of the Future: From the New Sociology of Education to a Critical Theory of Learning,* London: The Falmer Press.

Index

Fabrication of documentation 54

Fazzaro, C.J. 144

Fielding, M. 4, 181

Filer, A. 173, 259

Fink, D. 60, 61

Flick, U. 5, 6, 8

Flutter, J. 1

Flyvberb, B. 202

Foucauldian – *see also* Foucault i, 28, 147, 164, 170, 197, , 217, 228

Foucault, M. *iii, iv, vii*, 2, 3, 18, 19, 44, 45, 46, 47, 48, 49, 50, 54, 59, 61, 64, 68,
  69, 76, 80, 84, 147, 149, 167, 168, 172, 173, 180, 181, 183, 185, 188, 190,
  193, 196, 197

  inter-related dependencies

    extra discursive 173

    inter-discursive 173, 190–192

    intra-discursive 173, 183

      environmental use of space and time 183

Frameworks and Standards 9, 26, 35, 41, 42, 56, 63, 65, 99, 113, 127, 129, 132,
  133, 151, 168

  1988 Education Reform Act 51

  1990s education 129

  2003 Inspection Framework 55

  2005 Inspection Framework 45

  CfE and major changes 99

  Higher Level Teaching Assistant (HLTA) 150

  Initial Teacher Training 26

  Inspection framework of 2005 (OfSTED, 2005) 63

  National Agreement (DfES, 2003) 150

  National Literacy Strategy (NLS) 157

  National Numeracy Strategy (NNS) 157

  Qualified Teacher Status 26

  Qualifying to Teach 26, 27

Frazer, E. 127

Freire, P. 144, 145

Fullan, M. 92

Full-time equivalent (FTE) staff 150

Furlong, J. 24, 25, 151

Further Education (FE) 199, 200, 201, 202, 203, 204, 205, 206, 209, 214, 215,
  216

Author Biographies

Gert Biesta (www.gertbiesta.com) is Professor of Education and Director of Research at the School of Education, University of Stirling. His research focuses on the theory and philosophy of education, the theory of educational and social research, citizenship education and democracy, adult education and lifelong learning, and the professional formation of teachers. He is editor-in-chief of Studies in Philosophy and Education and co-editor of Other Education: The Journal of Educational Alternatives. He is co-director of the ESRC-funded Teacher Agency and Curriculum Change research project (2011-2012).

Geoff Bright, (publishing as N. Geoffrey Bright) is a visiting research associate at the Education and Social Research Institute at Manchester Metropolitan University. Currently writing up a PhD on the ethnographic study referred to here, his background is as a steelworker and rail worker in the 1970s and 1980s. Later he became a trade union, community and adult educator and, more recently, was a senior development manager in children's and youth services in Derbyshire.
Correspondence: Geoff Bright, Visiting Research Associate, Education and Social Research Institute, Manchester, Metropolitan University, 799, Wilmslow Road, Didsbury, Manchester M20 2RR, United Kingdom.
Email: g.bright@mmu.ac.uk .

Hugh Busher is a Senior Lecturer in the School of Education, University of Leicester and teaches on Masters and Doctoral programmes. He researches into the interactions of people, power and culture in the development of mainly school-based learning communities and the representations of students' and teachers' voices in particular policy contexts. He recently published, with Dr Nalita James, *Online Interviewing* with Sage.

Dr Hilary Cremin, a senior lecturer in the Faculty of Education at Cambridge University, researches, publishes and teaches in the areas of conflict resolution in schools and communities and citizenship education. An editor of the British Education Research Journal, she chairs the Forum for Youth Participation and Democracy, an international cross-disciplinary and cross sector forum for debate, research and impact on policy and practice. Recently completed research investigated the civic action and learning of young people from Socio-economically disadvantaged communities (funded by the Society for Educational Studies) and Restorative Approaches to conflict in schools (funded by the ESRC).

Irene Garland lectures on a range of undergraduate and postgraduate courses in education at Sheffield Hallam University and has a particular interest in qualitative research methodology. She gained an Economic and Social Research Council funded PhD from the University of Sheffield in 2008 with a thesis which focussed on workforce reform in schools. The research explored the boundaries between teacher and teaching assistant roles at a time when these roles were in a state of flux. Her research interests are in professionalism within the education workforce, and the application of Bourdieuan constructs in education research.

Paul Garland is currently Programme Leader for Research Degrees in Education in the Faculty of Development and Society at Sheffield Hallam University. He gained his PhD from Leeds University in 2001, with a study of the impact of GNVQ curriculum reforms on FE lecturers. His research interests include professionalism and the professionalisation of teachers; the work of Habermas and its application to postgraduate pedagogy; the experiences and trajectories of doctoral students in education; and research methodologies for education. He organises Erasmus Intensive Programmes on research methodology for education doctoral students through a network of Higher Education Institutions across Europe.

Vanessa Hayward is currently a doctoral research student at The University of Nottingham. During her time at the university she has gained research experience through involvement in various projects within the School of Education. Vanessa is also a youth support worker at a Derbyshire youth project, providing support and informal education opportunities for 11-19 year olds. Before coming to The University of Nottingham she successfully completed her PGCE in Post Compulsory Education at The Nottingham Trent University.

Moira Hulme is lecturer in educational research at the School of Education, University of Glasgow. She has coordinated a number of research projects funded by the Scottish Government, General Teaching Council of Scotland and Learning and Teaching Scotland. Commissioned studies include research on pupil participation in Scottish schools, professional culture amongst recent entrants to the teaching profession and stakeholder perspectives on the new school curriculum, Curriculum for Excellence. Moira is a member of the Executive of the Scottish Educational Research Association and co-convenor of Network 3, Curriculum Innovation by Schools and Teachers of the European Educational Research Association.

Bob Jeffrey has researched, with Professor Peter Woods and Professor Geoff Troman, the work of primary teachers since 1992. They focused on the opportunity for creative teaching and the effects of the reforms of the 1990s in England on this form of pedagogy and teacher identities. In the 2000s they developed this focus to learners and their opportunities for creative learning including a nine nation European study from 2004-2006. He has also worked closely with Anna Craft developing research and promoting creative teaching and learning in the educational research community particularly through BERA and through a nationwide seminar series from 2004-2005 and they edited a Special Issue on Performativity and Creativity for BERJ in 2008. He has been a co-leader of two recent ESRC studies into Primary Teacher's Careers in Performativity Cultures and into the effects of performative and creative policies on primary schools – 2004-2008 together with Professor Geoff Troman of Roehampton University. They have published extensively including a great many methodology articles focused on an ethnographic approach including a focus on cross cultural approaches. Bob is co-founder of the Ethnography and Education journal and now edits it, co-organises an annual ethnography conference in Oxford as well co-editing a book series www.ethnographyandeducation.org . He has recently retired but holds an Honorary Research Fellow post at Exeter University.

Michalis Kakos is a lecturer in education at the University of Leicester where he leads the PGCE (ITT) course in Citizenship education. Previously he has been employed as research fellow in the Centre for Citizenship and Human Rights

Education (CCHRE), University of Leeds and in the Centre for Research in Inclusion and Diversity (CREID) University of Edinburgh. Michalis' research interests include: intersubjectivity, self-conceptualisation and identity in adolescence; institutionalisation in education; 'normality', 'abnormality' and special education. Michalis has taught in Primary schools, Pupil Referral Units, Special, Grammar, Comprehensive and Preparatory schools in Greece, USA and the UK.

Ian Menter is Professor of Teacher Education and Director of Professional Programmes in the Department of Education at the University of Oxford. He has previously held posts at the Universities of Glasgow, Paisley, North London and the West of England. His research interests lie mainly in teacher education and education policy and he has carried out a number of 'home international' comparative studies within the UK. He is an editor of the British Educational Research Journal and co-convenes the Teacher Education Group and a UK wide research group on Curriculum, Assessment and Pedagogy Reform in the UK.

Kevin Orr is a senior lecturer in the School of Education and Professional Development at the University of Huddersfield. Before moving into Higher Education, he taught in Further Education (FE) colleges for sixteen years, mainly on English for speakers of other languages (ESOL) courses and in teacher education. Kevin's research continues to focus on FE and on vocational and professional education more generally and he is co-convenor of the Post-Compulsory and Lifelong Learning special interest group of the British Educational Research Association. His current research includes a study of the work-based learning of architects.

Jane Perryman is a senior lecturer in education at the Institute of Education, University of London. She is currently the Course Leader for the PGCE Social Science. She also contributes to the EdD and various master's courses and supervises doctoral students. Before working in Higher Education she was a secondary school teacher and head of department for 10 years. Her research interests are accountability and performativity in secondary education, school leadership and management, and how schools respond to policy.

Mark Priestley is Reader in Education in the School of Education, at the University of Stirling, where he is Director of the Curriculum and Learning research programme. His main research interests concern the school curriculum, and especially the processes of curricular change. He is currently principal investigator of the Economic and Social Research Council funded 'Teacher Agency and Curriculum Change' research project (RES-000-22-4208), and chair of the Editorial Board for the Scottish Educational Review.

Sarah Robinson is a Research Fellow at the University of Stirling currently conducting research on an ESRC funded project on Teacher Agency and Curriculum Change in Scottish schools. Sarah completed a PhD at the University of Western Australia carrying out an ethnographic study of how an educational bureaucracy works and responds to change. Her interest is in exploring the beliefs and values of the policy actors who work inside educational systems where reforms are initiated. She has worked in the UK, Denmark and Australia.

Pauline Sangster is a senior lecturer in the School of Education, University of Edinburgh. Recent publications include research investigating: listening in classrooms from wider sociocultural rather than narrower individual psychological perspectives; English as an additional language (EAL) provision in Initial Teacher Education (ITE) Programmes, and EAL policy and practice in secondary schools; the teaching and assessment of writing in primary and secondary schools; student teachers' knowledge about, and awareness of, language; and analysis of post-lesson talk between student teachers of English and an experienced tutor employing narrative research methods. She is currently the Director of the School's PhD Programme.

Pat Thomson PSM PhD is Professor of Education, School of Education, The University of Nottingham and Director of the Centre for Advanced Studies (faculties of Arts, Humanities and Social Sciences). Her research focuses on arts, creativity and change in schools and communities; she also workd on doctoral education and academic publishing. She edits Educational Action Research Journal and currently blogs about writing and research on http://

patthomson.wordpress.com/. Details of books on http://www.amazon.co.uk/
Pat-Thomson/e/B001IXNYV0

Geoff Troman is Emeritus Professor of Education at Froebel College, School of
Education at Roehampton University, London and Director of the Centre for
Research on Education Policy and Professionalism - CeREPP. Previously he was a
Research Fellow and Associate Lecturer in the Faculty of Education and Language
Studies at the Open University. Geoff is foundation Editor (with Bob Jeffrey,
The Open University; Geoffrey Walford, University of Oxford) of the Journal
Ethnography and Education published by Routledge, Taylor & Francis Group. He
taught science for twenty years in secondary modern, comprehensive and middle
schools before moving into Higher Education in 1989. Throughout his time in
schools he carried out research as a teacher researcher. His Ph.D research was an
ethnography of primary school restructuring. Geoff maintains a research interest
in Education Policy, Ethnography, Ethnographic and Qualitative Methodology,
Comparative Qualitative Studies, Sociology of Education, Teachers' work.